WHY WE SUCK

DR.
DENIS LEARY

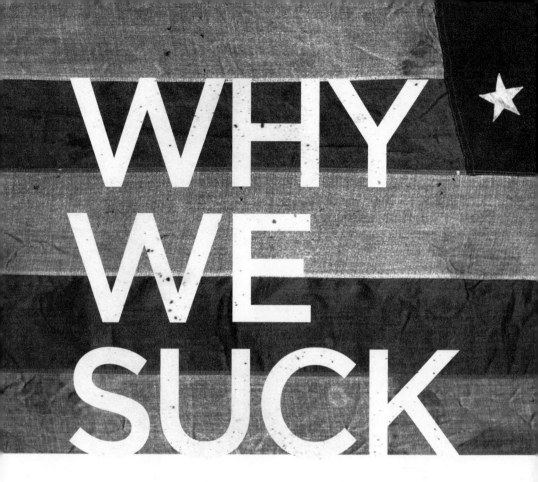

WHY WE SUCK

A FEEL GOOD GUIDE TO STAYING FAT, LOUD, LAZY AND STUPID

VIKING

VIKING
Published by the Penguin Group
Penguin Group (USA) Inc., 375 Hudson Street, New York, New York 10014, U.S.A. ✴ Penguin Group (Canada), 90 Eglinton Avenue East, Suite 700, Toronto, Ontario, Canada M4P 2Y3 (a division of Pearson Penguin Canada Inc.) ✴ Penguin Books Ltd, 80 Strand, London WC2R 0RL, England ✴ Penguin Ireland, 25 St Stephen's Green, Dublin 2, Ireland (a division of Penguin Books Ltd) ✴ Penguin Books Australia Ltd, 250 Camberwell Road, Camberwell, Victoria 3124, Australia (a division of Pearson Australia Group Pty Ltd) ✴ Penguin Books India Pvt Ltd, 11 Community Centre, Panchsheel Park, New Delhi – 110 017, India ✴ Penguin Group (NZ), 67 Apollo Drive, Rosedale, North Shore 0632, New Zealand (a division of Pearson New Zealand Ltd) ✴ Penguin Books (South Africa) (Pty) Ltd, 24 Sturdee Avenue, Rosebank, Johannesburg 2196, South Africa

Penguin Books Ltd, Registered Offices:
80 Strand, London WC2R 0RL, England

First published in 2008 by Viking Penguin,
a member of Penguin Group (USA) Inc.

10   9   8   7   6   5   4   3   2   1

Copyright © Killarney Ink, LLC, 2008
All rights reserved

Illustrations by Patrick Campbell. Illustrations copyright © Killarney Ink, LLC, 2008

Photographs courtesy of the author.

LIBRARY OF CONGRESS CATALOGING-IN-PUBLICATION DATA
Leary, Denis.
Why we suck : a feel good guide to staying fat, loud, lazy and stupid / by Denis Leary.
    p.   cm.
ISBN 978-0-670-03160-3
1. American wit and humor. I. Title.
PN6165.L43 2008
814'.54—dc22   2008025027

Printed in the United States of America
Set in Chaparral Pro with Gotham
Design and stain illustrations by Daniel Lagin

"Just remember, kid—it's all bullshit."

—ROBERT MITCHUM, WHISPERING INTO NICK NOLTE'S
EAR AT THE ACADEMY AWARDS

DOCTOR'S NOTE

I'd like to point out that all of the facts and allegations and medical science spoken about in this book have all been thoroughly researched. By me and my staff. Which means—just me. I didn't make footnotes and I'm not listing any evidence. That shit just takes way too long. You wanna find out if what I say is true IS actually true? Google it. That's what I did. The things I didn't bother to Google? They happened to me firsthand. Good luck and good reading.

Dr. Leary

ACKNOWLEDGMENTS

I'd like to thank everyone who ever told me to go fuck myself. It's why I fell in love with my wife, who bears more than a fleeting resemblance to me—except she's far prettier. And is a girl, obviously. And she's funnier than I am. And smarter. And somehow fell in love with me when I was broke and barely owned the sneakers on my working-class Irish feet. I owe everything in my life to Ann and my two terrific children—Devin and Jack. Let's face it—the only reason I wrote this book is because both of them wanna go to college. So thanks for helping to further their education by purchasing this fine piece of literature. Wow. I wrote a whole book. Well, it's SHAPED like a book. Anyways—enjoy.

SECRET HIDDEN MESSAGE PAGE

I have never been fat. But I have been—and oftentimes continue to be—loud, lazy and stupid. So put down the Pop-Tarts and listen up a little. I'm trying to help us here.

CONTENTS

A SECOND NOTE FROM THE DOCTOR

Just in case you still do not understand (and given the condition of this country and the people we place into elected office, I think there are whole cities full of morons who couldn't beat a bag of hammers in a game of Scrabble out there) let me make it simple for you:

This is a comedy book.

Which means it's meant to be funny.

So when I say something in here I am offering up my opinion, my slightly exaggerated take on people, places and things and very often a twisted take on reality.

In other words: it is parody, satire and poking fun.

If you are mentioned within these pages and your first reaction is to call a lawyer?

Good night and good luck.

Because there are endless things you can buy in America—but a sense of humor isn't one of them.

We got pills and potions for your head, face, fears, tits, ass, anxieties, colon, kidneys, alcohol addiction, drug jones, heart, lungs, lips and attitude—but we don't have anything that can make you laugh at yourself.

Otherwise—before you read this book?

I'd prescribe a fist full of it.

Once again,

Dr. Denis

SPECIAL THANKS

I'd like to thank Lydia Wills for her support and finely tuned interest. I'd like to thank God—if only because I am so sick of hearing rappers with criminal records longer than their extended-length Hummer limousines do it at the Grammys. But I'd also like to thank Satan—who never gets enough credit for his wonderfully inspirational work with everyone from Judas Priest to The Rolling Stones and seemingly every other talk-radio honcho and Bush administration member. I think I speak for all comedians out there when I say without Satan and his many evil minions, we wouldn't have such a wealth of great targets to aim at. I also must thank Patrick Campbell for his fabulous artwork that will make you laugh out loud later on. But I can't thank Patrick without mentioning his wife Kerry and their son Wyatt, who stopped by the apartment and my office many times when Patrick and I were working. I must also thank Wyatt for puking on the kitchen floor instead of the living room rug. And last but not least I'd like to thank my editor Josh Kendall for his bright advice and deft suggestions and all the lively and lovely girls from Penguin who first came into the offices at Apostle—my production company—and said "you gotta write a book." They sparked my interest. I have to thank two key people at Apostle as well—Bartow Church and my assistant Anna Urban, both of whom I drove nuts with requests for celebrity post-autopsy toxicology results and lists of political trivia etcetera etcetera. And I must thank the one man in particular who made this whole thing happen: my production partner Jim Serpico. After the Penguin girls had

SPECIAL THANKS

pitched their idea and left, Jim said "if you're ever gonna write a book, this is the time and these are the people." Then he kept kicking my ass to make my deadlines and reading drafts and telling me what made him laugh and what didn't and telling me time and time again that I only had such and such a number of months left and why don't you push that subject a little further and when are you gonna have that chapter done and you only have eight weeks you only have three weeks you only have four more days and I think this cover is the best cover and I'll tell you why. He's the hardest-working guy I have ever met and he's funny and he's sharp and he's really really really smart and he's made every project we've ever worked on better simply by being involved and God how I hate him. Thanks, Jimmy. You slave-driving sunuvabitch. I'd also like to thank my recently departed Irish Wolfhound Clancy—the biggest dog in the history of the world. Let's put it this way—when I had a cup of coffee in the morning, so did he. THAT'S how big he was. And I gotta give kudos to my new dog Lulu—she picked up right where Clancy left off. Only she doesn't drink coffee. But she did sit at my feet under the desk each day and look up at me yearningly with her big brown eyes, as if to say—when the fuck is this book gonna be done, asshole?

It's done, Lu. Let's go get us some squirrels.

PROLOGUE

Put this book down.

Right now.

Do not buy it.

Stop reading.

Now.

Why are you still reading this?

Okay.

I warned you.

Now I will beg you, beseech you—in short, do everything possible in the limited format of this medium to get you to buy any other book within reach right now (if this book was a gift and you are at home or on a plane or sitting in a hotel room somewhere I would suggest grabbing a newspaper or a magazine or even your laptop) because this book is going to piss you off.

If you are a woman, you will soon be livid.

If you are a man, you are going to be filled with a burning rage.

If you are a kid—meaning anyone under the age of eighteen—you will soon be filled with shock and awe.

Scratch that.

If you are under the age of twenty-five you will soon be filled with shock and awe.

If you are a fan of Oprah—good luck.

If you hate Oprah or Oprah tends to drive you insane—you too will need some assistance.

This is not a book for the faint of heart or the politically correct or the weak or the extreme right wing or the left of center leftist Democrat or nuns or any other members of any organized religion or New York Yankee fans.

I am warning you—I am not here to make you feel all warm and fuzzy or superior to everyone else or all soft and gooey inside. I am here to debunk and declassify and otherwise hold up a brutally honest mirror to our fat, ugly, lazy American selves.

I am here to explain how we can and must thin the herd and extricate the stupid and eradicate the obese and take Rush Limbaugh's head and make a bong out of it.

Senators, psychopaths, fence-sitters (all three of those may sometimes be the same person), celebrity assholes (hello), presidents, centerfielders, centerfolds—everyone is up for grabs here.

Because I'm sick of it all.

I'm sick of low self-esteem and fake fat-suit-wearing female talk-show hosts and extreme makeovers and *Cats The Musical* and cats in general and steroid-laden home-run hitters and Paris Hilton and *Grey's Anatomy* and Reese Witherspoon movies and Paris Hilton's himbo boyfriends and celebrity rehab and Dr. Phil and Terrell Owens and almost anyone else you can think of.

This country—including you and most of the people related to you by birth or marriage or both—is populated by beings who have been so blessed for so long that they have become almost completely immune to any interests other than their own.

Open ass—insert head.

THAT is the mantra with which most of America lives each and every day.

THAT'S what should be printed on the plaque beneath our beloved Statue of Liberty. Along with the following:

Welcome to America where I'M not fat, I'M not stupid, I'M not the problem—YOU are.

Americans have been so isolated geographically, financially and psychologically for so long that we don't even see reality in the mirror anymore. Everyone has bought so far into their own bullshit—backed up by other jerk-offs and human jack-o'-lanterns on TV—that the truth has been distorted into a believable fantasy world: I can't be overweight, look at the tub-a-lard sitting next to me. The food I eat can't be bad for me 'cause the commercial on TV says it's actually healthy. I'm not addicted to these doctor-prescribed drugs, the drug company discovered a disease that I have and then invented these pills to cure me.

Responsibility, research and actual factual thinking have gone out the window. If most people in this country see something on TV it must be true/news/necessary/important. Therefore, when things go wrong—how can the innocent citizen/TV watcher be at fault?

I spill a vat-sized "cup" of morning coffee onto my giant cellulite-dimpled thighs at the take-out window and suffer third-degree burns because it was hot and I desperately needed to wash down the two-ton doughnut I just manhandled into my gaping mouth—do I blame myself and go on a diet and start working out?

No.

I sue McDonald's because the take-out window kid who handed me the cup of joe—who's from Bumfuck, Mexico, and has been in this country all of eighteen weeks and only knows the English words "can I take your order, please," "would you like fries with that" and "go Yankees"—didn't warn me that the coffee was the same temperature as the air in the hut he grew up in was every single day of his childhood.

Open ass—insert head with flame-red tongue.

My kid is the size of an out-of-shape NFL offensive lineman, has what within two months might become a full-blown Fu Manchu mustache and is already smoking two packs a day and watching Internet porn even though SHE is only twelve years old.

Do I put her on a diet and make her start working out?

Fuck no.

I sue McDonald's because they make shitty, hormone-and-chemical-filled food that she eats every single day three TIMES a day because I'm very very busy living my selfish extended adolescent life and don't have time to:

A. Cook her normal food.
B. Monitor her free time.
C. Stop smoking pot and drinking so her easiest sources of alcohol and marijuana dry up.

Open ass—insert thick, self-medicated head.

An out-of-shape and overweight guy in Denver, Colorado, claims he developed lung cancer because he ate microwave popcorn with artificial butter flavoring. He loved when he would pull the bag out of the microwave and tear open the top and it would go "WHOOF" and he would stick his face in and inhale the aroma. You can just hear him sucking in the sweet sweet smell of all that great fake butter, can't you? Just like Homer Simpson: Ooooh—buttery fake butter. After whiffing up the cloud of chemicals, this moron on a mission would proceed to scarf down the entire bag and then—that's right—start the whole process all over again. He admits to snorting and scarfing two bags a day so let's do the actual math and add the two more bags he won't admit to because he probably figures four bags a day would just be really embarrassing so what we have here is a guy who ate and sniffed so much fake butter that he developed the same cancer that people who work in the plant where they manufacture the fake butter did—people who make thousands of bags of pretend popcorn every single day.

Should he blame himself for his lazy butter-assed slovenly ways?

Nope.

The popcorn factory workers filed a dangerous workplace/permanent health damages lawsuit and he decided to ride their cancer coattails all the way to the bank.

Let's up his total to at least five bags a day. Whatever the actual number might be I'll guarantee you one thing right now—you don't wanna be THIS guy when you're sitting down in the lung cancer chemotherapy waiting room. 'Cause when the guy who worked in a coal mine for twenty-seven years or the fireman who spent decades pulling people out of asbestos-ridden burning buildings asks how YOU got lung cancer the last word you wanna mention is "popcorn."

Open ass—insert fake butter bag.

And I don't wanna hear the words "misogyny," "racial profiling" or "politically incorrect."

I'm talking common goddam sense.

Misogynistic means you hate women—it doesn't mean you hate women because you are trying to tell them what they do not want to hear.

Like yes, your ass IS fat.

Or no—most heterosexual men do NOT find Renée Zellweger attractive.

AND—it's not possible that every single pair of shoes or every dress you decide to buy can be on sale. Maybe four hundred and seventy-nine dollars is the ACTUAL price and "marked down from seven hundred" is what they teach the salesclerk to tell you.

Danica Patrick—the much-heralded and publicized and ostracized and cursed-about-by-men female race car driver finally won her first race in 2008. Legions of women all over the earth were quoted in happy, feminist quotes about female power and female challenges and equal rights and equal abilities. Danica cried as she accepted her trophy and was photographed in all of her glory and joy. But the picture that was most often seen the next day was Danica in a bikini. From her pages in *Sports Illustrated*'s Annual Swimsuit Issue. In which she looked very very hot. Now—we can all agree or disagree about that picture and its placement and why she took it and are women objectified and blah blah sexist blah—but the truth is if you ask most men if they are attracted to a woman who can drive faster than them you will get either a no or a big fat maybe. But if you ask most men if they mind a woman who looks like Danica does in a bathing suit beating their brains out on the track? The answer is—not at all. Especially if she's WEARING the bikini while she drives. Hell—I'll sign up right now and ride shotgun. As a matter of fact—I wish there were a whole race of female race car drivers who drove like cheetahs on crack and looked fine in a swimsuit issue—I think the ratings would go through the roof.

But that will NEVER happen.

If you are a woman reading this, odds are Danica will win another few races but not you. Or your daughter. Danica is an anomaly. You and your daughter most likely are not. Even if you somehow managed to convince yourself that you were Danica Part Deux and passed every physical and mental challenge in your path and got sponsored and suited up and officially entered and placed on the track—you would never win a single IndyCar—EVER. Even if all the other male drivers were involved in an incredible crash that left them literally without the wherewithal to circle the track, you would be unable to maneuver around and between all the burning and airborne debris fast enough to see the checkered flag.

Especially if you have or plan on having kids.

Why?

Because there's an instinct built into the female DNA—if a woman is still of natural child-bearing age—to protect herself and not risk the future of her children, whether they exist in egg or embryo or live germ-factory form. Potential kid, kid in the oven or kid already running around. It's why most women don't wish to get into fistfights or shoot animals or fly airplanes into tall buildings—unless it's to protect or feed or avenge the lives of their own children. You wanna win the Daytona 500? We would have to strap your firstborn into the shotgun seat of a lead car driven by a crazed ex-boyfriend on a revenge ride from hell or your current lover while he was under chemical influence and give either of them a fifteen-second head start and then and only then would you be headed for a victory lap. And the winner's circle celebration would probably involve breast instead of bottled milk.

It's absolutely commonsense fact: girls like to dance and boys like to hit. That's why girls become cheerleaders and boys become football players.

Girls play mommy and boys pretend to kill each other. Girls like pretty clothes and boys like fire trucks.

For women, their list of hot men includes a dad who waits at the corner bus stop with his toddler son and places him on the bus with a kiss atop the head and waves goodbye as the bus drives away. This man could be thirty pounds overweight and wearing a goofy hat. Women will still find him sexy.

For men—a mom doing the same thing—placing her toddler on the bus with a loving kiss and a wave—would be just as hot and sexy. As long as she was built like Giselle Bundchen and wearing a leopard-print thong.

I know it's awful. I know it's incredibly simple and stupid and sad.

But it's true.

As a matter of fact—you could skip the kid and the bus and just have Thong Mom walk down to the corner and stand there—same difference for straight men.

A recent online poll by *Woman's Day* magazine came up with these results:

When asked which they would rather have—Jennifer Aniston's body or a million dollars—78 percent of the women chose the money.

If you had asked men—78 percent would have chosen Jennifer Aniston's body—as long as they could press it right up against their own.

As a matter of fact—if they had asked men—they would have found that most men WITH a million dollars would gladly give it up for the CHANCE to touch Jennifer Aniston's body. Or just to see her naked.

Maybe that's the difference between men and women.

One of them, anyway. Here's another:

Ninety-four percent of the people in this country who visit, pay and place heavy stock in psychics and what they have to say are women. The other 6 percent? Gay men.

Women go to psychics to find out what the future might hold for them in terms of true love, their children, former lives they may have lived, where their dead father/boyfriend/best friend might be.

Straight men? If psychics are capable of seeing into the future—why the fuck can't they give us the score to next year's Super Bowl.

That's it for men. Very cut and dried, very black and white. We'll discuss that and many other issues between men and women between these covers.

By the way—bipolar? Bullshit. Every single woman I have ever known has been bipolar for SOME part of her life—one week here, nine months there, ever since her mother stopped calling—something. When I was a kid, bipolar meant either the twin axis ends of the earth or maybe a bear who swung both ways. Now it's an excuse for every other girl whose hormones are conducting a human body remake of *Raging Bull*.

They didn't have bipolar when I was growing up. If they did—my mom would've been called TRIpolar. She could smack one kid with a wooden spoon, ask a second kid if she was retarded and give a third kid a sweet little kiss on the head—all within four and a half seconds. And ya know what? Each one of us almost always deserved what we had coming.

And that's another thing I don't wanna hear ever again—dysfunctional families. That one is officially off-limits. Done. Retired forever. Has anyone ever heard of a FUNCTIONAL family? Who? When? Where? The Jacksons? Nope. The Osmonds? I don't think so. You wanna know what a functional family is? One where no one ends up killing everyone else. You can't have four or five or fifteen people live together in one place WITHOUT war and envy and greed and anger and theft and every other available weapon.

You disagree?

Then you gotta be a chick.

Open vagina—insert head.

I told you this book was gonna tick you off. Let's face it—the raw truth hurts.

Like this fact: I don't know a living man on this planet who DOESN'T have attention deficit disorder or spends at least twelve hours of each day thinking about his penis.

I didn't know the guy personally but I would bet my left ball that even Jesus thought a lot about his johnson. Hey—he could probably make his do special tricks. If I was the Son Of God, special dick tricks would probably be the second or third thing I'd be spending my time on after I found out about my secret identity.

That's a lie.

Who am I kidding? It'd be the first.

Here's another lively topic:

It says somewhere in the piece of paper that this great country of ours was founded upon that all men are created equal.

Bullshit.

All men are created equal as long as they don't wanna blow each other.

And then decide to keep on blowing each other long enough to fall in love.

And then suddenly express a desire to formalize that relationship by getting married.

It's apparently okay to have sex with other guys as long as you keep it secret and have a wife who somehow doesn't know AND you are either the pastor of a church or a sitting senator or both. In Larry Craig's case the term "sitting senator" will more than likely get a laugh out of you—as will the term "wide stance."

Yup—there is a real fear in America that gay marriage will somehow up-end heterosexual unions and throw the entire moral fabric of the country into a tailspin—no pun intended.

I know several gay men and gay women involved in very committed and honest relationships with other gay men and gay women that would put a lot of straight married couples to shame. They are monogamous and caring and devoted and affectionate.

Besides—why shouldn't they get married? Why should straight married couples be the only ones who never have sex, argue incessantly over what to watch on TV and walk around on a daily basis harboring a deep and bottomless well of resentment and anger pieced together brick by murderous brick over years and years of both real and imagined slights and emotional warfare and wallpaper choices? Shit—I say marry every gay and willing couple off right now. Mark my words—just like the rest of us—within eighteen months at least half of them will come running back to court begging to be released from such an endlessly mind- and libido-numbing fate.

Open ass—insert the Bill of Rights.

Here's another inarguable factoid:

Racial and ethnic stereotypes exist because they are TRUE. For instance—don't tell me the Irish don't love to drink. I AM Irish. We invented whiskey, for crissakes. You know what whiskey means in Gaelic? Water of life.

I rest my case.

Of whiskey.

On YOUR politically correct goddam lap.

Years ago I wrote a piece for the *New York Post* about the St. Patrick's Day Parade in which I made fun of the fact that most of the Irish and a few Puerto Rican guys I knew would annually—which means every single fucking year—spend the unofficially holy day painting their faces green and getting drunk and then beating the living shit out of each other after an argument broke out over who had better pitching, the Yankees or the Mets.

The Irish Defamation Society threatened to file a lawsuit against me for perpetrating an awful and ruinous myth about Irish Americans.

Several weeks went by and no lawsuit emerged. Why?

Because they soon realized that all I had to do was call up any local news channel and request footage from ANY St. Patrick's Day Parade held since the invention of the television camera and there in front of our eyes would be green-faced Irish Americans in a drunken punch-up with their own cousins and best friends and actual brothers—many times right in front of St. Patrick's Cathedral. The Puerto Ricans and the New York Mets didn't enter the equation until they both started playing baseball during the 1960s. Otherwise?

Case closed.

The right to bear arms and the right to vote and the equal rights amendment and freedom of speech and every other piece of paper evidence you wanna throw onto the pile may guarantee you the right to spout stupidity (see Newt Gingrich, Mel Gibson, Barry Bonds et al.) but it also guarantees that the rest of us don't have to buy into it.

Ya wanna build a giant fence to keep all the Mexicans out? Fine. Who's gonna build the fence? Where are we gonna get our cheap Mexican weed? Who's gonna host *The Dog Whisperer*?

Our country has been so driven into debt by a drug-addled, inbred, dry drunk of the Republican revolution—a man who ran an oil company into the ground (do you know how hard it is NOT to make money off of oil? My daughter's Chihuahua could pull it off)—that we are now borrowing money from China.

China.

The same country that tried to KILL our dogs with poison dog food three years ago.

China.

Where there are seventeen BILLION people and eight automobiles.

China.

A country so corrupt that if I lived there and typed the words "CHINA SUCKS" as I did just now? Within a day I would have disappeared off the face of the earth, leaving my wife and the only child we are allowed to have—and our three bikes—to fend for themselves.

We will delve deeper into each and all of these matters during the next couple of hundred pages.

And I do so as a doctor, ladies and gentlemen.

That's right.

Dr. Denis Leary.

You don't believe me?

Here's a photograph of the actual degree I received from my alma mater Emerson College on the afternoon of May 16, 2005.

Suck on that, Dr. Phil.

Or as I like to call him—Dr. Full.

Hey—I don't know what his actual weight was when he started pushing his diet book, but let's just say he was more than a little puffy and really not what I would call an authority on that particular subject. Hell—he might as well have written a book on how to stop being bald while he was at it.

Let me point something out—Dr. Full doesn't even have a license to practice in the state of California, which is where he tapes his daily talk show.

Let me point something else out—if I needed to go on a diet, I'd want the guy selling me his diet book to not only be thin but actually be in shape—is that too much to ask?

But this is America—where if you're on TV—especially if you appear on Oprah—you MUST be some kind of authority.

Well, I haven't been on Oprah but I DO have my own TV show and a degree that calls me a doctor. So here's my point—if Dr. Full can write a diet book then I can sure as hell write a self-help book. And that's really all I'm trying to do here—help you to help yourself AND make a shitload of money while I'm doing so.

Because I really do believe we live in the greatest country on earth but—just like that fixer-upper you get a very good price on—there's still a lot of work left to do.

We live in a country that's still very very young, as countries go, and I think the whole idea of the American Dream has been convoluted and undone.

We live in a country where the first pictures of Brad Pitt and Angelina Jolie's baby were sold for over four million dollars. Shit—for THREE million dollars I'd sell you the pictures AND the kid.

We live in a country where Rosa Parks had the courage and conviction to sit down long enough to start a revolution that led to Al Sharpton screaming racism every time Barry Bonds gets indicted for taking performance-enhancing drugs in order to break a home-run record set by a black man who didn't even have the benefit of Advil.

A country where—once upon a time—the Presidential Medal of Freedom was given to people who fought for civil rights and equal rights and other matters that made a genuine difference and real contributions to a better future for everyone on the planet. Now it goes to guys who so botched the War on Terror that the president has to accept their resignations before they squirm off into the shadows to lick their wounds.

We used to honor our living war veterans with respect and bury the dead heroes with dignity.

George Bush The Second avoided Vietnam through privileged connections, shot down the brave deeds of another privileged son—John Kerry—who volunteered to serve, came home with medals on his chest and made the mistake of thinking the best man might win when he ran against a guy whose administration was caught cremating dead American soldiers from Iraq in a pet cemetery incinerator.

Because it was cheaper.

Open ass—insert Oval Office.

It's time to tear down the walls of the stupid and the inane and the politically correct and the righteous and the pretentious and the bald and tell them how much they suck and how fat they are and how everything in the Bible is NOT necessarily true and no your hair will never grow back and yes you look much older without it and no—women really don't find bald guys attractive unless you're Mark Messier or a multizillionaire or both.

It's time to shave your back and pay attention to your kids and buy a bigger-size dress and stop wearing spandex until you lose a hundred pounds.

Skinny jeans are meant for skinny people. In case you don't understand the term "skinny"—if your ass doesn't fit into a seat at the ballpark or hockey rink or football stadium—yer fat. Too fat for skinny jeans.

What would Jesus say? What I just said. Only louder.

And his hands and feet would be bleeding so he'd probably be in a very pissy mood.

So listen up.

I'm trying to help you here.

It won't be pretty. But it will be goddam funny.

Strap yourself in.

It's gonna be a bumpy-assed, roller-coaster-on-fire type of ride.

No helmets allowed.

CHAPTER 1

WHY EVERYONE HATES US

s being America. This is just a partial posting. Many of these subjects will be discussed in much further detail as the book moves along.

But I wanted to give you a starter kit. A little menu tasting of the who, what and why when it comes to the rest of the world and the things about us that burn their proverbial balls.

A lot of them are things and people and events that many of us—like our fellow humans in the world—don't get or support or even have the slightest interest in. But for some reason they fill up our magazines and televisions and radio waves until they are chock full to spilling over with incredible pulsing chunks of unbelievably stupefying activity. And like a train wreck or multicar collision or Mickey Rourke's most recent face— we just can't turn our eyes away.

ANNA NICOLE SMITH

It's never pretty when you die in a pool of your own puke.

But when you're a mom and you die in a pool of your own puke AND you have a newborn baby—ya can't really blame postpartum depression.

Brooke Shields may have done many strange things after the birth of each of her kids, but lying facedown in her own vomit and trying to swim upstream was not one of them.

In Anna Nicole's case there were obviously several different wiring problems gone wrong. She may set the first public example for Babies Who Are Better Off With Their Birthmoms Absolutely Erased.

Anna Nicole may also be the ultimate example of what happens when white trash gets money. And she serves up a great argument against taking strippers out of the strip club. Listen, go ahead and watch them wiggle, watch them giggle and jiggle and strut their stuff—give them each all the singles and wolf-whistles you want but please—we beg of you—please do not bring the dancers home. It's like taking King Kong off the jungle island and dropping him into the middle of midtown Manhattan—nothing good can come of it.

Let's face a few facts about Anna. Pick any angle.

Her fabulously idiotic persona that—ingeniously—seems to have been created out of her actual penchant for pure moronitude built on a foundation of her own absolute genetic idiocy.

Her "I'm, like, really really really in love with him" marriage to a 109-year-old multizillionaire businessman that involved more than likely only one partial erection and then several years of undone hateful relatives and continuous litigation.

Her giving birth to one child while a second fully grown child already scarred by his exposure to his mother and a worldwide reality TV show audience—not to mention several hundred forms of prescription and recreational drugs—basically dies in the recovery room. Of a drug overdose. Which was probably a good thing because let's be honest—he was only facing a future full of "Mom, have you seen my methadone?" afternoons.

And when it came to drugs, Mom set a goddam house record. In the fridge of her Indian-owned hotel mini-bar they found several powerhouse forms, in amounts large enough to mollify a small horse. These were the various drugs found in her system at the time of her death: Ativan (an anti-anxiety pill); Klonopin (an anti-seizure medication); Robaxin (a muscle relaxant); Soma (another muscle relaxant—I guess she was bigger than we thought); Topamax (another anti-seizure medicine—maybe she was so worried about the first anti-seizure stuff she took, she was afraid the fretting might cause a seizure in itself, so she superseded that seizure-mania with a backup plan); Benadryl (to ward off any sniffles); HGH (wow); Nicorette ('cause God forbid you smoke around the baby); Tamiflu (is it possible to feel a little achy with all of this other stuff in your system?); methadone (just in case the Tamiflu doesn't work); and Noctec (another sleeping medication—hey, you try lugging those two tits around all day); vitamin B-12 (just in case she gets a little sluggish while she's sleeping); Tylenol (probably just found a white pill on the hotel room carpet and swallowed it out of habit); and that good old standby—Valium.

Wow. That's what she took the day that she died.

Happy Mother's Day, mom.

And, perhaps my favorite—narcotic lollipops. Which are used for kids who have cancer.

Narcotic lollipops—these alone give the Islamic world a sudden urge to strap on bombs.

Great name for a band, by the way. Ladies and gentlemen, please welcome—Narcotic Lollipop.

Where did the narcotic lollipop come from?

Good old-fashioned American ingenuity folks.

You know kids—they hate medicine. So when they are really terribly horribly sick and absolutely need to take heavy-metal medicine—some genius doctor devised a way to put the dose inside a piece of candy glued to the top of a stick. The kids lick their little hearts out and fall into a pain-free, blissful, semi-coma state.

Wish they'd had these things when my kids were small. I woulda stuck those suckers in their mouths every single waking moment—which woulda been only about fifteen minutes a day, by the way. They would have spent most of their lives in dreamy McDreamland.

As did Anna Nicole, apparently.

Yup. She out-Elvised Elvis.

Elvis may have ingested drugs in myriad forms—mostly pills—and eaten his way through most of the peanut butter, bacon and bananas available on this green globe during his lifetime, but he never ever EVER took goofed-up candy from a cancer-stricken baby.

Would he have—if they had been invented sometime during his four decades on the earth? You can bet yer ass. The King woulda been the Kojak of the rock 'n' roll universe. But, alas, he died too soon. On the toilet. Which is literally only a couple of steps above where Anna Nicole ended up.

And then there are the men in her life, or as I like to refer to them—The Scumbags On Parade.

In no particular order:

(Ah, what the hell—let's put them in order of their proximity to the dead, bloated but always bronzed-with-skin-bronzer body):

- ★ Her scumbag lawyer, who the real Howard Stern should be currently taking to court for defamation of character by name association. This guy apparently had no other clients, lived in adjacent hotel rooms whenever Anna Nicole was in a hotel or upstairs in a guest bedroom at whatever abode she may have been renting or owned and his legal advice consisted of making deals for semi-glorified Girls Gone Wild videos featuring only one giant Orca-type girl—namely, Anna Nicole. As well as drunken, drugged and reeling casino appearances. And drunken, drugged and reeling public appearances. Last time I checked, that doesn't make you a practicing lawyer. But it does put you right at the top of the Celebrity Pimping List.

- ★ Her pretty boy ex-boyfriend who also claims to be the father of the child and is an actor slash model slash—what, exactly? Whore? Parasite? Yeah. Put those two words on your résumé, pal.

- ★ And then there's the crème de la crème of the douchebag brigade—Zsa Zsa Gabor's twenty-seventh husband, who—while Zsa Zsa spends each day in a catatonic state being wheeled around her Bel Air mansion—was out carousing with Anna Nicole and who knows who else, which may just be his personal business except he made it public knowledge that they met for sexual trysts in hotels all over the country. Now—I don't know exactly how much Zsa Zsa is worth, but it's obviously not enough to keep this male version of Anna Nicole away from the media or the pile of money Anna Nicole's wheelchair-bound spouse left behind.

These are just three more elements of the low-rent high-lush life Anna lived that were left behind. At least Marilyn had *Some Like It Hot* and *The Misfits* and *The Seven Year Itch*.

What's Anna Nicole's legacy?

Her gaining seven thousand pounds while bingeing her way out of the death of her aforementioned lover/human ATM card and then taking an over-the-counter form of methamphetamine and losing all seven thousand pounds and then some and serving as a spokesperson/swimsuit model for this legalized speed.

PLUS the rumor that the eventually victorious dad Larry Birkhead (insert your own joke about his name here) and the evil Howard Stern guy were apparently videotaped going down on each other in a fabulous and hopefully very very funny 69 session—a rumor I have actually prayed to God is true. If there is a God I'm sure he has helped Larry and Howie to spend some of that dead lover cash-cow cash in exchange for the original copy of said video. THAT would be—at the very least—a tiny little sliver of sweet karma pie delivered almost immediately after the judge handed the kid they hope grows into another cash cow over into their greedy and supposedly gay grubby hands.

Anna Nicole and her two lover/liar/blow job buddies are a walking talking eating breathing advertisement for why America makes everyone else in the world angry.

By the way—we could replace this profile of Anna Nicole with so many other people—from Paris Hilton to Terrell Owens to Britney Spears and any guy she has married or even had sex with.

Not to mention—if we ever get to pick the initial hostages/innocent victims taken during a future American soil invasion, men who had sex with either Paris, Anna Nicole or Britney should be first up. And hand jobs definitely count.

GEORGE BUSH JR.

That's right.

Junior.

Fuck this Herbert Walker blah blah blah bullshit.

Looks like a junior talks like a junior walks like a junior.

Junior.

Junior brain junior brawn junior bullshit.

His father fought as an actual jet fighter pilot during World War Two and after a real live fight to the death in the sky crash-landed off the edge of a navy airship into the Atlantic Ocean and crawled up the side of the ship to safety.

Junior dressed up like a jet fighter pilot and pretended to land a plane on the deck of a navy airship and then changed into a suit and announced the victorious end of a war that then went horribly wrong and lasted LONGER than the war his father fought in.

Junior.

Nuff said.

BRITNEY SPEARS'S VAGINA

Whether you've seen it or not.

Whether it was actually her very own God-given pooch or just a Photo-shop configuration or not.

You know what I'm referring to.

That fact—along with the idea that so many millions of us either over-heard a watercooler discussion of her muff or were actually the insti-gators of a "Britney's pussy" confab—is immediate grounds for foreign antagonism.

And it's not just an anti–pop star snatch hunt here.

The idea that in a civilized, free society there are supposedly grown men actually getting paid to find untethered and free-ranging celebrity hair pies, photograph them and then sell them to magazines apparently watering at the mouth for hot naked Hollywood gash can only mean one thing—well, maybe two things: there either is no God or not only is there one, but His idea of divine balance is an indiscriminate act of unjustified violence one second and then a naked celebrity coochie shot the next.

Because let's face the real facts: I may personally have no interest in Britney's bush, but you come up with a flash pic of Heather Locklear's or Sienna Miller's or Meryl Streep's and not only am I in—men all over the world are hard-charging to the Internet and their local magazine racks. Hell—Meryl Streep would send a lot of WOMEN running after those shots, if only to check out what Oscar-winning pussy looks like.

And that's why Muslims hate us. Not because they hate pussy or celebrity pussy photography. Just the opposite—they love it just as much if not more than we do. They just can't get their hands on it as readily as we can.

BRITNEY SPEARS'S HEAD

See preceding section on Britney's vagina.

Only in this case, the little-known Tarzana, California, hair salon she suddenly stepped into—demanding they shave off all of her hair before grabbing the shears and performing the task herself—at first discussed her condition as if they actually gave a shit about her. Words like "concerned" and "sad" and "hope" were being bandied about. But come the bright new light of the following morn?

They were selling her shorn locks on eBay.

Along with the empty can of Red Bull she left behind.

And her blue Bic cigarette lighter.

All available to the highest bidder.

In the newspapers that same day the shop owner's husband was quoted as saying some—and I emphasize the word "some"—of the proceeds from the sale would go to charity, possibly—and again I emphasize the word "possibly"—including Locks Of Love, which supplies wigs to kids with cancer. He also was quick to point out that the tresses from Britney's naked skull were the ONLY authentic Britney tresses available for sale.

Wow.

Imagine how much her pubic hair would be worth on eBay.

And which kids' cancer charity would "probably" receive "some" of the profits.

Britney Spears is a national train wreck who leaves the entire Western world looking suspect in her wake:

A. all the housewives and postfeminist pulpit bangers who buy the magazines with all the pictures of the hair and the hair salon and the vagina (with a gold star over the important bits) in them.

B. the paparazzi who not only take those unbelievable photos but the one or two who have apparently started having sex with her since the children were taken away and she blew a serious gasket.

C. the college and high school kids who—upon hearing that on the night she locked herself in the bathroom of her mansion with one of the kids when the cops came to take them away and place them back into the protectively tattooed arms of K-Fed—the night when she was photographed and videotaped being led out of the house while strapped on a gurney looking wild-eyed and insaner than ever— she apparently had been drinking a combo of Red Bull, vodka and NyQuil. Yeah. NyQuil. These college and high school kids immediately started having parties at which that concoction was not only served in great numbers but was given various nicknames: Purple Drank, Wake-Up Call, Britney Stinger, Good 'n Crazy, The 911 etcetera etcetera.

D. Dr. Phil/Full and his holier-than-thou visit to the hospital to "help" Britney after she snapped and his claim immediately afterward that he was hosting an hour-long episode of his talk show where he and Britney would have a sit-down and he would help her turn the whole messy thing around and get her back on the right track. Which would've been nice. But she changed her mind. And he was still going to use her name to sell the episode until an uproar arose and everyone started calling him a media whore/ambulance chaser etc. Which gives you some hope for the American people. Until you stop to realize if Britney HAD appeared on the program it would more than likely have been the highest-rated show on TV all year.

Believe me when I tell you—it's not just the Muslims who look at such information and immediately begin building bombs.

Anyone talked to China lately?

By the way—get Billy Ray Cyrus on the phone and tell him to start stockpiling that rehab money right now. You wanna talk about bipolar? Billy Ray's daughter performs LIVE IN CONCERT as Hannah Montana AND Miley Cyrus. And she's only fifteen years old. You don't need a calculator to figure out the math on this one. Christ—you could do it on an abacus.

By the way—if you don't know what an abacus is—throw this book into the trash can right now.

YOU

I don't mean you personally.

Unless you are fat, loud and wear low-slung hip-hugging jeans with your fuchsia thong underwear and two inches of backfat, a half inch of side-slop and what looks like white jelly but is in fact a whole extra ass hanging off your stomach and over the front of those jeans. Which are six sizes too small.

Or you insist on eating at McDonald's even though you're in Paris, France—not Texas.

Or you think black socks and sandals are the zenith of summer style.

Or you refuse to have your back waxed before the family trip to Europe.

Or you're over the age of thirteen but still just LOVE Adam Sandler movies.

Or you spend your entire tour of the British Museum going "Ewww—I just saw some dead dinosaur bones—can you believe I'm in London'n yer still in Cincinnati but we're both still talkin' live to each other?" into your cell phone.

Or you spent four months bitching about Janet Jackson's tit and how it ruined your children when she exposed the nipple during the halftime show at Super Bowl XXXVIII but didn't blink an eye during the five hundred and sixteen erectile dysfunction/"get a hard-on for a whole weekend" pill commercials.

Okay.

I take it back.

I do mean you.

MTV'S *SWEET SIXTEEN*

If you haven't seen or heard of this particular program you either spend far too much time sitting alone reading or suffer from a severe case of autism. If the first case applies—wake the fuck up. If your condition includes the second case—congratulations. You've been spared.

Not only does this program make a fine, upstanding and fairly normal red-blooded American like myself want to gather up every teenage girl with raging hormones and absolutely no sense of real-life limits, stick 'em in a pair of standard-issue fatigues and drop them chuteless into the middle of the Iraqi desert, but what's a day at a warm and breezy beach compared to what would lie in store for their parents.

Ya plant carrots ya get carrots.

In between bouts of whining and texting and whining WHILE texting and soporific party-planning and stomping their Jimmy Choo–clad feet because their dads didn't book 50 Cent for their party these denizens of designer clothes and high-end vodka, these future mental vacuums harangue their moms about seven-thousand-dollar place settings and gold-engraved invitations.

No jobs. No discernible talent. Not even one good blow job available from the entire batch.

They are living breathing Bermuda triangles.

Loaded with cash but not one iota of interest in anything other than the mundane.

Problem is—the terrorists get basic cable too.

TRUMP VODKA

The Donald doesn't drink.

At all.

Ever.

But some brilliant business guy came up with the idea for Grey Goose vodka—a smooth, sensational drink that would be distilled in its best form and become the best vodka in the world and be delivered into your hands in the most gorgeous bottle you could imagine.

Years later he sold the brand for over one billion dollars.

The Donald couldn't keep himself away.

He came up with an okay vodka that is distilled in an okay form but comes in a gold-plated bottle that is worth far more than the drink itself.

He went on CNN and told Larry King that even though he hadn't tasted the stuff himself, the people who worked for him guaranteed it was the best-tasting vodka ever made. And oh, yeah, boss—by the way—no one ever makes fun of your hair.

See, no matter what you might think about extreme Islam and its fevered believers, one thing you can take as a guarantee is this: they have a really truly madly deeply held passion for the things they love/hate. In other words, if they do not drink beer the last possible idea they would come up with is Muslim ale. Unless every bottle contained a secret hidden explosive device that was ignited by the opening of each individual cap.

And how many times could that work.

Maybe once.

Except in my family at Xmastime.

Then—maybe—somewhere between the second six-pack and the fourth dead uncle—we'd be bound to figure it out.

BILL CLINTON / BLOW JOBS

One of the big downsides of the Monica Lewinsky scandal as far as men were concerned was this—the highly acclaimed and heavily leaned upon "blow jobs don't count" rule that so many men had loved and lived by as a way of not really cheating on their wives/girlfriends was not only on full public display but became everyday fodder for discussion with almost every woman you knew—cousin, friend, spouse, sister, daughter, mother.

It's the one thing men will never forgive him for.

But had he not gotten caught—most men, including myself—along with a large bevy of women—would have agreed with the basic idea: balance the budget, orchestrate a healthy and robust economy, keep our country away from war? Free blow jobs.

Talk about an incentive. If every president knew—if he had it in writing—that a balanced budget meant a free blow job? Take my word for it—there would no longer be a federal deficit.

I'd even take it a step further. JFK slept with Marilyn Monroe and Angie Dickinson—the two hottest chicks on the face of Planet Hollywood during the early sixties.

Let's run with it, baby. Lower taxes? Tag Tyra Banks. Unemployment goes down? So does Sienna Miller. You win a war while in the Oval Office? You get to bang Halle Berry. And if Halle or Sienna or Tyra or whoever has a problem with the whole idea—hey, it's for the good of all mankind.

Let me tell you something. George Bush Junior looks like he hasn't gotten laid—never mind a blow job—since he quit drinking and snorting coke. If you guaranteed him that Sharon Stone would suck his testicles on Tuesday afternoon the war in Iraq would be over on Monday morning. He'd be sitting at his desk with his pants down watching a director's cut DVD of *Basic Instinct Three*—the widescreen edition.

The point I'm trying to make here is this: most of the world never understood the anger and unrest over the Monica Lewinsky deal because the idea that a world leader would receive oral satisfaction from a surrogate in a historically significant location made perfect sense to them. The conquering hero, the triumphant tribal chief blah blah blah. In France, Greece, Italy, Ireland, Turkey, Turkistan—everywhere else on this green globe—no one gives a crap who their leaders end up in bed with. All they care about is results—food, family, shelter. That's all anyone should care about.

We finally get a leader who not only solves most of our financial problems but is intelligent and compassionate and is not only interested in foreign policy but seems to have a pretty good sense of how to go about dealing with it and what do we do? Fry him up over a late-night snogfest.

Even terrorists like blow jobs.

And I'll go one step further: I'm sick and tired of being sick and tired of right-wing, clean-living, religious fundamentalists trying to run this country. It seems to me that the less fun the president has the more trouble our country gets into.

JFK? Womanizing, cigar-smoking, beer-drinking, boat-loving guy who scared the shit out of the Russians and Castro and started the Peace Corps. Nixon? Staid, isolated, intellectual monogamist who hated half the people who were breathing and the limits of the Constitution. LBJ? Lunatic pussyhound with a penchant for bourbon who gave us welfare and signed the civil rights bill and when he screwed up in Vietnam decided to get the hell out of the way. Bush Jr? You get the idea.

I think every presidential candidate—man or woman—from here on in should have to prove that they not only drank but smoked weed and tried blow and had casual sex while in college and maybe even beyond. In other words—they were fairly normal, just like the rest of us. No blow, no booze, no weed, no sex? Guess what? No federal matching funds. You want my vote? Show me some pictures of you in a rum punch–stained bedsheet at a college toga party. Forget some bullshit behind-the-scenes-developed middle-of-the-road policy on stem cell research or the future of the Middle East—I want to hear how many Twinkies you ate after the Halloween bong hit competition during your sophomore fall term.

Now Bush Junior apparently performed many of these actual tasks but decided to cover all of them up. No dice, folks. You gotta be proud of them. Cut to the chase and avoid all the bullshit. Like Obama. Did he do blow. Yup. How do we know. He told us. Weed too. Now that's the kind of candidate I like. Made mistakes. Owns up. Probably also wore ridiculous pants and had shitty haircuts too. Get the point?

Forget your grade point average and your congressional voting record—I want Polaroids of your ass etc. on display during some drug-and-sex-fueled youthful indiscretion. And we wanna see them in *People* magazine. DURING the campaign. Released by your own staff. Make it personal—not presidential. One of the great things about JFK was the fact that he was funny. As was Reagan. As was Clinton. And if the leader of this country doesn't find his job funny—believe me, we're fucked.

KATIE COURIC'S EVENING NEWS

The day of her debut as a network news anchor her third story from the lead was about Tom Cruise's baby.

She led with a report about the war in Iraq.

The second story dealt with the skyrocketing price of gas at pumps across the country.

And then—Tom Cruise's baby.

Poverty? Nope.

Genocide in Darfur? Not yet.

A possible cure for cervical cancer in preteen American girls?

Nope.

Tom Cruise's baby.

That's what the news has come down to in this country—with minor variations on any given night:

MONDAY

Wildfires continue to rage in Southern California.

President Bush to visit the Middle East.

Gwyneth Paltrow chokes on a raisin.

TUESDAY

Hurricane Carole set to hit the Florida coast.

Mitt Romney wins Republican primary in Michigan.

Nicole Kidman's face doesn't move.

That's all I'm asking for—throw in a curveball. I know that no one in America is really reporting vital facts and true information anymore. It's all showbiz. Anderson Cooper only looks forward to being live on location in New Orleans or Malibu so he can climb out of a monkey suit and wear a tight-fitting T-shirt that shows off his pecs—so let's have some fun with it all. Make some shit up that catches us off guard or—even better—makes us laugh.

And you wonder why half of the audience gets their news from *The Daily Show with Jon Stewart*?

THE DOUBLE QUARTER POUNDER WITH CHEESE

Most of the people on this planet have massive problems finding enough food to eat, yet we not only throw away more food in the course of a single day than they might see in their entire life spans—we also have obese pets. And books about obese pets. And sidebar segments on national news programs about how to put your obese pets on a weight-loss/workout regimen. Meanwhile—most of these pets that are eating too much dog and cat food actually ARE food in other parts of the world—so while we are desperately trying to slim them down there are families of eight in Africa who are dreaming of roasting them on a rusty spit over an open flame. They hate us and our pets. We make no sense to them.

Not to mention The Food Channel.

FIFTEEN-MINUTE ABS

A lot of people on planet Earth spend every waking hour of each and every day "working out"—walking twelve miles with ceramic jugs on their heads to get clean drinking water and another twelve miles back. Hunting and searching for scraps of rice. Or killing and skinning and deboning what we would call pets for dinner. Or chopping branches and wild brush in order to rethatch the rooftops on their meager huts after the most recent monsoon/hurricane/tsunami left them sleeping under the stars. This is when they aren't working for slave wages under the scrutiny of whatever dictator/communist regime currently runs their country while they work seventeen hours a day to make Nike sneakers that cost pennies to produce and sell at your local Foot Locker for slightly less than five hundred bucks. Meanwhile—we buy aluminum- or titanium-tubed gizmos they made for Suzanne Somers to sell to us so that we can tone and firm up our oversized thighs and ass cheeks. Then we wonder why the ones who can't get here to live just wanna watch someone—anyone—blow us up. Hmmm.

NASCAR

Most of these people have never been IN a car even though they live in countries absolutely polluted with deep, thick, unbelievably rich oil and gas preserves. And we have rules in place so that if Kasey Kahne or Jeff Gordon tries to sneak jet fuel into his gas tank we can fine him—just so they don't have an unfair advantage as they race around a circular track at two thousand miles an hour for half a day in order to win a couple of million dollars.

Look—I'm like you—I like to see car crashes as much as the next guy. Especially when it doesn't happen on a highway I'm driving across and therefore affects my commute. And especially when it's in a controlled situation that includes high-def cameras so I can watch the crash replayed in digital slo-mo from seventeen different angles.

But let's face the facts—in many places other than America and Europe—this may be the biggest example yet of profligate waste and arrogant expense. One tribe saunters along through 27,000-degree heat under a desert sun on top of a thirsty camel in search of moisture and food while down in Daytona Beach well-fed white hillbilly guys with leather jumpsuits on ride multicolored road rockets 500 miles to nowhere.

Tennis, anyone?

How about golf?

REHAB

They've never even heard of it.

Until rich white American celebrities started "entering" it.

They drink red wine with lunch and dinner and live to be one hundred and sixteen years old.

We have celebutards who can't make it past age nineteen without downing eleven-hundred-dollar bottles of champagne and vodka while blowing eight balls up one orifice and sucking weed and x through another.

Been drinking without wearing panties for six to eight months?

Rehab.

Image declining because of late-night drunk-driving arrests and numerous public pukefests?

Rehab.

Wanna kick that nasty heroin/cocaine habit and get back in the good graces of the studio execs who won't hire you for that next big movie or TV show?

Rehab.

Why—we can even cure your homosexuality. Ted Haggard did three weeks in a rehab center and came out claiming he was back in love with women.

What a deal. Go gay for as many years as you like—hell, throw in an addiction to methamphetamines—and whenever you feel the need (or you get outed in the press by a male hooker/drug dealer, whichever comes first), get back in the good graces of the public AND your wife by spending three weeks in a glorified spa and pop out the other side drug free and no longer desiring anal sex with men.

Talk about worth the price of admission.

And then—once again—there's Britney. She did one day in Eric Clapton's Crossroads rehab facility and then checked out. A week later she did a day at Promises in Malibu before checking out. Then she checked into a third rehab joint about a week later. She was a little confused at first, apparently she thought "one day at a time" was meant to be taken literally. Thirty days in thirty different rehab centers in thirty different cities. Hey—she spent most of her life on tour, so can you really blame her?

ICE CREAM

You scream I scream we all scream.

Yup. One of the first food items welcomed back onto the streets of Afghanistan after the fall of Osama et al. was—you guessed it—ice cream.

Even terrorists love it.

And we have the best.

Hands down.

Hence—one very simple reason for them to hate us even more.

Häagen-Dazs.

Ben and Jerry's.

Maybe that's the key to peace on earth.

Instead of dropping bombs we drop half pints of Chunky Monkey and Cherry Garcia and good old just plain chocolate.

Somebody get the Dove Bar people on the phone.

ANGELINA JOLIE

Okay. It's not just Angelina.

It's Angelina and Madonna and Rosie and Meg Ryan and whoever else in the female acting world fits the following requirements:

- Fame
- Cash
- Raging hormones
- A private jet

That's it. That's all you need. Those four simple items will allow you to fly into any Third World country and scoop up a black or brown or yellow baby, sign a couple of autographs and then head on home.

Where you can name the kid according to whatever whim strikes you. No need to adhere to the kid's actual ethnic or national background.

Chinese boy? Name him Johnny Boy.

African girl? Name her Ellen.

Totally up to you.

Now I have a cousin who adopted a Chinese kid years ago and named her Colleen. Which is well within her rights as the adoptive mom. But she wasn't famous or rich and didn't have a private plane so it took her THREE GODDAM YEARS to pull the whole thing off.

And why is it always white actresses flying in and scooping up?

Oprah flew into Africa in a private plane—with cash and fame and more than likely a SHITLOAD of raging hormones—and she started a school for African kids.

Why aren't black actresses flying into piss-poor white countries and nabbing parentless little pink children and jetting them back to the Hollywood Hills?

Grab a so-white-he's-almost-transparent white boy out of the Belfast slums of Northern Ireland, jet him off to a mansion in Bel Air and call him Jamal. Or Kaleel.

Never happen.

And you wanna know why?

'Cause caustic see-thru white kids with new names don't make for good press.

OR fashionable appearances.

I think a lot of these kids are like Gucci purses or Jimmy Choo shoes—not only are they cutting-edge accessories.

They're on sale.

THE WESTMINSTER KENNEL CLUB DOG SHOW

We've already discussed what most of our household pets are considered in other countries.

Throw in a full week's worth of dogs that have personal groomers and personal trainers and individual walkers and their own hotel rooms?

Death on a leash to a terrorist.

DR. LAURA AND MIKE AND MIKE IN THE MORNING

I like Dr. Laura.

I really do.

Besides the dirty pictures she took when she was young and foolish (and let's face the fact—weren't we all) in which she is actually very hot, she has grown up to piss people off. And by people I mean the morons with cell phone service who call up to complain about how their mom won't listen or their boyfriend doesn't wanna have sex anymore or their husbands want dinner on the table at such and such a time and her in a pink thong and high heels and they feel like they are not appreciated and blah blah blah and Dr. Laura comes thisclose to calling each one of them a whiny, self-obsessed, deaf and dumbass bitch. Over and over again. Which is what I wanna say when I listen to them. I love Mike and Mike in the Morning as well—when it's just the two of them OR the two of them and a sports expert discussing sports. Once they get into the cell phone calls from ingrate assholes on their way to work but unable to make it there without wondering how the Yankee pitching staff or the Islanders' goaltending or Eli Manning's left hamstring is gonna work out—I wanna grab a gun and take no hostages. This is a running, screaming, constant commentary on why we need to thin the herd on our own before the terrorists do it for us. Let's make it this easy—if you feel the urge to call Dr. Laura and ask whether you should stay in your current relationship even though your boyfriend has told you he doesn't love you and he's moving out and you weigh too much and he's banging your sister AND your best friend—and Dr. Laura tells you to get out now and you still don't wanna go? Save us all the trouble and swallow four bottles of aspirin. Better yet—make that sleeping pills. Maybe she'll even send you the prescription for them. If you really really actually for certain no bullshit now

I'm serious here cannot drive to work without finding out what an ex-lineman and a nerdy little Jewish guy think about Brett Favre's ballsack? Drive off the highway and into a lake. Now. Otherwise we may have to place a suitcase bomb in your garage long before an angry Muslim fundamentalist does.

ME

What terrorists and communists and dictators hate most of all is guys like me. Guys who make a living writing the kind of stuff you are reading right now. Humor, comedy, satire—these are the first things to go out the window in any society ruled by an iron fist or organized religion. Remember the uproar in Muslim countries over political cartoons lampooning the prophet Mohammad a couple of years back? Their first response was, of course, abrupt and absolute violence and when that was ridiculed they decided to publish their own Hitler and Bush Jr. cartoons. Which, of course, weren't funny.

In America, you have the freedom to say/paint/sing/dance or film whatever you want, and within your chosen medium you can satirize/denigrate/lampoon/cajole or blister any place, person or thing. Except Jesus.

Oh boy—stay away from Jesus.

I still remember years ago when Rudolph Giuliani was mayor of New York, an up-and-coming painter no one had ever heard of had a showing at a gallery in the city that included a piece in which the Virgin Mother was either urinating on Jesus or vice versa. I can't remember—which probably shows just how lapsed a Lapsed Catholic I truly am. Giuliani held a press conference and announced that such a piece of so-called art would never be displayed while he was the boss of the Big Apple. Much press coverage and many lawsuits ensued. Giuliani's approval rating shot through the roof. The Catholic Church went crazy. And considering how crazy the Catholic Church is to begin with—well—nuff said. I love an organization that says you can't paint an abstract portrait of Jesus or His Mom because that would be sacrilegious but hey—if you happen to see the face of Our Lord The Saviour or His Mom in a grilled cheese sandwich or in a bunch of random wood knots on a bathroom door or even in the wet birdshit-ridden bark of a public golf course maple tree—it's a miracle!

Call CNN! See if we can get Anderson Cooper down here—even though he's gay and we believe Jesus hates him!

I met Jesus once at a party in Boston sometime during the summer of 1985. He slipped out of a cloud of smoke in the living room—full beard, long hair, flannel shirt, scabby hands, the whole nine yards (I figured the flannel shirt was his way of fitting in a little). He walked up to me and said "Hey—they orderin' pizza or what?" I was so stunned, I didn't have the chance to tell him I think so but lemme ask you about the whole hellfire and damnation thing and whether The Clash will get back together or not because he kinda snarled at my silence and disappeared back into the crowd. My first reaction was shit—he better not hit on Ann (then my girlfriend and now my wife. By the way—I trust my wife now and I trusted her even then but, c'mon—we're talking about the Son Of God here. Even though she hates beards—who knows what tricks he has up his Holy Sleeve). Later when the pizza came I saw Jesus grabbing a slice and heard someone call him Doug and realized that in fact he wasn't the Messiah but a stonemason cousin of the guy throwing the party AND I'd had about seventeen beers and eight shots of Jameson's. So there ya go. Ya see what ya wanna see.

I was raised under the thumb of organized religion—I did twelve years in a Catholic school. The beauty of it was, the nuns and the priests and the monsignors and the bishops pretty much forbade laughter in the classroom and the hallways and in the church itself and all that led to was us laughing and giggling. When they published the list of banned books and records and movies in the church newsletter every Sunday, guess which books and records and movies we immediately sought out.

So—talk about simple math—because of Giuliani's public outrage and the front cover stories in the *New York Post* and the fact that it takes weeks to get the legal system lined up—the painter's little-known show became a sold-out sensation. Yup—it was good old-fashioned American-style capitalism gone wild. No one talked about whether the art was good or bad or even worthy of an admission price. It was all about the Benjamins and that most basic of human itches—curiosity. Not to mention that the people who were the most outraged by the moral fecundity of the art—a guy who was probably already in the process of cheating on his second wife and a church built on the concrete foundation of hiding and transporting pedophiles—were both standing on very soft and unstable moral ground. But he got the attention every politician craves and they—more than likely—saw a spike in the green cabbage their dedicated Sunday churchgoers drop into the basket each week. It was a win / win situation for the mayor AND the pope. Meanwhile—I got a five-minute routine out of it that I performed onstage and as a guest on David Letterman and Jay Leno. See? What a great system.

Stand-up comedy and comedy in general is the ultimate form of free speech because you get to poke holes in all the pretentious bubbles politicians and pundits and popes and pretenders try to float over our heads.

Every single album and DVD and television special and book—most likely including this one—that I have ever put on public sale has been banned or scorned or both by the Catholic Church. And—in the nineties—by Tipper Gore. She made them put an explicit lyrics/language sticker on my CDs and DVDs. Guess what happened? The sales quadrupled. So here's to hoping that—as you read this—the Catholic Church is warning teenagers and kids everywhere NOT to read *Why We Suck*. And just in case they are somehow not offended by and/or banning it yet—let me make sure they do. Sorry. This'll just take a couple of lines here:

JESUS WAS A GIANT HOMO!

TIPPER GORE'S A DYKE!

See? That didn't take too long. I may have just spiked the sales of this book by several thousand copies. I didn't take time to overtly offend the Muslims because, well, they actually BLOW YOU UP when they get pissed.

That's why—for all of its faults and fat pets and celebutards and warmongering figureheads—this country is still the best chance humanity has. There may be a lot of noise and news conferences and finger pointing but—in the end—you pretty much get to do or say whatever the fuck you want. Whether you are an idiot or a true sage—it doesn't really make a difference.

I'll take five Anna Nicole Smiths for every Martin Luther King. And if Reverend King wants to sleep around while he's sacrificing his life in the name of a world-altering civil charge—hey, line up the ladies.

Loud, stupid and overeating will suffice as long as we also have the funny, the fierce and the intellectual.

C-SPAN versus pay-per-view porn.

NPR versus Howard Stern.

Monster Truck Races versus the national Scrabble competition.

I want it all and I want it available 24/7.

Let the terrorists have their seventy-two virgins.

I'll take an actual, experienced hot forty-seven-year-old mom.

And a pizza.

CHAPTER 2

YOUR KIDS ARE NOT CUTE

eah yeah—we know. We all know. Your kids are special. They are talented and gifted and smart and gorgeous and endlessly cute and full of unbelievable inner light and extraordinary ability. They walked early talked early have expansive and unique motor skills and they should be kid model/stars. They have the most beautiful eyes and the most plump little red cheeks and the tiniest little toes and they are so endlessly fascinating that you just wish you could eat them all up in one big happy bite.

Yeah well—here's another headline: they also suck.

A lot.

To anyone outside of the precious inner sanctum that includes you, your spouse, the kid's grandparents and some of the tiny dimwit's classmates—your kid sucks so bad he or she is a living breathing vacuum of suckitude.

Everyone else hates him/her.

The dog. The cat. The other kids in the family.

The aunts, the uncles—even the godparents.

I am an uncle and godparent. I know of what I speak.

Yes, the kid may sometimes be cute and maybe even—every other odd time—on occasion—even almost bearable.

But most of the time he/she is a whining sniveling selfish thieving angry violent midget who not only makes a baboon look like a major intellectual but also uses his/her small size to advantage full well knowing no matter what evil he/she decides to create—my mommy and daddy will think it's cute.

Here are the actual facts: your kid is a gimongous germ factory. A walking talking coughing pants-pissing snot-snotting shit-directly-into-whatever-outfit-I-happen-to-be-sporting sniveling crying where's my mommy noise machine.

They have no sense of the real rules or how to behave or who not to puke on or what not to throw absentmindedly in any given direction that happens to strike their tiny unmanageable pealike brains.

When they want something they want it now. Right now.

And they have no idea what sharing is. Mine mine mine. Me me me. Mine, me, mine, me—me me me me me. What's mine is mine and what's not I will steal. Or break. Or hide.

They will defecate happily into their trousers and then walk around acting as if—literally—their shit don't stink.

As a matter of fact the only reason they shit in their pants is because THEY HAVE PANTS ON—otherwise they would shit directly onto whatever surface they happened to be standing over—the floor, the couch, the sidewalk—you name it.

The only thing separating children from wild jungle monkeys IS pants. Kids have them. Jungle monkeys don't.

To children—the world is their immediate and utter personal oyster. They do not know that all cookies are not THEIR cookies. That too many cookies can kill you. That cookies—or the elements involved in making them—cost money. That in order to gain cookie money you must have a marketable skill that results in your getting paid cash at the end of the week—thereby allowing you to not only purchase the cookies and/or the items needed to make them—but, in fact, giving you the power to eat all of the cookies bought/made yourself or decide to disseminate them amongst several other humans and animals who are either:

A. Nice to you

B. Listening to you

C. Painting your house/shoveling the snow around your house

D. Somehow related to you and too small to perform the duties required to get the cookie money but have had the rules explained to them and behaved well within the boundaries of those rules—one of which is finishing all of the normal food on their plate on this particular evening before being allowed to have a cookie.

Children are born without knowledge of cookies and playthings. When they first arrive the only sustenance they know of and seek is the milk they find at their mother's tits. But once they get a taste of the real fun stuff—BAM! Just like junkies—they become bottomless black holes waiting to take advantage and fill themselves up with sugar and chocolate, surround themselves with every single toy imaginable and make themselves king of the hill they happen to live on.

And why wouldn't they be selfish black holes?

They have lived inside a soft, warm, pouchy round sac in which they were fed endlessly and floated in a near constant sleep state for nine peacefully pain-free months.

Then someone unplugged the juice and yanked them out of dreamland right smack out into a cold hard world. Sometimes with a hard fast slap on the ass.

Why wouldn't they think of anyone but themselves?

It's like the old joke about men: you spend nine months waiting to come out of a vagina and the rest of your life trying to get back in.

So this whole theory about children being born as innocent and sinless vessels waiting to be ruined and overcome by the darkness and anger and hatred of an already evil world is a total crock. Kids are born as pure, untempered one-way evil beings. They get that umbilical cord cut and all holy hell breaks loose. First it's just the tits—which they almost never manage to relinquish. Then once they get a good look around while sucking on those nipples, they instantly become what they are born to be:

round mounds of unending, unblinking and eager chaos who will use their newly discovered cuteness to curry favor and gain more access to people and things they wish to eat, gnaw, lick, damage, hurt and break.

They will walk up to other kids—most times their own blood relatives—and violently attack them. Biting, whacking, kicking and screaming.

They will take sharp toys and jab them into the face of the family dog.

They will grab the dog's tail and try to yank it off.

They will lie about anything and everything all the fucking time—like Richard Nixon on crack. Odds are if you have kids what you hear all day every single day is some version of this: I didn't break that I didn't hide those I didn't shit my pants I didn't piss in the corner I would never ever, Mom! he's hitting me again, Dad! she's looking at me Ow Ow Ow Ow Ow Ow and so on and so forth and blubbedy blubbedy blah blah blah.

At some point in every day that passes, you will also witness many of these lovely and memorable moments:

Amazing little Ashley—dressed in her diminutive Vera Wang dress, accented by her Kenneth Cole kid patent leather shoes and the Paul Labrecque Salon tiny highlights in her hair—will yank the largest snottiest green snot out of her tiny evil nostril and then calmly deposit the pulsing glob of mucus into her angry mini-mouth. And then consider the taste as if she were consuming a dollop of the world's finest French wine.

Joyous bundle Joshua—such a tough little tot in his tiny Wrangler blue jeans and his lit-at-the-heels Nike King James kicks will offer up his impossibly angelic, heart-melting Hebrew smile mere moments before whacking the new baby kitten across its whiskered fluffy face with a hefty plastic baseball bat. His only regret? That the baseball bat wasn't made of wood. Or better yet—aluminum.

Cute and yummy Chase—sporting his Baby Gap khakis and his color-coded Baby Gap oxford blue polo—looking so much like his tall, preppy trust fund–encrusted papa—right down to the barely there slivers of comb-over hair—will suddenly stop socializing and stand in the middle of the living room with a strange, fuzzy focus ambling across his cute-as-a-button face. Then—a mere five or seven seconds later—the stench of crap and an acrid plume of urine will fill the room. Yes. He has in fact laid a giant Baby Gap load—along with enough piss to jam a juice box—into his don't I look like my dad one-hundred-and-fifty-five-dollar pants.

Elusive and oh such a handful Elizabeth—who refuses to keep her clothes on!—runs naked through the house screaming gay little screams and stopping only to roll around the floor so free and unashamed and full of boundless expressive energy—like a newly minted dance member of a jazzercise class she rambles from room to room until she stops to eat a bite of her dinner—look how she uses her fork—just like a grown-up little girl—and everyone is smiling at what a character she is—until she turns to her baby brother and stabs him in the head.

Stabbing screaming puking farting pissing shitting crying complaining whining moaning kicking angry goddam jellyfish.

That's right. Jellyfish. It may be the most inhumane trick they can pull out of their awful, incredible bag of tricky little tricks: The Jellyfish Move.

Those dirty filthy spineless mini-criminals.

The Jellyfish Move is a gift given only to the very small.

A true super-power that God imbues them with—apparently as a self-defense mechanism to avoid being captured and killed by angry parents and other adults whose patience has been worn down to the very bare barren marrow of their giant bones.

After the stabbing or the spilling or the screaming or the crying or all four combined into one elongated and loud private or public tantrum they run away on their vicious pudgy legs and once you actually corner them and manage to get your hands on them—finally grabbing ahold of their fat-filled midget arms—they become—literally—spine-free.

They squirm and collapse onto the floor or the sidewalk and suddenly—no matter how hard you try—you cannot lift them up. It's like trying to hug a bucket full of steam. It's as if you are trying to gather up two armfuls of slimy squiggling eels. No matter how hard you try—how hale you may hug—how gainful the gather—you cannot get a handle on them. They slither and slather and wiggle waggle out of your grasp and leave you cursing first under and then above your breath.

Twelve minutes later you stand there with sweat pouring down your brow and your face contorted into a bleak mask of Halloween terror—lips pursed, teeth grinding—and you finally break down and go to give them a nice hard whack on the ass and guess what—you miss because the human amoeba has somehow swaggled its ass out of your aiming area.

That's when you snap. You start chasing them as they slither and slather down the hallway—aiming and whacking and missing by so much your arm almost flies out of its socket.

And if you find yourself lucky enough to make some good, solid, sudden hand on ass contact—guess what again?

It works.

It sends a blood-rushing, breath-stopping shock right from their ass up into their elbows and out of their wickedly wide-open eyes. First there is a moment of absolute silence and then—of course—they start to cry. That's the key moment—when they squinch their eyes tightly shut and begin to howl you gotta grab 'em before they begin the amoeba dance again. Grab 'em and whack 'em a second time and carry them off to bed. This, of course, is all based on the fact that the tantrum has occurred in the private inner sanctum of your own home.

Because if it happens in public? All bets are off. You get a kid who wants to pull The Jellyfish Move in a store or in a restaurant or God forbid out on the sidewalk and pushes you to the point where you have to whack him or her on the rear end? Get ready for almost every passerby to call you out as a bad parent or to shun you like you bear a scarlet letter on your chest or to beckon a nearby officer of the law and claim themselves a witness to child abuse. And once a kid realizes you can't get away with hitting him or her in public? Those tantrums will happen over and over until the toy or piece of candy or place they wanna go is handed over in a split second. They will cry and kick and jellyfish their way to every little thing they want.

And you deign to tell me they are angels.

You dare to call them cute.

Hugs not drugs?

Bullshit. I say drugs. Drugs with a capital D and plenty of them. Drugs in all kinds of colors and flavors. Foolproof kid-type drugs that look and taste like candy and ice cream so they greedily suck them down like the one-way elves they are and end up getting knocked on their self-centered pink-cheeked hair-free little asses.

They wanna use the dreaded Jellyfish Move and become immobile unassailable amoebas? Good. Let's ply them with sweet-tasting sugar-coated chemicals that will make them pure putty in our nonsilly gi-normous parent hands.

We owe it to ourselves and all the innocent, childless people on planes, trains and other forms of public transportation.

CHAPTER 3

PLEASE DRUG YOUR CHILDREN

 know I know—you find it distasteful and dangerous and just plain wrong. Give drugs to my kids? you say, What kind of a mother/father do you think I am? But what you are really worried about is this: how can I do it and know for a fact that my kids won't slip into a coma and somehow send me to prison for life when all I really wanted was some peace and quiet.

Hey—calm down. It's fine. Better than that—it's legal. Besides—it's not like you're asking them to teethe on a lead paint–covered choo choo train outsourced by Toys R Us from the bowels of China. These are good, solid, FDA-approved American drugs. The very same ones you take yourself in big tired parent-type doses.

Slip the little brat a simple shot—NyQuil actually comes with an actual plastic shot glass—of a basically harmless and not to mention very patriotic over-the-counter medicine that will not only taste good but within fifteen minutes have him or her sound asleep and dreaming about sugar plums. Or video games. Or high school shooting sprees—whatever the hell it is that children dream about these days. Meanwhile, you and your better half can tear each other's clothes off and have at it or just sit down in front of the TV and absolutely ignore each other while watching some good old-fashioned American-style sex and violence.

Now if you find yourself still hung up on a morals hook here—let's get very specific. We all know that a completely exhausted kid is a kid who still has at least two or three hours' worth of kicking and random screaming left. And the final stretch of random screaming is often the worst—it's the Daytona 500 of guttural effects. After nine o'clock at night—when a kid gets on that endless crying jag treadmill—you will hear sounds emerging from the tiny beast that even Bigfoot would run away from.

I'm talking noises coyotes can't even make. Forget howls. We're talking yowls. Yelps. Caterwauls. Peals of terror so highly pitched that entire shelves full of glassware may explode—not to mention synapses in your own brain.

So if you don't relish the idea of shopping for new dinner plates and coffee mugs while one side of your face is frozen and you are dragging your limp left foot behind you—give the little shit a dose of NyQuil. Or Benadryl. Two great forms of morphine in a bottle that has been so watered down you don't need to have a discussion with a doctor to get it. Just walk into any drugstore or pharmacy and pick up as many bottles as you want. And stop worrying about the side effects—that's why they make CHILDREN'S NyQuil and PEDIATRIC cough medicine. Smaller doses for smaller kidneys and smaller brains.

Why do you think they make these products in kid-friendly flavors? To make it easier to get it down their goddam gullets, that's why. Hey—I think they should chock these products full of all the vitamins and daily nutritional supplements every kid is supposed to ingest on a day-to-day basis and make them taste like every type of food kids love—cheeseburger flavor, Chicken McNugget flavor—pizza, popcorn, fudge—you name it. That way we could feed and drug them at the exact same time and keep them under control for the first three to ten years of their uncivilized, unruly, bad-smell jammed little lives—just long enough for us to get regular sleep and enough free time to do what we want—travel and watch football and read and jerk off. Then—once the rules have been ingrained in their thick-and-only-getting-thicker skulls—we slowly wean them off the baby drugs and up onto the adult doses of antidepressants and alcohol and recreational drugs we adults need just to get through life as it has to be lived.

Now maybe it's the product names that are putting you off. Maybe it's the ny in NyQuil or the dryl in Benadryl. That's a pretty easy fix. Would you like it better if we called them LoveQuil and BenAsleep? Or even better maybe QuietQuil or PeaceQuil. Or just cut right to the chase and name them after what YOU have to gain from putting them into a parent-induced mini-coma: Sexadryl.

When I was a kid—oh yeah, there are definitely gonna be a lot of those types of speeches in this particular chapter—my parents gave us whiskey when we were sick. First sign of a cough or a sniffle or a sneeze or a sore throat and they got a nice hot toddy down your throat. Hot toddy being a cute kid-friendly name for Irish whiskey heated up on the stovetop. Two minutes later we were fast asleep. Supposedly fighting off the onrushing effects of the flu. I don't remember whether my parents tricked us into drinking hot toddies even when we weren't feeling sick but hey—that's another positive example of just why you should be drugging your kids. Twenty, thirty—even forty-five years later they won't remember a goddam thing.

Although I do bloody well remember getting whacked on the ass by my parents and the reason I remember was because it hurt. And whatever it was I had been doing wrong—lying, cheating, stealing, biting, whacking—or all five things at approximately the same time?—I stopped doing right away once they whacked me.

I also have a scar worth about a hundred stitches on my left arm that runs from the bottom of my palm all the way up my wrist—halfway to the elbow. How did I get it? Fooling around with my older brother in front of a glass door in the kitchen of our apartment. He went one way and I threw a left jab and my left arm went right through the door.

By the way—you can go through a glass window or door and not really do any damage—it's when you pull your appendage BACK THROUGH the same glass window or door that you get cut. You also bleed—a lot. I don't even know how many stitches that gaping hole required but you know what? I never punched my way through a glass door again.

Once, in the living room of our apartment, my brother and a gaggle of cousins convinced me to wrap a towel around my neck like a cape and pretend I was Superman, which I did. Then they convinced me to stand on the back of the couch and pretend it was a window ledge on The Daily Planet building, which I did. Then they convinced me to jump from the window ledge over the coffee table (which was doubling as a newspaper truck parked in front of The Daily Planet building) and save Lois Lane (my cousin Betty Ann) from the clutches of the bad guy (my brother Johnny, of course). Needless to say, that was the day I learned that I couldn't fly. I landed on the edge of the coffee table, taking several stitches in the face. Did I ever try to fly again? Nope. Done deal. The quick trip to the emergency room, the blood, the pain, the giant numbing needle in the lips—more than enough to convince me I was born an earthbound creature.

The same theory works with any other form of pain for kids—burning a hand on a stove, getting your tongue stuck to an icy mailbox or a frozen fencepost—feel it once and you never wanna feel it again. It's human nature. I'm sure Jimi Hendrix made a mental note never to puke in his sleep again right before he choked to death.

You have to hit kids. You have a responsibility to do so. Just to show them who's in charge and to remind them that there are boundaries that need to be respected.

Besides—when they are very very small they have diapers on—which means their asses are padded and pretty much pain proof. As they get older and lose the diapers they may actually get used to the ass whacking and become somewhat immune to the pain. That's when you have to change it up a little.

CHAPTER 4

I HAD SEX WITH KATHIE LEE GIFFORD (AND SHE WAS AMAZING)

ust wanted to make sure you were still paying attention.

If you went right from the table of contents to this chapter—you screwed yourself.

Because I didn't sleep with Kathie Lee Gifford. But in the first chapter of this book—"Why Everyone Hates Us"—I mentioned you by name.

So anyways—back to raising kids:

I called my mom just now to gain her perspective on what is necessary in terms of hitting or not hitting children. Let me describe her to you: if you put Mary Tyler Moore, Mother Teresa and Joe Pesci in a blender, set it on high and let it mix up to a fine, thick chocolatey shake—out would step my mom. She's eighty-one years old but looks like she's sixty, has the energy of someone in their early forties and will kiss you one second, kid you another and threaten to kick your ass the next. I love her. For many reasons. Some of which you are about to witness:

[the phone rings several times]

Hello.

Hey Ma.

Johnny?

No. It's Denis.

Oh, Denis. (laughing) How are you?

I'm good. Hey Ma—

Mrs. Timmons died of cancer.

Who?

Mrs. Timmons, down the street. Remember I think you and Tommy Barolli egged her house one time?

That wasn't us. I told you—

Dead as a doornail. Smoked four packs a day. Same thing with Mr. Willoughby from up on Edlin Street. He had horrible cancer.

Is there good cancer?

That's not funny, Brian. Quit that smoking.

It's Denis, Ma.

I know who it is. Uncle Jerry's got terrible pain in his back again God help us that that's not some kind of tumor or something and do you remember Jimmy Hanrahan used to work with Daddy?

Big Jimmy?

Yes. The father.

Yeah.

He has brain cancer.

From smoking?

No—he never smoked. Never drank either. Straight as an arrow Jimmy Hanrahan.

What about Little Jimmy?

The son?

Yeah.

Oh God. He died last year. Terrible cancer.

So—is there a difference between the terrible cancer and the horrible cancer?

(stop making fun of me) Denis.

(still making fun) Ma.

What are you calling for?

I'm just wondering—when we were kids—how often you and Dad used to hit us.

(suspicious) Why?

I was just curious.

Well—your father one time when you kids were small Johnny forged his name on some paper at school and the nuns called up about it and I told Daddy that you know he had to set an example with all these kids because this could be the beginning of some bad behavior here so we got all you kids gathered up in the hallway and he took Johnny into the bathroom and I think he used his belt but anyways he gave him a good couple of whacks in the bathroom with the door closed and I think the message got across and that was that.

I remember that.

You do? Well then I guess it did what it was supposed to do. Kids are the house that they come out of Denis—whatever goes on inside that house that's the way the kids're going to behave when they go out into the world.

Dad used his belt—what would you use when you hit us?

Whatever I had in my hand. I dunno. I really had to hit you and Betsy. The two of you—you two were always getting into some kind of cadology.

Okay.

Okay?

Okay, Ma.

That's it?

Yup.

You know Brian Leary hasn't had a cigarette in almost fifteen years now?

I know.

He rides bikes all the time in races.

I know.

Okay then, honey—thanks for calling.

Okay, Ma.

Bye.

CLICK.

(Let me just take a moment here to note: the word "cadology" was one my mother threw around the house on a daily basis. Cut the cadology, knock it off with the cadology, yer not kidding anyone with that load of cadology—these were just a few of the variations we heard throughout our lives. We just assumed it was an Irish word. My parents had learned Gaelic when they were in school and my father was very fond of the word "ammodon"—our spelling—which as far as we could tell was Irish for asshole or jackass because everyone he referred to as an ammodon was, in fact, an asshole or a jackass or a clear combination of both. Cadology sounded like it was connected to science and maybe a behavioral science but that would seem out of character for my mom. After this conversation with her I looked it up in an online dictionary. Nothing. So I tried the big giant hulking eight-pound *Webster's* dictionary I keep at my feet when I'm writing. Nothing. Now I am beginning to believe my mother just made the word up—a pleasant and lilting term she decided to toss around perhaps just as a way to confuse us. I check Merriam Webster Online. Nothing. I Google the Google Thesaurus. Type in "nonsense." Cadology does not come up. I change the spelling—codology. Merriam Webster Online—nada. Big Hulking Eight-Pound *Webster*? Nope. My Irish-English Dictionary? Not a chance. English-Irish? Forget it. Irish-English and English-Irish Online? Not there. I even went to *Encyclopaedia Britannica*—which is a goddam encyclopedia from fucking BRITAIN—where they pretty much invented words. No codology. Finally I call my sister Ann Marie and get her husband Neil—who I will speak further of much further on—and he says that my Ann told his Ann that I'm working on the book but that reminds him about my cousin Ann who we have to call Nancy because there are too many Anns in the family on this side of the Atlantic but anyways Nancy whose Ann ran into my cousin Betty Ann who was talking to one of my Aunt Anns in Ireland and she had just used the term "codology" in reference to her daughter Ann's baby Mary Ann and that's the point at which my head almost exploded. So Neil went to a website called World Wide Words while he was telling me this because he said whenever my mother uses a word that he doesn't know he skips all the normal sources and goes right to this place and sure enough—there it was:

Codology.

H. V. Morton in 1930 wrote that codology was "a science unknown to us in England which involved individuals or entire villages performing a joke, hoax or parody at the expense of an Englishman. Derives from the term 'cod' which is Irish for 'bunk.'"

So it was, in fact, a science. A science of bullshit that my mother was clearly trained to identify and defame. Goddam those British bastards. If they had never invaded Ireland then the villagers would never have had to come up with what was essentially a clever game to employ when wishing to evade questioning and the giving up of important information and it wouldn't have been handed down from generation to generation so my mother would never have witnessed it being used as a child and therefore become privy to all the nuances and tricks and nervous tics and tells involved in the process of putting one over on somebody else and I, most importantly of all, would have gotten away with a lot more shit. Other favorites of hers included rigamarole, hooliganism and cahoots. All three of which—along with codology—were fired at us, I realize now, whenever we did try to lie, cheat, steal and/or bullshit our way around her set of rules. Dammit. She knew what she was talking about. Okay—back to the beating.)

I have definite and vitally bright images of that beating in the bathroom she is referring to—so gathering us around to watch Johnny getting dragged in there and the sounds of him getting hit with that belt more than certainly did their job. After that, I don't think my dad ever had to administer another belt beating—all he had to do was threaten to take it off or begin to unbuckle it.

And I distinctly remember how my mom would whack us on the knuckles with a hair brush or a wooden spoon or even a dough roller—whatever she happened to have in hand when we got on her nerves. She was like a Ninja Mom—suddenly springing on you with a fork or a can of Spam or a whole cucumber. My mom was like Rachel Ray on steroids: she would be chopping up some carrots one second and then furiously mugging you with a Crock-Pot cover the next.

My dad? All my mom needed to say was "Wait until your father hears about this." Yeah—that's right. Until he HEARS about this. Most kids receive the "Wait until your father gets home"—which usually meant you had at least a few hours to come up with a different story or maybe move a few facts in the story around a little bit. Embellish. Rehearse. But my dad was a mechanic and he worked in a garage about five minutes from the apartment so all Ma had to do was pick up the phone and about seven minutes later he was headed up the back stairs—removing the belt from his pants as he did so. Your ass would start hurting just watching him.

Let's put it in plain, blunt verse: if someone punched me hard in the face every time I lit up a cigarette I'd either have to start smoking while wearing a football helmet or just quit smoking. The same Pavlovian dog rule applies to kids—anything they get hit for doing you can be damn sure they will not wish to do again. No pain? No gain.

The state of Massachusetts recently considered a bill brought by its Joint Committee On Children that would become the country's first ban on corporal punishment of kids. It cost several million dollars.

(This reminds me—by the way—of the study done two years ago—again costing millions of dollars—to find out that being in a rock 'n' roll band actually shortens your life span. Yeah. They had to spend that much to figure out that being in a band increases your alcohol and drug intake and places undue stress on the heart, lungs etcetera etcetera. Not to mention being married to Courtney Love. That REALLY shortens your life span. Especially if there's a shotgun in the house.)

So Taxachusetts actually spent millions of dollars of taxpayers' money and an unbelievable amount of absolutely wasted time to figure out that whacking kids on the ass or across the back of the head not only makes them cry—it strikes the fear of God into them. This is roughly equivalent to spending seven million dollars and sixteen months to find out that sticking your hand in a fire not only hurts like hell—it sears the flesh and almost certainly guarantees you will never ever ever ever do it again.

What the fuck is getting a good hard kick in the ass or a sharp swack across your skull SUPPOSED to do? Make you ask for more? For every action there is an equal and opposite REaction—in this case? Whatever the fuck you just did wrong you sure as hell won't do wrong again.

Unless you actually LIKE the pain, in which case the physical abuse becomes a defendable form of medical research: your honor, by smacking my son several times over the course of the last three weeks I was able to discover that he is, in fact, some kind of pain freak.

Shit—when I was a kid even school wasn't a safe haven. The nuns would whack you with any weapon available—a ruler, a stapler, their hands. I had a nun wallop me across the back of my head one time because I couldn't come up with seven of the ten commandments. She hit me with a Bible. I asked her if thou shalt not hit a kid with the holy book was one of the seven I had missed. The class laughed. She hit me with the Bible again. It was worth the pain.

Even if the nuns hit you for no good reason your parents always took their side. "They wouldn't be hitting you unless you were doing something wrong! They're nuns fa crissakes! They're married ta God!"

My mother always took the side of the nuns AND the priests. Of course, my brother Johnny and I didn't really give her any reason to think we were innocent of any given charges. If there was a stupid plan to be hatched—egging the convent or stealing a priest's wallet or drinking the holy wine (I wanted to see if it actually made me act more like Jesus, which—if He was a giggling, sneaky, bumbling mess—it did)—my brother and I were, generally speaking, somehow involved. And once we established that kind of reputation, my mother's trust was pretty much broken beyond resolve.

It always cracks me up when you see the mom of some guy who's been accused of some horrible crime on the TV news. No matter what the guy may have done or how guilty he may seem there's always one person left on God's green earth who thinks he's not guilty—his mom. Murder, grand theft, fraud—you name it. The guy could be convicted and rotting in jail and after everyone including his wife and kids had given up and decided he was guilty—his mom would always feel the opposite. If O.J.'s mom were still around she would be telling anyone who asked and even those who didn't how her son could never have murdered Nicole.

Not my mom. Whatever the charges brought happened to be—even if they accused me of assassinating the sitting president—point a camera in my mom's face and the first thing she would say is "he did it." Followed by "And I'll bet if you dig a little deeper you'll find this is just the tip of the goddam iceberg. I'm sure he's got something to do with this whole global warming crap. I wouldn't put anything past this kid. He's trouble with a capital T. I wouldn't be surprised to find out HE was the one who killed O.J.'s wife."

Most moms I know and have met feel that the women who marry their sons will never measure up to expectations. Not my mom. She couldn't believe I came home with my wife. I think—for the first couple of visits anyway—she thought I was drugging Ann or possibly even blackmailing her. Of course, she's right. Not about the drugging. About the chances that I would have won the heart of a woman as bright, funny and beautiful as my wife. The odds were very much against me. I really had to turn on the charm. And the drugs didn't hurt. I'm kidding. I've often thought if my wife and I ever got divorced, I'd have to fight the courts for visitation rights—to keep my mom from visiting Ann.

Of course we want our kids to have a better life than we had but in this country things have gotten out of control. My parents were born and raised on farms in County Kerry, Ireland. They literally made the proverbial five-mile trek to school on foot every morning and the same five miles back every afternoon. When my mom told my wife about this my wife asked, "Didn't your dad ever come and pick you up?" My mother said yes, which led my wife to exhale a sigh of relief.

"He'd come out and meet us in the fields and lift each of us up and give us a hug and then we'd continue on our way home." He came out to LITERALLY just pick them up and spread a little welcome-home love and then he'd continue working in the fields. He was a farmer. Feeding his eight or ten or whatever number of kids he had. He probably didn't even remember how many kids he had. I can't even remember how many aunts and uncles I have on my mom's side of the family. I'm amazed that she can. They grew up in a world where death, disease and destruction lay in wait around almost every single corner. And they only had about five corners—down in the village. Once you got onto the road out of the tiny town—they didn't even have corners. Just long and winding dirt roads with ditches or turf bogs on either side. Trees? Hah. Trees were for pussies.

There was nothing except the dark wet sky and the cold hard ground and an assortment of atrocities in between as you headed the seven miles back to the farm. How any of them survived is a mystery to me.

My mom once brought a box of ancient black-and-white photos from Ireland in the 1930s and '40s—when she was growing up—over to our house in Connecticut and flipped through them in front of my wife Ann and me—telling us what eventually happened to each person pictured. It went something like this:

FLIP:

That's Mary Aberdeen from the Aberdeens two farms away. She got kicked in the head by a horse when we were ten. Died right there on the spot.

FLIP:

This is Fiona Something Or Other. She got this fever and was never the same. She became like retarded almost. Then she fell into a fireplace when we were fifteen.

FLIP:

This guy here was lost in the ocean. It just swallowed him up one night. He was walking along the beach just minding his own business and— then he was gone.

FLIP:

This would be my second or third cousin—she was a Burke I think— and she got what they would call multiple sclerosis now or whatever Jerry Lewis is always on about with those kids and she got married and had some kids of her own and then she was in a wheelchair but she could like stand up and walk around a little bit and then one night all the kids were in bed and she had a couple of drinks and she got up out of the wheelchair to throw some more turf onto the fire and then she fell into the fire and that was the end of it.

FLIP:

This was a fourth cousin of your father's who got a pitchfork in the eye.

FLIP:

This was a friend of your Uncle Jerry's who got split into two pieces by lightning.

FLIP:

This lady here was someone's aunt who got some horrible growth on her leg and never told anyone and then when it burst she got run over by a car.

FLIP:

This man was a great friend of your grandfather's who fell out of the hayloft in the barn and got trampled by a horse and then got cancer and then fell into a fire. Do you see how lucky Mary Aberdeen was now?

FLIP:

This man dropped dead.

FLIP:

This lady disappeared.

FLIP:

This man got melted.

FLIP:

This young boy on the bike was like a midget or something and then didn't he grow up to be a great big strapping man until he got hit by lightning out in a field and then he shrank up and was kind of bent over for a long time after until he got the cancer and then he died.

FLIP:

This man had no fingers.

FLIP:

This man had been out in the fields at night and was found in a bog with his head bashed in.

FLIP:

That lady went to bed one evening and woke up dead.

FLIP:

This lady died last year and now her whole family is dead.

And on and on it went. Ann and I sat riveted as the parade of tragedy and manifest destiny unfolded in front of us, wondering just how many Irish people had perished in day-to-day disease diagnoses and accidents and some who apparently had just been smited from above in mysterious circumstances versus those lost during The Great Potato Famine. We could barely keep count of the faces as they flashed by, one old photo after another. It gave me a rush of sense memory from when I was a kid—my mom constantly warning of the sudden possibility of lurking danger and immediate payback for the slightest of sins, not to mention how people could just be turned into instant piles of smoking ash.

I know that growing up in my day I had seventeen cousins here in America and two sisters and a brother and we all lived near each other and every time we went on vacation or just to the beach there were about eight or nine kids in the back of my dad's station wagon and there were no seat belts and at least four kids in the way way back and the window was always all the way down because the car had no air-conditioning and the entire car—the floor, the side panels, the dashboard, the roof—every single part of the car was made of steel and since you weren't strapped in whenever the car hit a pothole or any other bump in the road your head bounced off the roof or the side or the floor or if you sat in the way way back maybe even all three one right after another and we thought that was FUN because no matter what you did to someone else back there my father couldn't reach you unless he threw something at you from the front driver's seat and if he did that he usually hit one of the kids in the middle row instead and by the way if you fell out the back window onto the highway they didn't turn around to go back and get you or make a sudden stop they kept right on going 'cause it was just one less mouth to feed.

I remember a Green Hornet cane that turned into a knife and a kid named Matt and another kid named Patrick and a toy Batman motorcycle that shot missiles but my mother says I never owned either one of those toys and Matt was a pain in the ass and there was never anyone in this family named Patrick except your Uncle Patrick so if there was another Patrick shouldn't she remember? No wonder they never took pictures. It was like the Mafia with children.

And by the way the station wagon was marine green with a painted-over gas company decal on each door because my dad bought it secondhand and retooled it himself because not only was it all he could afford but they never had cars when he was growing up.

My dad grew up with a shitload of other kids on a farm adjacent to the one my mom grew up on—real storybook romance territory. His mom died giving birth to the last kid. He only went to school until he was twelve and then he had to go to work to help feed the rest of the family, along with my Uncle Patrick. One of the kids—who would've been my Uncle Matt—died from something when he was five. No one even remembers what disease he died from—they didn't have enough time or money to find out. They pretty much just buried him and kept on milking the cows. Hey—he's lucky he got a grave. In those days you had as many kids as possible because you figured some would die, some would get killed and the rest would still be able to carry stuff. You got a cold back in those days—you could pretty much kiss your ass goodbye. My dad grew up the hard way. When he decided to come to America, he was given what all the Irish who were headed across the pond got—something called A Living Wake. That's where everyone who knew or was related to you gathered themselves down at the village pub and placed whatever money they could manage into an envelope for you—which they gave to you with their solemn goodbyes because odds were very much against them ever seeing you again. So my dad got on a big boat and two weeks later landed in New York City with thirty-seven dollars in his pocket. Almost enough to buy a cup of giant fagulated coffee and a pumpkin cream–filled muffin at Starbucks in today's terms.

So if you wanted to complain about ANYTHING in our house—you were up shit's creek without a paddle. There wasn't a single solitary complaint you could make about your clothes or your toys or your situation that my mom and dad couldn't dial right back down to the basic facts of life—hey, yer lucky yer even here.

NOT TO MENTION the house they lived in had no electricity and the toilet was a shack out in the backyard. My older brother Johnny and I lived in the attic of a three-decker and my parents and everyone else lived in the third-floor apartment. When my dad got enough money to buy a ranch house in a better neighborhood Johnny and I lived in the basement. We went from dwelling above the rest of the family like strange, pink-cheeked bats to dwelling in the bowels of the house like strawberry blond goddam rats.

The attic sucked 'cause we had to walk up three flights to get to the apartment and then another steep flight to get to the place where we slept. The basement sucked because we slept right next to the boiler room and the water heater would kick on and off and make one helluva racket. So when we did something wrong and my mom or my dad said "Go to your room!" it was a genuine hard-ass punishment.

Today? My kids each have televisions and giant computer screens and electric guitars and sofas and their own individual bathrooms and Xboxes and PlayStations and stack after stack of DVDs and CDs and video games. As a matter of fact when the kids get into trouble my wife and I say "That's it! WE'RE going to your room. You guys go sit in our bedroom and read actual books."

When I was growing up we had three TV channels and there were a handful of movie stars and only one or two kid stars plus Lassie and Mr. Ed and a dolphin who answered to the name Flipper. No one in my neighborhood ever even dreamed of being on TV. Not even me. Wasn't an option.

We knew Lassie AND Flipper were both smarter and better off than any of us could ever hope to be—not to mention the talking horse. We had

clothes on our backs and homework to do and were expected to have paper routes by the time we were twelve and shovel snow off sidewalks in
the winter and paint apartments in the summer if we wanted money in
our pockets. I got a job in a diner twenty-five yards down the block from
the local hockey rink as did my older brother my two sisters and almost
all of my cousins and that was considered a choice place to work because
they gave you free food at the end of your shift, which was very handy
because in the house I grew up in there were no late meals. My mom
served supper at six sharp and if you weren't there to eat it you just didn't
eat. My dad worked two jobs so he would come home from his day job
around four in the afternoon, take a quick nap and then eat dinner at six
and go to his night job. What did we have for supper? Guess what. Supper. Meaning, whatever the hell she decided to cook that day. She served
it hot and when they placed the bowls on the table you had to grab as
much as you could and start forking it away 'cause once it was gone that
was the end of it. No special meals for anyone. You didn't like what she
was serving up you didn't eat. Plus—we lived in an Irish household so
forget about food that tasted good. If you could taste it at ALL you were
way ahead of the game. If you downed a forkful of potatoes and they
tasted like dogshit your tastebuds did a goddam kitchen table jig. Irish
people eat as though they were doing penance—it's punishment for your
sins and just a way of laying a foundation in your stomach for all the
booze that's about to follow it down your gullet. Here's an example of a
few traditional Irish recipes my mom cooked up for us:

CABBAGE POTATO CHUCK ROAST

14 sticks of butter
Pinch of salt
Cabbage
Seven hundred potatoes
2 pounds chuck roast beef

Place chuck roast, potatoes and cabbage into a very large pot of already
boiling water. Boil for five hours. Turn heat down to a simmer. Drop in 14
sticks of butter and pinch of salt. Let boil for one more hour. Then another
fifteen minutes. Then a couple more minutes. Make sure all germs and taste
have been boiled out. Serve.

Here's her Thanksgiving recipe:

TURKEY DAY

47 sticks of butter

Cabbage

Six thousand potatoes

Fifteen cans of jellied cranberry sauce

65 boxes of Shake 'N Bake Stuffing Mix

Jar of Skippy Peanut Butter—Creamy Style

Two celery sticks

Five carrots

Some peas

Pie

One giant—and I do mean giant—turkey

Boil several really huge pots of water. Take all the stuff out of the inside of the turkey. Begin cursing in Gaelic. Stick the Shake 'N Bake Stuffing stuff into turkey. Slather turkey with melted butter. Place in oven with heat as high as knob will turn. Clean rest of house for one hour. Throw potatoes and cabbage and peas and carrots into boiling pots of water. Eat some pie. Dip two celery sticks into jar of Skippy Creamy Peanut Butter and eat. Check turkey. Probably not even close to being done. Begin cursing in English. Baste turkey with tons more butter. Place back in oven. Open the fifteen cans of jellied cranberry sauce and combine into one giant heap of cranberry sauce on a large table platter. Eat more pie. Call relatives in Ireland and gossip/slander etc for half-hour. Check turkey. Begin cursing in Gaelic/English mixture that sounds like a third and almost completely separate language. Serve large amounts of whiskey and beer to guests who have already begun to arrive. Serve pie. Check turkey. Still not done. Clean up kitchen for half an hour. Threaten to begin making peanut butter and cranberry jelly sandwiches unless drunken jackasses stay out of the goddam kitchen. Check turkey again. STILL not done. Threaten to move back to Ireland—include "If I never see another turkey again it won't be soon enough for me" speech. Remove potatoes etc. from pots. Place in bowls. Smell turkey burning. Curse. Serve.

Fridays were special because as Catholics we couldn't eat meat. So that meant my mom had to break out one of her fish recipes. Like this one:

FISH

One loaf Wonder Bread

8 sticks butter

Cabbage

Seven hundred potatoes

Six boxes Gorton's Frozen Fish Sticks

Two large bottles ketchup

Place fish sticks in flat pan in oven. Turn knob up as far as it will go. Place cabbage and potatoes in large pot of already boiling water. Wait twenty minutes. Take fish sticks out while middle seems to still be frozen. Pour ketchup over them until they disappear beneath a sea of red. Wait another hour for flavor to evaporate from cabbage and potatoes and they are soft to the touch. Make sign of the cross. Serve.

We never went hungry. We never were at a loss for drama and the men were absolutely never ever allowed or expected to cook or clean up. Our job was to shovel and bang nails and fix flat tires and kill mice and rats and giant insects. We played football and baseball and hockey right there in the street. No helmets no shin guards no crying. You got hit with a puck or a stick or a bat or a ball you walked it off and kept on playing.

Everyone had scars and broken bones and some kids even had strange dents in their heads and some kids stuttered and other kids lisped and some had weird walks—everyone had something wrong with them and nobody's parents could either afford to get them fixed or had the time to even do so. You sucked it up and kept moving forward. You couldn't do your homework you flunked out quick and went to work pumping gas.

It was the natural order of things—the food chain in action—the way God meant things to be. Those who could run faster got ahead quicker and the weaker links in the chain got eaten by the enemy.

Shit—I was late for work right after school one day so I ran across the street against oncoming traffic and got nailed by a Buick right on my left ass cheek—and if you think I have no ass now just imagine how small it was when I was fourteen years old. It was basically all bone. Anyways— the good news was I bounced right back up and the traffic came to a stop—including my bus—and I not only made it to work on time but I had no desire to sit down for the next two weeks.

And like I said before—that was when the front ends of automobiles were still made out of steel, not these pussy-assed plastic bumpers they have now.

I wasn't the only one, by the way—lots of kids got hit by cars and half the time the drivers were drunk. EVERY adult was drunk back then. It wasn't against the law to drink and drive. And there were no cupholders in cars—so if you wanted to drink and drive you had to be able to balance the goddam beer can or whiskey bottle and drive at the same time. Come to think of it—that's how they probably gauged whether or not you were too drunk to drive back then—if you dropped your drink—time to get out and walk.

And there was no rehab in those days—none at all. If you were Catholic, you had Lent—forty days at the tail end of winter when you could give up anything in service to Our Lord Jesus—who supposedly spent forty days in the desert with the devil whispering sweet little nothings into his holy ear. As a sign of your devotion to His noteworthy struggle, Catholics are meant to conduct a fast from one of their favorite things—food, sex, candy—whatever you might find enjoyable and hard to stay away from. Believe me, most Irish Catholic men spent that month and a half on the wagon. Jesus resists the temptation offered by Satan—the Irish resist Bushmill's and Budweiser. I'd call it just about even.

My brother Johnny got clipped by a drunk driver while he was delivering papers on his bike. He was in the hospital for a couple of days and then he came home. But for those two days? There was extra potatoes and meat for everyone else. The food chain in action. There were no airbags no seat belts no helmets no Ritalin no Adderall no special ed classes no learning disabilities no tutoring no nothing—you had to be a REAL retard to be considered a retard. Talk therapy in those days consisted of my mother saying "That homework better be done by dinnertime or you are gonna have to deal with your father!" Everybody got hurt and stabbed and shot in the face with BB guns and bitten by dogs and slapped by their parents and fed shitty food—no one was smart or good-looking or gifted or unique. The toys alone would kill or maim you.

One time I was cutting through the alley between Tommy Mullaney's building and ours when I heard my brother shout "Hey faggot!"—his usual way of saying hello. I looked up to see Johnny and his best friend Cliffey DeCoursey down at the other end of the alley with a brand-new toy in tow—a bow and arrow. Not a TOY bow and arrow, an actual, real live bow-and-arrow set you would use to go hunting for venison. Now, Cliffey DeCoursey's parents deciding to give him a real bow and arrow as a birthday present would—in this day and age—be either the foundation for a record-setting lawsuit by my parents or the beginning of a foster child investigation or both. But in those days it just made Cliffey and every other kid in the neighborhood think they were cool. Anyways, one millisecond of a nanosecond after I heard the word "faggot" and stopped and glanced up—which probably says something about my own self-esteem—my brother let the arrow go and I am telling you THUNK! that's how quick the arrow stuck itself in my skull. Two inches above my right eye—I still have the scar. Cliffey went one way and Johnny the other and I was left standing there like some kind of horrifying William Tell Overture.

I climbed the alley fence and ran up the three wooden flights on the back of my building—the arrow still in place—and ran into the kitchen where my Uncle Jerry put down his beer and yanked the thing out of my head— at which point I started to howl and he said "It's out goddammit yer fine so shut up!" My dad said I didn't need stitches but my mom went into a what if he's brain damaged now and he's not that bright to begin with monologue so he and Uncle Jerry drove me to the hospital where they did the usual here's a piece of candy because this is gonna hurt like hell routine and they sewed me up and then we drove home fast because it was close to dinnertime and my father got really pissed because no one could find my brother or Cliffey and my dad and Mr. DeCoursey had to go house to house and building to building looking for the two escapees until they finally found them an hour or so later hiding in the basement of Tommy Spencer's building which led to a very entertaining and rare double ass-kicking up the entire block, which I watched with relish from our third-floor window.

And after dinner that night, in the living room while we were watching TV, my father sat down in his favorite chair while I sat on the floor and we both watched the Red Sox game on the TV. He handed me a bowl of ice cream and he had his own, and after a couple of spoonfuls he very calmly and evenly taught me the moral of the story by saying this:

Hey Dinzo.

Yeah, Dad?

The next time your brother—or anyone else for that matter—calls you a faggot?

Yeah.

And you look up to see that your brother—or anyone else for that matter—is shooting an arrow at your precious, pink little Irish face?

Yeah.

You know what I want you to do?

What?

Duck, goddammit—duck!

It was always your own fault—you were supposed to learn how to survive no matter what the situation was. Boys will be boys will be boys—we were expected to shoot arrows and throw rocks and God help us if we ever got our hands on REAL guns because every stick or twig or baseball bat we could get our mitts on became a PRETEND gun in very short order.

My son Jack had a friend in grade school—nice kid. His parents were very politically correct and had made up their minds not to preordain any kind of stereotypes onto their daughter or son by buying her dolls or him trucks—you get the idea. So one Christmas—which wasn't really Christmas in their house, it was Christmas and Kwanzaa and Hanukkah and some other bullshit holiday all combined into a two-week celebration that might as well have been based on Seinfeld's fictional Festivus— Jack's buddy asked for one of those giant air-pumped water guns that looks like a plastic AK-47 on steroids. Instead, they sat him down and had a long discussion about nonviolence and the life's work of Gandhi and Martin Luther King and blah blah blah and on Xmas/Kwanzaa/ Festivus morning the poor kid woke up to find an incredibly expensive and intricate balsa wood creative design workshop his parents had imported from Denmark. When I dropped Jack off with HIS air-pumped AK-47 plastic water gun on steroids, both kids looked extremely disappointed. But to their credit—they had a great time that afternoon. Because the first thing Jack's friend made with his Danish balsa wood design center was the biggest, badass balsa wood AK-47 you have ever laid your eyes on. They pretend-shot at each other and the kid's environmentally overconcerned, tiny carbon footprint–pushing, organically soaped-up and shampooed parents all day long.

These half-wit parents today think they can legislate every single tiny dangerous detail out of the protected lives of their dainty little children. What they can't manage to keep away from the kids on their own they will beseech the rest of society to outlaw, banish and reform.

Bad language on TV shows, Janet Jackson's left nipple during the Super Bowl—bullies, mean girls, brawlers and all the other badasses need to disappear.

Personally—seeing Janet Jackson's left nipple on TV wasn't anywhere near as offensive to me as the four million ads for Viagra and Cialis and all the other "how to get a hard-on" pills that rolled out every other minute during the same game OR Janet's co-star Justin Timberlake and his next-day "I didn't know nothing" protect-his-own-skinny-ass-and-leave-the-girl-hanging defense. Chivalry? He not only never heard of it—I doubt he even knows how to spell the word.

One brown tit sent everyone running for moral cover while the phrase "an erection lasting longer than four hours" was pummeled into the formative brains of our tiny, little children.

I love tits. Real tits. Big tits, small tits, perky tits, floppy tits—I don't think it's possible for American kids to see ENOUGH tits. And what are we afraid will happen if they do? One of the first things our kids ever saw—after the birth canal and the face of the doctor who delivered them—were two juicy, chock full of mother's milk tits. Tits that brought them nothing more than comfort and pleasure and nourishment and fun. As far as kids are concerned—tits are the best. Tits and candy. As a matter of fact—before they discover cupcakes and other sources of man-made sugar—tits ARE candy. Never mind all the cartoon violence and cutesy, idiotic Teletubbies—there should be a channel on TV that is all tits all the time—TIT TV. In France, Africa—half of the goddam planet, for God's sake—women sunbathe topless and no one even thinks twice about it, but here in America—during a full three-hour broadcast of organized violence between grown men hopped up on illegal drugs and human growth hormone—we are desperately afraid that our sons and daughters might see a fleeting ever-so-quick GLIMPSE of a pop star's teat.

We suck. We suck really really bad.

By the way—if the tits don't kill our kids, the bullies will.

Let me tell you something about bullies—we need them. They teach your kid how to survive. How to plan a trip to school that includes every available navigational option so he doesn't have to run into the kid who wants to kick his ass.

Mean girls teach your daughter what it will be like in any workplace full of women she ends up dealing with later in life—the jealousy and envy and catfighting and backbiting. It is an early education. Why? Because that's the way girls are.

Boys? Boys will beat the living crap out of each other for one reason and one reason only—because they are awake.

CHAPTER 5

BULLIES R US

et me tell you a couple of bully stories.

When I was a kid, there was a bully in our neighborhood named Bobby Burns. He used to walk around in the summertime wearing a denim jacket with no shirt on underneath—like a discount Roger Daltrey. (In those days, everyone thought Roger Daltrey was cool. Tanned, long blond curly locks, no shirts, open denim jackets, sometimes with fringe, lead singer of the Who—who could be cooler? Just to put some perspective on the shelf life of cool, years later—in the nineties my son Jack—age nine—saw a video of Daltrey sporting that look and said "Wow. What a dork." So good luck with the ultra-baggy jeans, giant T-shirts and baseball hats cocked sideways, kids. Take plenty of pictures.)

Anyways—Bobby Burns was short and muscle-bound and for some reason hated my guts. Probably because I was taller than him. I was taller than most of the kids my age by the time I was fourteen. Also, I could actually put several words together and form a sentence—which Bobby had some trouble with, which led to his grunting and giving the finger a lot, which led to his repeating the fifth grade three times. He wasn't bright, Bobby. He was shaving before he took algebra. He drove himself to eighth grade. He was old enough to join the navy during his freshman year in high school. (Me and my friends came up with a million of these, by the way.)

Long story short—Bobby kept taunting me whenever he would walk by and my friends and I were playing street hockey or football on my block—grunting and giving me the finger and at least once challenging me to a fight because I was "bigger" than him. Needless to say, I was basically scared shitless of Bobby—as were all the kids in the neighborhood.

Rumors flew, of course, that Bobby was thirty-seven, that he had been in jail, that he had killed a guy and—the scariest rumor of all—that Bobby knew Kung Fu. Keep in mind that this was in the early seventies, when Kung Fu was considered a secret form of the martial arts that meant you could fly through the air and kill a guy with a karate chop. There was a show on TV about Kung Fu, a special G.I. Joe with a Kung Fu grip and a number one hit song called "Kung Fu Fighting." Kids being kids—reality had been massively displaced by a monster dose of gossip and fear until we all believed Bobby was a vicious, insurmountable superhuman force.

One day he walked right up to me and my friends and said—to me—"Hey Faggot—tomorrow if I see you on the street—I'm gonna kick your ass."

And then he swaggered away.

My friends were quick to back me up.

You better move, Dave Minor said.

Canada, Barry Gay said. They got plenty a hockey up there.

Yeah, John Dourville added, or you could live in the basement in my house—no one ever goes down there.

We should call the cops, Mark Zambini said. Kung Fu is against the law.

Andy Zambini cut a huge, smelly fart.

These were my advisers.

We spent the rest of the day throwing rocks and discussing why—with a kid actually named Gay on the block—Bobby Burns felt the need to call ME a faggot.

Barry said it was because beating up a guy named Gay was REALLY gay. Dave said it was because Barry was smaller than Bobby and therefore beating him up proved nothing. Mark Zambini said maybe your brother calls you faggot so much, Bobby just thought faggot was your actual name. John Dourville said his father had gotten his nose broken once and that his dad said it hurt like hell and it bled a lot and your eyes watered and then it hurt for like another five or six weeks or so and then after a while it was okay. Andy Zambini hocked a huge loogie onto the sidewalk. And I mean huge: several ants immediately became suspended in it. We stared at them for a while as they tried to wiggle out of the goo. By a while I mean about an hour and a half. We poked at them with sticks.

I went home, said nothing to my dad or my brother—who said pass the salt faggot at supper and got whacked across the head with a gravy ladle by my mom—then I went to bed, staring at the low ceiling of the basement and wishing I could just disappear.

I woke up the next morning and briefly considered pretending to be sick but after a couple of minutes I decided to get up and get it over with. If Bobby Burns was gonna kick my ass I might as well get my ass kicked as quickly as possible and carry on with the rest of my summer. I spent a couple of minutes staring at my nose in the bathroom mirror— imagining what it would look like moved over another inch to the side of my face. Then I went outside to meet the guys.

So I guess you didn't move, huh? Dave Minor said.

Or run away, John Dourville added.

Barry Gay piped in with this headline: my sister said a kid in her grade said that he knows a kid who used to go to school with a kid who knew Bobby Burns's first cousin and the cousin said Bobby killed one of their drunk uncles with a Vulcan Death Grip.

No one said anything for a second. The Vulcan Death Grip was a move that Spock used to kill people on *Star Trek*, which of course I never watched because I hated science fiction because it seemed like bullshit. Until now.

Needless to say, later that morning we were playing street hockey when everyone just froze, right in the middle of a scoring play. They all were suddenly looking over my shoulder and beyond me with fright in their eyes. I turned to see what they had seen: way down at the end of the block—Bobby Burns. Approaching.

I looked down at my feet for a second—gathering my thoughts—until I realized—my thoughts sounded a helluva lot like breaking bones.

Looking up, I could see that Bobby Burns was only about twenty yards away, cracking his knuckles, each crick of a finger echoing off the asphalt like a bullet's ricochet:

Crack.

Thwang.

Crack.

Zwing.

I could feel the blood leaving my body—apparently not wishing to get spilled.

As Bobby came closer, I could sense everyone else starting to move away from me—I think I even heard a couple of uh-ohs and maybe even some whispered prayers. One of the guys even moved the street hockey net out of the way. As if they didn't want it covered with my blood and intestines and stuff.

Within seconds Bobby Burns was right there in front of me. The hair. The open denim jacket. No shirt. His beady eyes looking up—glaring. He smiled his menacing, evil grin. Then—two things happened:

1. I didn't shit my pants.
2. Not shitting my pants made my lower lip—which had begun to tremble—stop trembling.

Then Bobby Burns yanked my street hockey stick right out of my hand and threw it behind him. It clattered across the road. Then—Bobby Burns called me a faggot and slapped me in the face. Hard. Really really hard.

Then, his left hand slowly began to move upwards—in what looked to me much like what I knew the G.I. Joe With The Kung Fu Grip's hand always looked like—ready to kill or hold a plastic grenade. Or maybe this was what Spock's hand looked like just before he tried to kill Captain Kirk.

Two more things happened, almost simultaneously:

1. I didn't shit my pants again.
2. I kicked Bobby Burns in the balls—so fucking hard that my foot almost split him into two separate halves.

No sound came out of his mouth as he doubled over in pain and stumbled sideways onto the tiny front lawn of Zambini's house. I thought that any second Bobby would spring up and stab me or shoot me or even worse— chop off my head with some crazy Kung Fu karate chop, fly through the air and scissor-kick my torso, slicing open my rib cage to reveal my beating heart to the entire WHAM! I jumped on him and started beating the living crap out of him. Punching and kicking and elbows and knees and punching and everything became one big blur and the next thing I knew my own dad and Mr. Zambini were pulling me off and telling Bobby Burns to get the hell up and go home.

Which he did—very very slowly.

Okay okay, he stuttered, awright.

He had drool running down his chin and a bunch of cuts on his Roger Daltrey chest and grass stains all over his jacket and jeans but—he was moving away.

My father had come running from our house and only saw the last part of what had happened—but he knew enough to say—out of the side of his mouth—"Good job. But don't say anything to your mother about this." And off he went. Mr. Zambini told us to get the hell off his goddam lawn. Then he went back inside. It was all over so fast.

As we watched Bobby Burns make his way down the block—bent and bumbling—Dave Minor summed up what each one of us was thinking:

What the hell did you do that for?

I dunno, I said. What just happened?

Holy shit, Mark Zambini said.

He's gonna kill you tomorrow, Barry Gay said.

He's gonna kill all of us, John Dourville added.

Andy Zambini didn't fart.

Or hock a loogie.

Or even belch.

He just shook his head and followed his father inside the house.

Wow.

That night I went to bed thinking my life—as I knew it—was probably over. My dad gave me a knowing look at the dinner table and instead of feeling proud—I was worried sick. The next morning I awoke, once again filled with a let's get it over with quick mentality. I met up with John and Dave and Barry and the Zambini Brothers. Everyone had long faces. We played street hockey, but every time someone thought they saw a figure off in the distance—we'd stop and look up—frozen with fear and a bottomless pit of dread.

Then someone would say It's okay—it's not him.

That must have happened ten or fifteen times that morning. But Bobby Burns never showed up. As a matter of fact—he didn't show up anywhere for a couple of days.

Maybe you killed him, Barry said.

Maybe he's buying a gun, Dave said. ·

Then—on the third day—down the block he came. As soon as we saw him, we all got Deaf Mute Fear. You know the kind? The fear so strong it starts out somewhere inside the marrow of your bones and emanates like a magnetic force out through your blood cells and into your veins and rumbles up and wraps around your arms and legs and neck and chest and leaves you unable to speak or hear anything except the pounding of your own pulse reverberating in your eardrums?

Ba-bump.

Ba-bump.

Bobby Burns was walking toward us.

Ba-bump.

Ba-bump.

I wanted to run but my feet refused to move.

Ba-bump.

Ba-bump.

From a distance, he looked angry—defiant. Uh oh.

Ba-bump.

Ba-ba-bump.

My heart was beating faster.

Ba-ba-bump. Ba-ba-bump.

Maybe that was Barry's heart.

Ba-ba-bump.

Nope—it's mine. Don't shit your pants don't shit your pants whatever you do DO NOT SHIT IN YOUR OWN PANTS.

Ba-ba-bump.

He's twenty feet away. Don't piss your pants either.

Ba-ba-bump.

As he drew closer I actually shut my eyes, figuring at least I wouldn't have to watch my own dismantling.

Ba-ba-bump.

I could smell him now.

Ba-ba-bump.

I sneaked a peek—to see if Barry and John and Dave and The Zambinis were still there and—much to my surprise—we were all looking at each other. Then we looked up to see Bobby Burns—walking just past us, waving a weak hello and saying "hey guys" and—get this—continuing on his way.

It took us more than a few seconds to mutter two or three heys back at him.

And then he was gone.

Wow.

We must have stared down at the empty end of the block for at least thirty seconds.

Later in the day he came back in the opposite direction and gave us a little head nod with a tight little smile.

We nodded back.

And that was it.

No beating, no knife, no gun—not even any Kung Fu.

Everyone made that jaw-drop, round-mouthed, wide-eyed holy shit can you believe it face. Then we laughed. Then Andy Zambini sneezed and as he sneezed he also cut a giant fart. We laughed. Loud and long.

Bobby Burns never ever threatened any of us again.

As a matter of fact, anytime he walked by he would wave that weak hello and say "hey guys" or just give us the head nod with a tight little smile. Turns out he had never been in jail never killed anyone and *Kung Fu* was just a TV show he watched like the rest of us. The Vulcan Death Grip? Bullshit. It was all hype. My boot to the balls was just what the doctor had ordered. It had shut up the biggest bully on the block and filled me with a new confidence. I couldn't wait for the next asshole who decided he was going to push me around—man, would he get his. The boot to the balls with absolutely no warning was gonna become the signature move I would use to establish my reputation with all bullies everywhere.

One day later? The opportunity quickly arose. I tried the same exact move on another guy who was bullying and belittling me and calling me a faggot and thought he was going to get away with it and you know what happened? He blocked my foot before it reached his balls and then beat the living daylights out of me. That guy was my brother Johnny.

That's right—I roomed with a bully. My brother wasn't an official bully—just a bully brother. He could handle himself well and was the kind of guy who would wander the streets putting bullies in their place—but when it came to me—well, brothers will be brothers, especially when they share a room small enough to be a walk-in closet for Mini Me.

My brother was way bigger than me and I drove him to the brink as often as I could. Here's one example: he would alphabetize his record collection along the floor against the wall on his side of the room and then—here's where he would fuck up—tell me that he had just alphabetized it and for me not to even look—never mind touch—any of the records. I would then wait until he left and immediately pull all the records out of their sleeves and put them haphazardly into other sleeves—a little process I like to call Anti-Alphabetizing. He would come home later, go to pull out

Crosby, Stills, Nash And A Whiny Canadian and instead end up listening to Iron Butterfly's *In-A-Gadda-Da-Vida*. Then the Iron Butterfly sleeve would produce Grand Funk Railroad. *Abbey Road*? Leon Russell. Leon Russell? Three Dog Night. Watching him struggle through the process—and this happened many many times—never failed to make me smile. And then he would threaten and chase and pummel me—which I never really minded. I would laugh and cackle and it would make him insane. He could kick my ass. So what. We both knew he didn't know Kung Fu or the Vulcan Death Grip. He would go back onto his side of the tiny room and painstakingly realphabetize the records and I would secretly plan how long I would wait before anti-alphabetizing them again.

What did I learn? Patience, pulling, pushing, and the great pleasure of anticipation—waiting for him to come home, knowing the records were all messed up. I learned all four of those things by aggravating my brother. Oh—and Vaseline. Let me explain.

Sometimes my brother would come home late—when I was supposedly asleep—so he would have to put on headphones to listen to the stereo. The big, giant, puffy seventies headphones you see in old movies? Uh huh. You got it.

Once or twice I coated the inside of those babies with Vaseline or this stuff my dad kept with his tools near the water heater—it was called Lava hand soap. And believe me when I tell you—it was aptly named. Lava came in a giant screw-top vat and was invented to wash away engine oil and valve grease. I think it was actually just volcanic spew that some guys at Mount St. Helens let cool down after an eruption and then shoveled into jars and slapped a label on. It made your hands feel as if they were melting. So you can imagine what it would do to your ears. It had a warning on the front: Do Not Put On Face! The way I figured it—technically speaking—the ears are part of the head.

I don't even think my brother ever figured it out. He'd usually be two sheets to the wind and fall asleep with the headphones on and some shitty music rejiggering his brain cells and wake up with greasy hair.

And the other odd time, ears that felt like they were on fire. I imagined him making a mental note to turn the bass down before he got under the sheets.

Oh the pure joy that brought me. What did I learn? Revenge, folks. And, of course, how to fall asleep with a smile on my face.

Here's a funny story that sums up my kidhood relationship with my brother. I was playing football in the school yard with some older kids I barely knew. I was covering this kid who went up for a pass and as I blocked it I also accidentally hit him in the face and as we both tumbled to the ground the guy starts punching me. A lot.

As I was trying to defend myself and/or grab a hold of his hands WHOMP! he was hit with blunt force and suddenly disappeared from view.

I sat up to see my brother sitting on top of the guy and holding his head against the ground by the neck and saying: Nobody touches my little brother except me, okay asshole? Hah? Ya got it? Hands off. Then he stood up and walked away. The guy lay there, desperately sucking air. I didn't know what to do. So—confused—I said That's right, asshole. Only he can beat the shit outta me! Then I turned to all the other guys—who also looked confused—and said Everybody hear that? Okay, then. Puzzled, they all nodded yes. Then we played more football. There were many many You okays? and Lemme help you ups from then on.

One more bully story: my good friend and writing partner Peter Tolan (*Rescue Me*, *The Job*, *Analyze This*, *America's Sweethearts*, Too Many Other Credits To Mention Not To Mention Some Insane Amount Of Emmy Nominations And Three Actual Emmys) was born in raised in Scituate, Massachusetts, in much the same circumstances as me including Irish (American) parents, nuns, priests the whole nine yards. We're both about the same age.

Peter's bully was a kid named Billy Noonan who would stand out in front of his house and refuse to let anyone pass unless they gave him money. He made threats and swore and spit and acted like a tough guy and pretty soon everyone was forking over their loose change and lunch money just so Noonan wouldn't kick their asses. His reputation grew. He killed a guy. He skinned a cat. He invented a new kind of Kung Fu (hey, I told you—Kung Fu was EVERYWHERE back then).

In order to get to school, Peter and every other kid had to walk past Noonan's corner—there was just no other way without walking an extra couple of very very long blocks so most kids just decided to give in and pay the vig and accept their fate. Then—one winter morning—there was a huge snow and ice storm. Walking the streets was like skating on a huge outdoor rink. Noonan put on a big, brand-new gangster-type overcoat and stood outside his house—as always waiting to taunt and spit and collect. As Peter made his regular turn onto the corner—along with a bunch of other kids—Noonan yelled "Hey Tolan—where's my money?" Peter sighed and very carefully—making sure not to slip and fall—turned and looked over at Noonan's outstretched hand. "C'mon, faggot. Fork it over."

Peter tossed a look at the other kids, shook his head in disgust and sauntered gingerly across the ice toward the bully. Then—something snapped. Peter had finally had enough. In his mind things had come this far and would now go no further. He was going to stand up to Noonan once and for all. Tell him where to go and how fast to get there. But there was only one problem—speaking of speed. Peter's feet were moving so fast in an attempt not to slip that he realized he was in fact gaining a great amount of gusto—too much gusto—he was heading straight at Noonan with no way to stop and so his brain stem sent the signal This Is It! Fuck Noonan! Kill Him Before He Kills You! He Has A Secret Kung Fu Move!

Much to everyone's surprise, instead of stopping and placing his lunch money into Noonan's grasp, Peter instead leapt forward onto Noonan's chest and as the bully fell backward Peter inadvertently—only because of gravity and other scientific relationships between two moving masses—raked his arms down the overcoat and ended up ripping the two pockets off as he landed on top of him.

The lunch money of many flew out—coins bouncing off the cold cold ice, dollar bills billowing out on the wind.

Thinking quickly, Peter got to his feet and tossed the two pockets down onto Noonan's very scared and shock-filled face. Where's your Kung Fu now, asshole? Hah? he said, standing over him. Then he made a very dainty, delicate retreat—the ice underfoot not allowing him the swaggering John Wayne exit he would have preferred.

"Look what you did to my cool new coat!" Noonan whimpered.

"Yeah yeah yeah," Peter replied, struggling to keep his balance.

All the kids watched in awe as Peter minced up the icy street with his head held high. Had the bully pushed Peter over the edge? Was this cold snowy morning's demand just the final straw in a long and seemingly endless battle? Was justice finally getting its due?

Nope.

Kung Fu and Spock's Vulcan Death Grip had just scared the crap out of an entire generation of kids—to the point where some kind of revolution was inevitable. Bullies everywhere had taken the power of gossip and TV and turned it against the masses, much to their own chagrin.

Noonan was never again to collect lunch money or even stand in front of his house spitting and taunting. Bobby Burns was reduced to just another idiot who forgot to wear a shirt. Noonan became known as No Pockets. Eventually shortened to just Pockets.

Those were the days. You fought your own battles and sometimes you won and sometimes you lost and sometimes Mother Nature actually stepped in to lend you a secret hand. Just getting from one place to another was fraught with peril and potential karate chops.

We were lucky to be alive and our parents reminded us of that almost every other day. Starving kids in China and Africa and Ireland itself. I can't count how many times teachers and parents would say think of the poor kids over in Vietnam—and they weren't just referring to the Vietnamese. Ray Kelly who lived in the building next door got drafted. Another kid two streets over joined up. In the working class it was always an option—you wanted out of the neighborhood—a fresh start—you probably couldn't afford college so you signed up with the army. And sometimes they just came and took you. Your number came up. Literally. It used to crack me up later in life when I'd meet people my age who grew up with money and they talked about Teen Tours—trips they took in the summer during high school where they visited Rome or Paris or the Swiss Alps. Yeah—we had Teen Tours too. To goddam Saigon. Or the Ho Chi Minh Trail.

We walked our skinny asses to school or down to the bus stop and it might as well have been the wild wild west: bullies on one corner, drunk drivers on the other and once you got to school you dealt with women dressed up like penguins who wielded wooden yardsticks as if they were light sabers and pedophile priests who lurked up and down every single hallway.

Nowadays parents show you videos or photos or tell you stories about how their kids are climbing and standing and saying such and such.

Hey—you wanna impress us?

Show us pictures of the kid falling down and getting stitches and stuttering to speak and swallowing nails or munching on a pigeon or just staring into the camera with scabs all over his head. Then we might be impressed. Show us a photo of the world's ugliest kid and say "hey, look—my baby looks just like an orangutan!" This would really lead to a round of applause.

First of all—they are SUPPOSED to start climbing and standing and grabbing and kicking—if they aren't, then take them back to the hospital and ask for a refund. And as far as him or her saying such and such—bullshit.

People other than the actual parents can't understand a single sound a kid is making. It all comes out as gibberish. Save us all some precious seconds and call us when the kid can say "I gotta go poop." No one—with the possible exception of the grandparents—really cares.

I'm tired of hearing the convoluted explanations of how special or talented or blessed with ability every single asshole's kids are today. I don't wanna hear how he tests in the something something percentile of his class or how she was judged to be blah blah blah by a panel of mathematics experts.

It's gotten so bizarre that some people are actually trying to circumvent the system and get their idiotic children DECLARED special-needs.

Parent pair after parent pair digging through books and trawling the Internet in search of symptoms that match up with their underachieving imbeciles.

A lot of them turn to the gold standard excuse—Attention Deficit Disorder. ADD. Holy shit. I was never diagnosed as being ADD but I'll bet if they tested back in the sixties I would've come up ADD-HD—High Definition. I can barely keep my focus long enough to stay on this subject. I mean—have you been reading this chapter or not?

Lemme give you an example.

I am truly, honestly going to stop typing for a moment and see whether I can think of something to say about attention deficit disorder and I will type the first two things that come into my head.

Here we go.

Gimme like—five seconds.

Okay—start counting.

- ★ Why do old people drive so goddam slow? You have had the experience—stuck in a forty-mile-per-hour speed zone on a one-lane road behind some brittle, ancient creature who's barely going thirty as he daydreams about LBJ. Meanwhile, YER in a rush but the old asshole's driving as if he's got all the time in the world. Hey—I got news for ya, shithead. Yer eighty-seven years old. Death is not only right around the corner—he might be riding shotgun. If I were eighty-seven years old—full well knowing I might have a heart attack or an aneurysm or if I cut a hard fart the wrong way it might actually blow an internal gasket and make my entire insides explode all over my leather 1994 Cadillac Seville seats—I would drive so fucking fast you would barely be able to identify my car if I ran you over. And what if I did run you over—what're they gonna do, give me life in jail? I'm eighty-goddam-seven! I think old people should be forced to actually drive the same speed as their age. Eighty-seven is your age AND your speed limit. You better hope I don't hit my late eighties or early nineties because I will guarantee everyone right now—you better get the fuck out of my way. I'll kill young people just for spite. And when I say young I mean anyone under seventy-five.

See? Wait—watch this:

- ★ Everyone talks about how crazy Tom Cruise is because he believes in Scientology—a religion based on the idea that aliens came to Earth many many years ago and created the human race blah blah blah. Yeah. That sounds pretty crazy to me. But not as crazy as the religion I was brought up to believe in—the Catholic Church—where we were taught that a chick got pregnant without having sex and gave birth to a guy who could walk on water and feed thousands of people with one loaf of bread and a fish. Hmmm. Who's crazy now?

See? Wait wait—one more:

★ They just announced on my desktop satellite radio feed that lame-duck President George W. Bush is going to sign into law a bill that will keep the mentally ill from being able to purchase guns. Great. At least Britney Spears won't be able to shoot herself in the head. Then again—neither will Kevin Federline.

I could keep going for almost forever.

★ Have you noticed that all the women Roger Clemens injected with his Hall of Fame semen started out very petite and pretty and blond and ended up—after the affair had run its course—far bigger with larger butts and faces? And that semen was supposedly steroid-free? I don't think so, Rocket Man. We don't need no stinking syringes—let's just do a Pap smear or two or three or—how many girls was it again?

Sorry. I'm stopping now. I think you get the idea—what was I talking about?

Oh—right. Attention something something.

All these Ritalin- and Adderall-addled kids are simply a result of their parents' wish not to have to pay more attention to them. If your son is unable to focus on his homework for longer than five seconds it doesn't mean he's got a learning disability—it means he's got a pair of balls. EVERY BOY EVER BORN has a short attention span—it's in our DNA. It's why God invented tits—so we would have something to focus on while women were talking to us about how emotionally unavailable we are. Tits, trucks, t-bone steaks and video games. That's what boys are built for.

By the way—if you think there isn't a direct relationship between forcing your child to take prescription drugs in order to do better in school and the current boom in prescription drug abuse in high schools across the country—then keep your head planted firmly up your ass. Three decades ago they were concerned about my generation smoking pot snorting coke and shooting heroin. Now? They have commercials on TV warning about how kids raid their parents' medicine cabinets to get pills. Give yourselves a big dumb round of applause, America—you've home-schooled your kids on how to get fucked up without even leaving the house. And better yet? It's free!

You wanna use ADD as an excuse for not doing well in school—then I want a do-over.

The same thing goes for parents who bring charges against all these high school teachers who are having sex with students. Hey—look at it as free sex education. With NO unanswered questions after the class. These teachers are giving your kids firsthand knowledge they will DEFINITELY use later on in life. In my line of work, all the crap I heard in science and math and physics and algebra went in one ear and right out the other— but head from my homeroom teacher? THAT would be permanently emblazoned in the very front of my frontal lobe.

Where were these teachers when I was in high school? I'd love to go back in time and learn how to feel up Sister Sharon—the real hot nun who eventually left the convent and married one of our lay teachers—Mr. Ridley. Ironic term for a teacher who isn't a priest in a Catholic school who ends up fucking a nun—a LAY teacher. In retrospect—man, was his title an apt one.

There are lawsuits flying left, right and center against priests in Catholic schools who sexually abused their students. I did twelve years in that prison and not one single priest even made a pass at me. Not even the priest who was involved in helping with the high school musicals. I mean, if there's gonna be a gay priest—THAT guy should be the most obvious candidate, no matter what school we're discussing. But not one pass. Maybe I should sue for lack of sexual attention. Maybe they had a negative affect on my self-esteem.

That's a whole separate ball of asshole wax: self-esteem.

CHAPTER 6

AUTISM SHMAUTISM

n my day self-esteem came from actual performance and a clear understanding of your place in the world. The facts were laid out almost from the get-go—if you wanted to be a model and you were a girl you had to be tall and thin. If you wanted to play baseball there was no goddam wiffle ball or a special "soft" pretend, fakey baseball set up on top of a standing tee—you had to learn how to hit an actual pitched HARD baseball. Which sometimes would hit you in the face if you didn't get out of the way fast enough. Which would break your face. Which would hurt like hell. If you wanted to be in a rock band you had to learn how to sing and actually play an instrument. While on drugs. Lots of drugs. If you were ugly then you were ugly and there was very little hope you were going to change the way you looked unless the baseball that crushed your face rearranged the bones and let you come out the other end looking like George Fucking Clooney. These were the cold, hard facts of life and your parents were in charge of supplying you with every single one of them.

There is a huge boom in autism right now because inattentive mothers and competitive dads want an explanation for why their dumbass kids can't compete academically so they throw money into the happy laps of shrinks and psychotherapists to get back diagnoses that help explain away the deficiencies of their junior morons. I don't give a shit what these crackerjack whackjobs tell you—yer kid is NOT autistic. He's just stupid. Or lazy. Or both.

I know a couple of autistic children and let me tell you something they both have in common—they are extremely bright and attentive and—much like Rain Man—have individual talents and abilities that would lay your empty little tyke's video game–addled soul to waste. A truly autistic child may be able to reproduce music he or she hears with perfect pitch—entire classical pieces, the rock opera *Tommy*, the latest hit Broadway musical—over and over again. OR tell you instantly upon hearing what your birthday is—what day it has fallen on every year for the last four decades. What the weather was on those days. Who the president was at the time. What the number one song on the radio was just before singing it note for note and word for word. THAT'S an autistic child. Not some fat-assed simpleton whose brain has been fried by television and the Xbox and no proper daily attention from his or her supposedly caring parents.

Maybe your kid is not autistic. Maybe he's just a dolt. And thank your lucky stars for that. Face the facts.

Autism is up and who knows why—parents who wasted time, their brain cells and a lot of healthy DNA on way too many recreational drugs is this doctor's guess—but I refuse to sit here and believe that half the idiotic offspring I come across even amongst my own friends and family are a part of that problem.

I recently heard an interview with the brother of acclaimed author Augusten Burroughs. This brother guy invented the gizmo that allows smoke and a small fireworks display to spazz out of electric guitars onstage. He did it while working as a roadie/techie for the band Kiss. Ace Frehley turned to him one day and said Hey, can you make smoke 'n shit fly outta my Axe while I'm playin' it? So this guy did so. Not a huge contribution to society but hey—it is what it is and he made a good living at it. The reason I bring this up is: the interview was about a book this brother had written because when he was about fifty years old he almost completely self-diagnosed himself as having Asperger's syndrome.

In the interview he said that all of his life people thought he was odd. He would talk to people but had trouble making eye contact with them and he knew—somehow, somewhere deep down inside—he was different. Because they wouldn't talk back. They would usually just nod and walk away.

Uh-huh.

Here's the textbook definition of the disease:

Asperger's syndrome is one of several autism spectrum disorders (ASD). Characterized by difficulty in social interaction and restricted, stereotyped interests and activities. People with Asperger's are not usually withdrawn around others, they simply approach others by engaging in a one-sided, long-winded speech about one of their own favorite topics.

Where I come from, we don't call a guy like that a victim of Asperger's. We just call him an Asshole Who Won't Shut The Fuck Up.

You wanna find people who don't think it strange or boring or mind-numbing to listen to you ramble on and on and on about what it takes to plug electronic boxes into electro converters and then into tubeless amplifiers THROUGH a remote-access special effects board and blap blappety blap until shit shoots out of a guitar played by a guy wearing fourteen-inch-high platform-heeled leather boots and a girdle? Here's the list:

1. The guy in the girdle
2. You
3. People with Kiss T-shirts on

That's it. You don't belong in the spectrum of autism disorders. You belong backstage with a shitload of AA batteries and a suitcase full of roman candles.

Long-winded and one-sided.

I heard the guy on the radio and believe me, folks, long-winded ain't the least of it. This guy had his head so far up inside his own ass he could be interviewed about his memoir and perform his own colonoscopy at the same time.

Odd? Yeah—you became a roadie for a rock band that dresses up in superhero costumes and wears twenty-seven pounds of makeup? Where and when is that considered normal. AND you made money at it? Sorry, pal. You don't get to make guitars blow up for a living and then stake a claim as some kind of social retard. Lucky? Yes. Rain Man? No. Not on my planet.

Two days later I hear another person on the same show—a chick who made a documentary about her brother—another Asperger's victim. This guy was incredibly smart and socially adept but for some reason couldn't keep a job or cook or clean or do his own laundry and therefore was still living with his parents at age forty-two. My cousin has this version of Asperger's. It's called Mikey Ain't Moving Away From Home syndrome. It's a disease that makes you suddenly realize—hey, I gotta good thing goin' here—rent-free—so my ass ain't goin' anywhere. Some guy tried it in Italy a few years ago and his parents kicked him to the curb. He actually took his parents to court—at the same age, forty-two—and the courts told him to grow up and move out. I know a ton of Irish and Italian guys who would still be living at home being waited on hand and foot by their doting mothers if their dads didn't one day decide to lay down the law.

But in America? It's not pure, unadulterated sloth or taking advantage of a good thing until it goes dry. No—here it's been coddled and studied and written about and fully vetted into a sickness. It can't be that your kid is just a lazy, potheaded, beer-bellied slob. No. He must be "special."

I think the parents don't wanna face the cold hard facts that their joining of the loins has produced a semi-retard with a nervous twitch so they jump on any available train—in this case the autism express—and blame good old Mother Nature. And of course they find a doctor more than willing to tell them what they want to hear for close to seven hundred dollars an hour—not to mention the special pills and potions. This doctor don't work that way. You bought this book so I'll consider that my fee and here is the answer to the questions about your kid: give up. The next Steve Jobs he ain't. Matter a fact—he ain't even gonna be the guy who goes to get Steve Jobs his coffee in the morning. If he keeps himself on the straight and narrow and doesn't get run over by a bus or go to jail—he MIGHT be the guy who cleans up Steve Jobs's office after Steve goes home to his mansion every night.

Now I know how hard it may be to face the truth when it comes to your kids. If it was easy to be objective about your own progeny don't you think Paris Hilton's parents would have hired a short bus and special security to transport their daughter/whore/celebutard out of the public spotlight? Damn right they would have. Instead—they pimped their second daughter out into the marketplace to try and juice more money. Because—I'm sure—they thought she was "special." Just like Paris is so "special."

Listen up, America—odds are, your kid is NOT special. Einstein? Special. Hitler? Very special. Your little jackass? Not so much.

Will your child leave his mark on the world? Probably not. A stain, maybe. A mark—that's probably a reach.

Jeffrey Dahmer left his mark. So did Jesus. And Babe Ruth. Your kid— c'mon. Let's get real. Unless he kills and eats twenty-five people or walks on water or hits eight hundred absolutely steroid-free home runs, he will more than likely live a boring, fat, stupid and uneventful life and then die from some horrible form of cancer. If he's a boy—ass cancer. If she's a girl—cancer of the tits or vagina. Them's the facts.

There will be another Adolf one day as well as another Albert and there are plenty of Osamas and Kennedys to go around, but you should really take a good long look in the mirror.

Odds are against your kid being smart or talented or good-looking unless you AND your husband/boyfriend/sperm donor are BOTH smart and talented and good-looking. If yer both morons—yer kids're gonna be morons. It's the old apple-not-falling-too-far-from-the-tree theory. If yer both fat-asses—yer kids're gonna be fat-asses. If you happen to be one of those couples they base shitty network sitcoms on—pretty, smart chick with dumb fat husband—more than likely you'll have two kids and— hopefully—one will be cute and smart and the other a lumpen chunk of meat. And all the government-approved, good American know-how kid-fixing drugs imported in dangerous plastic bottles from China won't help one bit.

Take a look around. Better yet—just drive down to your local mall. Grab a seventeen-dollar cup of ice cream dressed-up-like-coffee from Starbucks and watch all the hunchbacked, pasty-faced, acne-scarred, backfat-bearing, arms-too-short-to-box-with-the-God-who-supposedly-made-them creatures dithering and doddering along in their two-sizes-too-small designer jeans and hot blue spandex tube tops: these are not just your neighbors. This is what most of this country looks like. What makes you think your kids will be any different?

If you are white trash your kids will be white trash. Believe me—I know what I'm talking about. Just ask my wife. I may live in a beautiful country home with rolling meadows full of gorgeous horses and grass and indidgineous rock formations, but right here in my office as I sit writing these words? I am surrounded by framed photos of Bobby Orr and Cam Neely and Derek Sanderson and Carl Yastrzemski and numerous other baseball and hockey heroes. And I may have used the term "indidgineous rock formations" but only because a guy who did some work here once mentioned it and—hang on a second - - - - I just looked it up in the dictionary and indidgineous is spelled indigenous. See? Whaddaya expect from a guy who—right this second—is wearing a Red Sox T-shirt with mustard stains from a Fenway Frank eaten on the Green Monster seats at Fenway Park during the championship season of 2007 AND a pair of Boston Bruin sweatpants that are so old the drawstring has fallen out of its seam—it don't get much more white trash than me. Want more cred? When I was a kid we got ice out of a machine eight blocks away from our apartment. We put ketchup on spaghetti. When you outgrew your pants your little brother wore them. When he outgrew them they got mailed over to Ireland. I never had my own room till I moved out on my own.

Now my wife and I have spent a lot of time trying to educate and manner our kids so that they don't turn out like me. My daughter is smart and funny and gorgeous—just like her mom. She's also very embarrassed by her father most of the time—just like her mom. My son? Well—he's funny and smart and tall and—wears the same sweatpants I do. Only they have a Boston Celtics logo on them. And his Red Sox T-shirt has a ketchup stain.

Give up the dream of rearing someone who is going to cure any major disease or invent the next groundbreaking electronic doodad or even sing a number one song. Dial it down a notch. Aim for goals that may actually be within your child's grasp: the paper-hat-wearing manager at McDonald's. A driver for UPS. Secretary. Wet-nurse. Welder. Then—if things don't work out with union jobs—teach them how to count and they can always fall back on the safety net of crystal meth manufacturing. You can do it in your own home. Sure—there may not be a dental plan, but in the world of crystal meth—lack of teeth is not a detriment. It's actually a badge of honor.

For girls without a college education—the lap dance never goes out of style. All you need—believe me—is two tits, an ass and a vagina. Literally. If you didn't even have a head some guys might get a little skeeved out, but I'm telling you—a lot of other guys would be lined up around the block to get some lap action from the dancer who didn't talk. I'm not exactly the strip club type but I'll tell you this much—I've seen more than a few who had fantastic bodies and not so great faces and the exact opposite as well. Guys aren't in strip clubs to meet the next Miss America. The type of guys who spend money in strip clubs are the ones who don't have the balls or high enough self-esteem to talk to the pretty girls at work but just enough self-esteem to keep them from hiring a hooker.

The girls are usually the type lacking the self-esteem needed to keep them from peeling off in front of strangers, but somehow holding on to just enough pride not to fall into the fucking-guys-for-money trap. PLUS they've all been sexually molested at some point. As have most prostitutes. Usually by drunken male family members. Still interested, guys?

My advice to men who are thinking of going into a strip club would be this: don't. On second thought, go to the club. Just don't go in. Stand outside, remove all the cash in your wallet and light it on fire. Watch it burn until it's just a smoking pile of ashes. Then bang your head against the wall of the club several times—hard. Get in your car. Drive home. When you wake up the next morning, you will have achieved the same effect as if you had spent the night inside the club: no money, giant headache. What did you miss? Nothing. Smelly armpits, seven useless hard-ons and eighty-five horrible tattoos.

That's another lesson kids today should learn—tattoos may have been cool five decades ago when the only people who had them were sailors, inmates and lead guitar players. Now? Not so much. You wanna be a rebel nowadays? DON'T get a tattoo. Or a nose ring. Or a pierced anything. Everyone will wonder: what the fuck is up with that guy? He actually has nothing painted on or attached to his body except his limbs and his real skin. What a freak. Plus—for girls? You know what that insane snaky flower or some bullshit Chinese symbol or a set of angel wings above your ass or your pussy makes you look like? A stripper. Ask a drunk uncle to grab your tit and you'll be ready to roll.

Hey—The Drunk Uncles. Good name for a band.

Strip clubs—as a matter of fact—are basically live laboratories for low self-esteem. The dancers, the customers, the bartenders—everyone in there would rather be somewhere else. The dancers would rather be living normal healthy lives, the guys would rather be in a cheap hotel room with the dancers and the bartenders and bouncer would rather be actors or professional athletes. In expensive hotel rooms with the dancers.

Will performing in a strip club or selling drugs damage your child's self-esteem? You bet your ass it will. But low self-esteem is a disease every single kid in this country could use a little bit more of.

When I was a kid one day in grammar school one of the nuns was teaching us about what it took to become the president of the United States. After all the typical bullshit about hard work and dedication and blah blubbedy blah—she took a left turn into the Constitution and spiced it up with a little extra info—that as long as you were born in these United States and had all the other qualifications in place—ANYONE could become the commander in chief once elected. Hey—that was news to me. Up to that point the only things I had spent time dreaming of becoming were a Boston Bruin, a Boston Red Sock or the newest/youngest member of the Rolling Stones.

I walked home from school that day doing the political math in my head: I was born in America / I could—ostensibly—start working hard in school / John F. Kennedy had been the president and HE was Irish and Catholic. Not to mention the fact that he was FROM where I lived—Massachusetts. Not only that—when he was president he had one time driven through our neighborhood on his way to deliver a speech at Holy Cross—a college not more than twelve blocks from where our apartment was.

Needless to say, I arrived home with flashes of my future success illuminating my brain: people waving at me as I drove through their neighborhoods in MY motorcade; my mom yelling at the White House staff about leaving all their supposedly important papers lying around everywhere; me passing laws that would make huge differences in our society, for instance—declaring free candy and no more school for kids everywhere.

When my dad got home from work I ran right up to him.

What's up? he said.

I could barely wait to get the words out:

Sister So And So said that anyone who was born in this country has the God-given right to become the president of the United States.

That's absolutely one hundred percent true, he said.

And then she said that all you had to do was work hard in school and get a college education and get good grades and want to help people and change things and make this world a better safer place.

That's true too, he said.

And then you just get people to vote for you?

Yup.

And then if they do—you get to be president?

Yup.

(Wow. A rush of dreamy blood flooded my tiny blond head. I went in for the ultimate okay.)

So does that mean that I could become—one day—if I did all that stuff— the president of the United States?

There was a long pause. My dad looked down at me with a warm smile creasing his friendly face. Then, he said:

Hell no! Whaddayou—crazy?

Then he started to laugh as he gave me a big hug.

Hey Nars! he called out (that was my dad's nickname for my mom, whose real name is Nora)—Dinzo thought he was gonna be the president one day!

I could hear my mom's laughter bouncing off the dark brown paneling in the hallway outside the kitchen.

Then my dad leaned down and said:

You ain't ever gonna be the president, son. Because you gotta be born here, you gotta work hard in school AND—you gotta be rich. And we ain't rich. Now go get ready for supper.

And that was the end of that dream. Crushed like a bug under the immigrant boot of my no-nonsense old man.

Did it make me sad?

Yes.

Did it knock my adolescent self-esteem down a heavy notch or two?

Yup.

Did it lessen my faith in The Great American Dream?

You bet your patriotic balls it did.

But he was right. There wasn't a chance in hell I was ever going to have even a sliver of a micro-ounce of an atom's testicle of EVER getting elected to the highest office in the land where I lived. I had a better shot at growing TITS than I did living in the White House. Shit—speaking of shots— given my place in American society I was more likely to fire a weapon AT a presidential motorcade than I was to ride IN one.

So I sucked up that fact and started dreaming of being a Bruin or a Red Sock or a Rolling Stone once again.

My precious tiny self-esteem was dealt a severe blow that it desperately needed—a dose of hard-ass reality that more and more parents in this country need to drop on their own offspring: get a grip. Life sucks and is unfair and there are certain facts that will always remain hard, fast and true: pretty, thin chicks with small tits, minuscule brain waves and long long legs will become supermodels—all other chicks will demean and abhor and hate them even as they try to starve/binge/drug their way into the same set of shoes; the fastest, smallest little guy and the biggest dumbest angry guy will both make it into the same professional team sport—no matter what it is—because you can't hit what you can't catch.

My dad taught me in eight seconds what kids nowadays don't know even as they hit their late thirties: not everyone gets to do everything. My dad and my mom worked their asses off just to get to New York City and begin to live and work as illegal immigrants and they adjusted their dream as they went along because they had a family to feed. My dad was a talented musician—he played the accordion in Irish bands on the side when I was growing up. I've always had it easy with music as does my son Jack and I believe the talent comes from my father's side of the family and I'm sure Dad would have loved to make his moolah on the stage but it didn't work out that way so he became a mechanic. He loved working on engines too. He fed his kids. He bought a house. My mom stayed home and made sure we did as we were told. They both made sure we had our priorities all set straight but even more importantly they made our options crystal clear: that's why my dad cut right to the chase when it came to questions about what we could or couldn't "become." When I decided to give acting a try as a senior in high school, much to his credit my dad's response was to say it was known to be a rough road but that I should give it a try. He also told me we had no money for me to go to college and if the acting or college thing didn't work out he could always get me a job down at his company and that he could easily get me into his union. He then showed up at almost every play or show I did in college and as many as he could after I graduated—always coming backstage with a big smile on his face. When I was playing ice or street hockey in leagues as a kid he would show up for a whole game or part of the game almost every time and if I had a bitch about the coach he'd always give me the same response—HE'S the coach, not your father. Shut up and listen.

I'd say when it comes to self-esteem my mother said it best and way more than once to me, my sister Ann Marie, my brother Johnny, my baby sister Betsy, and any and all cousins from this side of the ocean or the other who tried to get above their station in this life.

Pick one:

> Just who the hell died and left you in charge, huh?
>
> Well, now—there's another county heard from.
>
> Why can't you be more like (insert smart faggy kid from school's name here)?
>
> Why don't you learn a lesson or two from (insert faggy cousin's name here)?
>
> No one asked you for your opinion mister/missy/smartass.
>
> Shut up, cut the cadology and go to bed!

You wanted self-esteem when I grew up? You had to earn it. The only rights you had were to eat whatever it was they put on the table and sleep in a warm bed and get free clothing as long as you showed up on time. And after you hit eighteen? Time to go out into the real world.

You want some self-esteem?

Then get up off your lazy ass and DO something.

Invent something, make a great catch, learn how to play the piano, cut the goddam lawn, shovel the fucking sidewalk, paint an interesting picture—anything except sit there whining about how no one pays any attention to you.

You know what kids learn when parents insist on making sure that everyone gets a trophy and everyone wins and nobody loses? They learn that losing doesn't suck. Which it does. Which is why no one wants to lose and be called a fucking loser. Jesus. You fall down you get up. That's how you learn how much falling down hurts and how much you never wanna fall down ever again. Christ. Modern moms are desperate to make sure their kids never lose, never get beat up, never get called fat, never get anything negative ever ever ever. It's okay for the kids to do whatever they FEEL like doing—never say no—just yes yes yes.

Another little story about self-esteem and all its iterations—confidence, wherewithal, ingenuity and advancement:

HOW I LEARNED TO ACT

When I was a freshman at Emerson College several of my best buddies and I were told we had to wait in line for the best parts because the juniors and seniors needed to play leading roles before they graduated. Basically that meant not getting onstage on a regular basis in a meaningful role for at least two or three years. Being an understudy, standing in the wings, hoping wishing praying plotting dreaming that one of the stars might maybe perhaps if possible suffer a broken ankle or a pinched neck nerve or a bout of laryngitis or just a full-blown onset of basic-ass stage fright.

But instead of cursing the darkness we lit it up—using the advice of one Dr. James Randall we formed The Emerson Comedy Workshop. Dr. Randall forced the Student Government Association to recognize The Workshop as a legitimate theater group and fund it, thereby allowing us to write all of our own one-act plays, variety shows, mini-musical parodies—whatever came to mind. We even ended up getting credit for all the creative work as well as the set design, lighting design, tech work et al. We did three to four shows a year. We were almost always last on the list for available theater space, but we would take whatever we were given—lecture halls, raw square spaces, even—in my favorite turn of events—a former church—and have to outfit it with a stage, lights, backstage area and seating. Our limitations always became a plus. Our shows were funny, exciting and always on the cutting edge and what began as what some people thought of as an impossibility became the hardest ticket in town—we sold out every single production for every show three theater seasons a year for three seasons running. The Workshop still exists a full thirty-two years later. I'm not telling you this as a form of braggadocio—I'm informing you how our generation of kids refused to accept the status quo. We rebelled and it paid off—big-time.

That's an example of the power of not taking no for an answer. As a matter of fact—taking no and turning it into a giant gleaming Yes. I learned everything I know about experimental original theater and comedy—from acting to writing to painting and building goddam sets—by not taking no for an answer.

Now—part two of the same story. Kind of:

HOW I BECAME A PUBLISHED POET

During the summer certain members of the workshop would travel and perform at other colleges and theaters in and around New England. In order to do so, we had to take jobs that kept us close to Emerson during the summer months. At the end of our junior year, a guy named Eagle — he was bald at age twenty, got hit with the nickname and nobody ever called him anything else but Eagle ever again—said he had a job as the assistant head janitor at the Atlantic Monthly Building. *The Atlantic Monthly* was and still is a well-respected magazine zoned in on intellectual discussions of cultural and political matters and its offices were located in several brownstones built side by side half a block from the Emerson campus. Eagle needed four guys to work the night shift as janitors during June, July and August. Adam Roth, Chris Phillips, Reagan Kennedy and I volunteered immediately. We'd never been janitors before but between the four of us there had been plenty of experience cleaning up odd puddles of beer, vomit, cheap vodka and just general leftover after-party ooze in the various hellholes we lived in—some of which Eagle had witnessed firsthand, which is to say we were well qualified. So Eagle hired us on the spot.

The pay was good but the best part was yet to come: our first night on the job, Sully The Head Janitor—classic Boston Irish guy, fifty-something, barrel-chested, redfaced with a nose that doubled as a Bushmill's bottle—explained that we were to be on time every evening at five o'clock and we were supposed to clean all four buildings in the following eight hours. However, he said as he handed each of us our own official Atlantic

Janitorial Staff short-sleeve button-down shirt (think basic bowling league red and blue), if we chose to work our balls off like slaves on cocaine, we could leave whenever the hell we got the work done.

After Sully split, Eagle said he guessed we could get through all four buildings in less than five hours if we worked like slaves on cocaine and didn't take cigarette breaks. And that's just what we did. Every night at five Sully would list off the areas where there may have been a large coffee spill or a water leak or an ink explosion and we would don our bowling shirts, grab our mops and buckets and run a full tornado sweep so swift and thorough it would have made Mr. Clean crap his tidy whitey pants. We were out on the town chasing tail and downing booze by ten-thirty almost every night. It was a dream gig.

After a few weeks we got so good we COULD take cigarette breaks—during which we started to take notice of all the office-type swag there was just piled up and lying around. It's amazing what you can convince yourself you absolutely need to have in order to survive—especially when it's stuff you have survived without up until that particular point in your life. Staplers, number two pencils, paperweights, letter openers, boxes of number two pencils, plastic coffee cups, paper clips, boxes of boxes of number two pencils, toner bottles, Sanka packets, Cremora jars, big boxes of boxes with boxes of number two pencils in them—you name it we took it. Hey—they were the big corporate giants and we were the struggling artists. We needed to write and draw and staple and sip Sanka with fake cream powder in it. At one point Reagan actually stole a rolling steel chair with some great swivel action in its legs. The rest of us decided that might be pushing the envelope a bit—although we had already pushed the envelope literally and figuratively by stealing thousands of envelopes over the course of our first month on the job.

One night during week five, Adam and I were in the editor in chief's office when he noticed something on top of the big guy's desk—a neat pile of typed pages.

Lookit this, he said.

What? I replied as I speed-polished a bookcase.

It's a bunch a poems.

What kinda poems? I said, waxing a coffee table by wrapping two towels around my forearms, spraying a shitload of Lemon Pledge on the table and flailing back and forth like a wounded trout in an Igloo cooler.

John Ashbery, he said.

(Now let me take a second to explain who John Ashbery was and is—an incredibly celebrated American poet who has won every available award, including the National Book Award, the Pulitzer Prize and, well—name one more important award and he probably has two of them. His work is dense with intellect and verbal dexterity. He will go down as one of the greatest poets in the history of the written word.)

He sucks, Adam said.

Yeah—I know, I agreed.

This must be some stuff this editor guy's thinking of puttin' in the magazine.

Yeah, I mumbled.

So.

So what?

We should get rid of this shit and put some of your stuff here instead, Adam said without even a hint of doubt.

Whaddaya nuts?

Listen ta me—this guy comes in tomorrow'n reads yer stuff—yer stuff is revolutionary, man—this editor guy's gonna read it and he's gonna flip out'n he's gonna publish it'n yer gonna be famous'n we're gonna be bangin' chicks from Harvard'n shit.

(Now, as dumb as that plan sounds please remember—we were both nineteen years old. We WERE dumb. Young, dumb and full of come. And bad poetry. I had been writing it for only about a year and a half and at the time, of course, I thought it was Groundbreaking and Important and Needed To Be Heard. Needless to say—I took the bait.)

You know two or three of your poems by heart? Adam asked.

(Of course I did. I couldn't remember the Our Father or The Latin Mass or any part of The Declaration of Independence or The Gettysburg Address beyond their titles, we the people and four score and seven years ago—but my own poems and Rolling Stone lyrics and the starting lineup of every Boston Bruin or Boston Red Sox team since I was about five years old? Those were all on the tip of my tongue.)

Let's go, I said assertively.

So Adam and I tore up John Ashbery's poems and tossed them into the trash and sat down at the desk of the editor's secretary and typed up two of my poems. This is what they were:

ONOMATOPOEM

Bang.
Bang bang.
Bang bang bang bang.
Boom.
Crack.
Bam.
Boom.
Shicka shicka shicka.
Poof.

FUCK

This.
Them.
That.
Us.
Is.
As.
Was.
Will.
Be.
And.
You.

We decided not to put my name on them—just to make the whole process an even bigger mystery. Then we tenderly stapled them together and placed them gingerly in the center of the editor's desk. Stared down at them for a long, long beat—imagining the great fortune they were about to bring our way. We literally shook hands and smiled at each other. Then, as a fitting gesture of trust and solidarity—we left the stapler behind.

Returning to our tornado sweep cleaning, we finished by ten-fifteen, hit the bars at ten-thirty and chased tail and planned plans and laughed and smoked and dreamed and laughed and went to bed and got up to rehearse with The Workshop and eagerly returned to work the following afternoon at five p.m.

It was almost five past five when the editor in chief of *The Atlantic Monthly* pulled me aside as I was once again donning my bowling slash janitor shirt down in the working-class bowels of the building. He said Adam had pointed me out as the source of the poems left atop his desk. He then congratulated me on owning—and I quote—"the most original young raw voice in poetry I have come across in almost a decade."

Wow.

Adam and I smiled beaming broad smiles as the editor and his posse of publishing elites led me upstairs where we shared flutes full of champagne and plans for my first book.

One month later "Onomatopoem" and "Fuck" made their debut in the magazine and three weeks after that I signed the deal to publish my first book of poetry with Harper Collins. It was called *Slap* and was nominated for Best New Book by The American Poetry Bank.

Which doesn't exist.

Because I just made up that happy ending to this little story of how I became a published poet.

What really happened was:

As I tugged on my shirt the day after we planted my poems, Sully entered the locker room for our daily dose of spills, blotches, wet patches and stains to clean up. The first words out of his mouth were "Who's the genius who left the crazy poems on the editor in chief's desk?" He looked around for half a second before spotting my upraised arm, which had been eagerly in the air since he had uttered the word "genius." I was more than ready for my moment in the spotlight. "Okay, asshole—turn in yer shirt. Yer officially shitcanned." Then he immediately continued reading off various dirty locations that needed special attention from the rest of the crew that night.

The dream was over so quickly I didn't even have a chance to ask a follow-up question. Sully headed out the back door and the guys all said how sucky my situation was and then they went off in search of dust and filth.

Within a few days I was working the switchboard of a swanky downtown hotel on the night shift and furiously spending the overnight hours writing more poetry. Why? So I could get better at it.

I was always one of those people who never took no for an answer. Whether it was girls or work or sports or acting, when someone told me I wasn't good enough I found another way to prove them wrong.

About three months after Sully made me turn in my bowling shirt, two things happened—out of pure spite I'd become a much better poet and ended up getting two poems published in another, more cutting-edge poetry magazine called *Ploughshares*. I was the youngest writer in that particular issue and one of the youngest they ever featured.

The other thing that happened was Adam, Chris and Reagan got shit-canned after Sully caught them trying to smuggle a whole desk out a brownstone side door.

I never tried to get my poems published again after that—I'd proven I could pull it off. I still write them for my wife and most of the time just for my private files and I love doing so, but in my heart of hearts I know the only reason I can claim to be a published poet today is because of Sully With The Bushmill's Bottle Nose. And the reason I became a successful comic is because of all the club owners who told me I was too edgy and the reason I became a working actor is due to all the acting teachers who said I didn't do what they told me to do and all of the casting directors who wouldn't cast me.

Every time I hear the word "no" I think "yes."

Every time someone says it's against the rules I wonder why the rules exist.

I don't run home with my tail between my legs—I bang down the door to find out what's on the other side.

And that comes from growing up with parents who made it clear that—within reason—you can be whatever you want to be in America but no one is just going to hand you anything, you have to go out and get it.

The harder you work, the luckier you get—that's one of the things my dad taught me.

You learn more with your mouth shut and your ears open than you do the other way around—he said that too.

Most people who are older than you are also a helluva lot smarter. That was another one of his faves.

No one owes you anything and being born into a free society means you get to say whatever the hell you want but it doesn't mean anyone has to listen.

Which is why I walk around now just wishing I could grab every other mouthy, misbehaved, spoiled and rotten little urchin I come across in airports and restaurants and just when I'm walking down the street—kids who are throwing snit fits in public as their disinterested or seemingly powerless parents stand off to the side and let the rest of us listen to the whining—I just once wanna grab them HARD by the flesh on their twiggy upper arms, that soft flesh that really really hurts—and I mean grab them bruise-inducing, five-finger-indentation-left-behind hard—and whisper Clint Eastwood–style right in their dirty little ear: Listen up and listen fast, punk, 'cause I'm only sayin' this one goddam time: yer gonna shut the fuck up right now and start doing what yer dumbass mom and dad say from here on in or a special van is gonna pull up one day and just pluck you right off the goddam street and drop your ass on a plane to Iraq where you will be dropped out of the sky with nuthin' but a parachute and a bag of white rice—no cash, no toys, no more SpongeBob SquareAss—ya follow?

I'd like to see how far their overinflated self-esteem plummets after that. Hopefully? Like a big rock in a backyard kiddie pool.

CHAPTER 7

FAMOUS DEAD KIDS

arents need to take back the control. Now. Half-assed moms and self-centered fathers should stop blaming everyone else and head back into the house. I'm not talking about two-income families where existing without both parents holding down jobs is an impossibility. I'm talking about houses where both parents had kids because it was almost a fashion accessory and then once the kids arrived, it became a constant battle over who changed how many diapers and whose turn is it to get up with the baby. Here's the bottom line: kids want their moms—almost all the time. You feel tired and unable to do anything else because the kids are a full-time job? Welcome to reality, asshole.

From caveman times to calendar date 2009—someone has to feed them and someone has to go get the food to feed them with. That's it. We—as fat loud lazy Americans—wanna watch our TV shows and drive our new cars and play golf and watch Internet porn and e-mail our girlfriends and text our BFFs and blah blah blah but BIRDS are still building nests and digging up worms and flying them back to the nest and dropping them into the mouths of the baby birds.

THAT'S HOW FAR WE HAVE EVOLVED—not even two inches.

You only get one chance to raise your children right and it's been said a million zillion trillion times but they grow up in less than a heartbeat and all the damage is done. We all get up in arms when another secretly planted webcam captures another Dominican or other illegal immigrant nanny suddenly up and slapping an innocent American baby but—quite frankly—what the fuck else did you expect? You want an underpaid stranger you've met maybe twice who barely speaks broken English to have never mind love but even an iota of empathy or a caring bone in her hand for a kid you don't have the time or desire to take care of yourself? They don't have nannies in the deepest dark areas of Africa—they have aunts and uncles and actual neighbors—the same thing I had growing up. That's what families and friends are for. Your dog is more likely to take care of your kid than a Third World worker in an entry-level position is. But in America we expect everyone to do the dirty work we find ourselves to be so far above—including wiping the fat asses of our own fat kids.

Kids have become a stepping-stone—especially daughters. The trash cans of Hollywood are lined with the litter of ex–teenage stars whose mothers wanted their own failed dreams to be fulfilled by pimping out their progeny. Lindsay Lohan's well-documented fall into drugs and drunk driving have proven one thing and one thing only to her party-hopping, publicity-mad mom: time for her and the other daughter Ali to get their own reality show! Dad just got out of jail so he has no say in the matter! Britney Spears melts down for over fifteen months on international TV and in wall-to-wall, seemingly moment-by-moment magazine coverage and what does her mom do? Write a book about being a great parent! Then her other daughter—who is sixteen—announces she's pregnant. Time to cancel the book tour? Hell no—let's make it happen right away because Britney's in the nuthouse and the heat is on! The only book I wanna read that's written by Britney Spears's mom is the one titled "How To Get One Daughter's Pussy Onto The Internet And The Other Daughter Loaded Up With Semen Before She's Even Old Enough To Drive!" Foreword By Family Friend Dr. Phil!

What would you guess—honestly speaking—the girls of the Kardashian family have in store for them? The oldest one has spread her legs and fondled her breasts in *Playboy* and one of them has gone down on and banged a rapper on a sex video that SHE HERSELF made available for sale and now their cosmetically enhanced biological mom and their ex–javelin throwing stepdad—who apparently went to the same plastic surgeon who fucked up Kenny Rogers's face—have the older girls and two sweet young innocent little ones tramping around in a reality show called *Keeping Up with the Kardashians.*

On one episode, mom and the three oldest girls agree to do a beachside photo shoot for a bikini line being sold by Girls Gone Wild impresario Joe Francis—who calls to make the offer from a jail where he is serving time for giving alcohol to underage girls and getting them to expose themselves and perform sex acts on each other while he videotaped them. Mom sells the girls on the bikini shoot by saying Joe Francis is guaranteeing the ad will be on a giant billboard on the Sunset Strip in the very city where the Kardashian family lives! Yay!

Here's another headline—the mother has a stripper pole in her bedroom and lets the girls practice their moves on it! Double yay!

I mean—this is so insane in terms of parents without brains, borders or any INKLING of common sense that all I can say is it's a dead certain lock the daughters will eventually never talk to their asshole mother again after a certain point—either because they simply have come to realize the entire planet finds them to be a joke or because they finally impaled mom and Bruce against a master bedroom wall with one of his old Olympic javelins.

It's five girls total so I'm gonna go out on a limb and offer up this fantasy Mix 'n' Match questionnaire—pretend it's eight years from now and try to peg the drug they will ultimately become addicted to and the occupation they are qualified to perform with the Kardashian daughter's name:

A. crack/whore   Kim

B. smack/whore   Kourtney

C. Oxycontin/whore   Khloe

D. cocaine/stripper   Kendall

E. Jesus/nun   Kylie

The annals of kids unleashed into the monster Hollywood machine who came out clean and still working on the adult side has two names on its list: Jodie Foster and Ron Howard. Case closed.

You wanna argue about it? Two words: Dana Plato. Two more words: Brad Renfro.

River Phoenix, Judy Garland, Mason Reese, Gary Coleman—I could go on forever.

Drew Barrymore.

I know she's clean now. But think about it—you only know her to be okay over maybe the last couple years or so, correct?

Right. Well guess what?

She just turned thirty-three.

Which means she's been high or coming down from a high or seeking another form of a high most of the time since right after *E.T.* came out.

Which was in 1982.

And she probably STILL doesn't talk to her mother.

Jennifer Aniston—as far as we know—fine. But still—as far as we know—doesn't talk to her mother.

Brooke Shields. Fine. A mother in her own right. But spent a big chunk of her lifetime not talking to her mother.

Enough with the girls? Danny Bonaduce.

Attempted suicide while shooting a reality show called *Breaking Bonaduce.* He would've actually killed himself until he came to realize the ratings would probably spike through the roof.

More boys? The OTHER black kid from the Gary Coleman sitcom. See? Don't even really know his name, do you? Gary Coleman's older brother? Come on. Think.

He was Willis. As in What You Talkin' 'Bout, Willis. Think for another second. His real name?

Ready?

Todd Bridges.

In Todd's IMDb biography, one section about the beginning of his career reads:

"It all began one day while watching Redd Foxx display his comic genius on the hit sitcom *Sanford and Son.* Todd, then six . . . exclaimed excitedly to his mother 'I want to do that!'"

Which is when his mother should have said "No problem, sweetie pie—once you turn forty-goddam-seven! Now turn that shit off and go do your homework!"

Instead she took him out of school and started carting him around to commercial auditions and his dad became his agent and they both became his pimps and blah blubbedy blah blah big hit show magazine covers *Tiger Beat* "omigod we love you!" groupies early promiscuity pot booze blow smack no hit show hates himself and his parents "omigod you look like shit! Look, it's that guy who used to be on that show!" shoplifting guntoting crackwhacking armed assault drink drive rehab.

Want some more boys?

The entire male side of the Culkin clan.

Macaulay and Rory and their failed actor dad/manager/pimp/moneywhore Kit.

Kit ran Macaulay's career into the ground in the brief span of three and a half years—from the breakthrough hit *Home Alone* in 1990 to the box-office triple flip-flop of *Richie Rich*, *The Pagemaster* and *The Good Son*, which all came out and died one after the other during 1993 and 1994.

His father had fought and won numerous battles over his kid's fees, his own fees and "creative control" over the films themselves. If ya wanna real glimpse into this guy's ego Google his website—it's got a giant list of his acting credits and his books and blah bitcheddyass blah.

After his career sputtered out Macaulay Culkin took legal action in order to be officially separated from his parents and was declared an emancipated minor. The nonfamous kids in the family—needing food and shelter, of course, and with no money to call their own—didn't.

Ya gettin' my drift here?

If I had taken my parents to court and asked for a legal separation from them and won? I'd have had to ask the judge to put me and my money in jail for as long as my parents remained alive because my father would have kicked my ass up and down the streets of Main South Worcester, Mass., shouting "I'll emancipate your skinny minor ass right now!"

In the case of Hannah Montana, whose real name is—let's face it, Hannah Montana at this point—we have a kid hellbound for a five-star career crash PLUS they have discovered that Hannah Montana back-packs made in China with pictures of Hannah painted on the back have lead paint in them and so if kids ingest the paint—they can die. First off—if kids are licking their Hannah Montana backpacks—let 'em go. Give 'em up. It's like a test run for future morons. Secondly—is there any way we can get Hannah to lick a few?

Lindsay Lohan's mom should not be repimping a second daughter while cell phone pix of her first daughter blowing some coke-addled ex-boyfriend are still circulating on the Internet. Lindsay's response? She doesn't remember. Which is evidence enough to signify why—whatever substances she was under the influence of at the time of the bj—she went into rehab. Could this happen to anyone's daughter? Sure. But unless she's famous the pictures don't get to travel all the way around the world. Lindsay's mom should be locked up WITH the dad, who now claims the reality show about second daughter/cokehead-in-waiting Ali was HIS idea and Mom even stole the title from HIM. Plus—HE was supposed to co-star. Come to think of it—let's make this a pay-per-view event—Lindsay's Ma vs. Lindsay's Pa in an alcohol and ego-fueled full-on cage match. Call it "Whose Fault Is It, Really?" And let the two vapid, empty, chemically enthralled siblings take the money and run.

Every other kid actor whose name you can think of and almost all of the ones whose names are escaping you can be qualified by one of three words: dead, addicted or well on their way to both. Okay—so it was nine words. Shoot me. Better yet—shoot their parents.

I've met a few of these people—Bonaduce seems like a nice guy and has a terrific sense of humor but he went through a real rough patch—for thirty-five fucking years. That's what fame does to a kid. He was paid to be the wiseass on *The Partridge Family* and the entire world was laughing with him not at him and then BAM! the show gets canceled, his balls drop, his voice gets deeper, his cock starts talking to him and he's not fa-mous anymore.

The ball and cock part happen to every teenaged boy but imagine what it's like when you're not making money for your parents anymore.

Everyone loves the kid who looks to be eleven but acts as if he or she is twenty-eight years old. Yay—Dakota Fanning! She's oh so cute and sooo precocious!

Yeah—okay. Reserve the rehab spot right now. Book her next nine movies AND a three-month stay at Promises in Malibu during the exact same phone call. She's eleven and a half but can drink like she's thirty. Delete her mom's number from her cell phone. Better yet—delete her mom.

Here's the right answer when your child points at the TV and says "I wanna do that!":

NO.

N - O.

CAPITAL FUCKING N. CAPITAL FUCKING O.

Forget what you want or what you didn't get to do or how much money you can manufacture or all your best-laid plans or your dreams of stardom or wanting your kid to like you.

No no no no no.

Embrace the power of no in all its iterations:

No Nada Nein Nyet Fuck no Shit no No fucking way Not now Not ever Never ever What did I just motherfucking say? Not as long as I live Not over my dead body Not even if hell freezes over.

These are the acceptable answers.

Here is a small sampling of the questions that get an automatic, loud, fast, no negotiation involved no:

Can I be on TV?

Can I get a tattoo?

Can I get my hair cut like Lindsay Lohan?

Can I get pierced ears?

Can I watch *The Sopranos*?

Can I have a sweet sixteen party like they have on MTV when I grow up?

Can I be home-schooled?

That's right—DO NOT HOME SCHOOL YOUR KID!

Danica Patrick, Race Car Driver

This is my favorite shot of my mom and dad—she's being cute and cool and he's being very sardonic.

My mother, when asked to recall this picture and who, what, where, when, etc., said, "That's me and Dad on the left and Aunt Bridie, Aunt Margaret and Uncle Timo on the right. The lady in the middle is dead and so is her husb──────── ─── 'one else in her family so don't worry about her at all." I love this sh─── ───── ─ and dad look so happy. As does the dead lady.

Me and my dad and a doll I stole from my sister Ann Marie and a
Christmas tree that would make even Charlie Brown wince.

Xmas 1965. Same tree apparently. It's grown a little fuller, though. Left to right: Me,
Jerry, Noreen, Ann Marie, and Johnny. You got one big present every year. Mine was a
Felix the Cat game I was way too proud of. My brother seems to have a Creepy
Crawlers molding tray in front of him, which I'm sure he used to try and melt my face off.

August 18, 1959. My brother Johnny, my sister Ann Marie, my dad and me. It's my second birthday. Johnny is already planning his first attempt to murder me.

This is me dressed up to go to the St. Peter's High School senior prom when I was eleven years old. I think my date was the girl on the right. After this night on the town, I did not drop out of school and move to Hollywood to become a pill-popping, drunk-driving, shoplifting, cocaine-addled celebutard whose acting career is over by the time he reaches the legal drinking age. Although that's what I had in mind. My parents wouldn't let me do it. Thanks Mom! Thanks Dad!

This is our family—My wonderful son, Jack, and my gorgeous daughter, Devin, alongside their fabulous mom. I know, I know—I'm speaking in cliché adjectives—but it's true.

This is the tux and tie I wore to the Emmys the year *People* magazine picked me as one of its "Worst Dressed." The fact that I was standing next to this gorgeous woman all night and someone managed to even glimpse what I was wearing still astounds me.

CHRIS HATCHER / PR PHOTOS

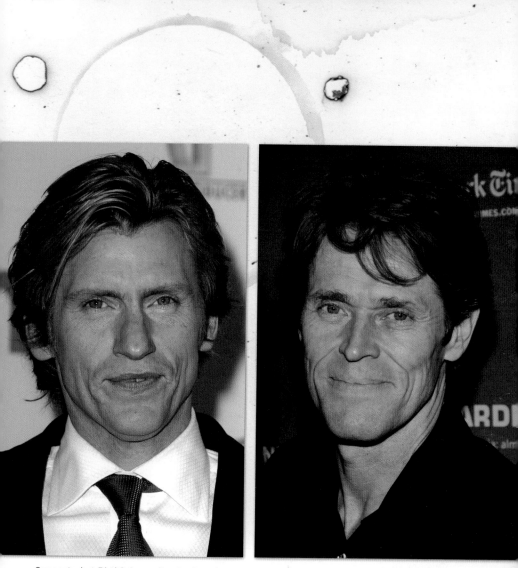

Seperated at Birth? According to *People* magazine—yes. That's me on the left and Willem Dafoe on the right. I don't see it. And I apologize to him if every time I hear, "You were awesome in *Spiderman*!" he has to listen to "Why the hell did you do *Operation Dumbo Drop*?"

Legislate This: That's Paddy Brown lying on top of a rescue rope to keep it in place for Paddy Barr—who then lowers himself a couple of stories down to rescue a man trapped in a smoke-filled window some twenty or so stories above midtown Manhattan. If you don't have the cojones to pull this off, you shouldn't become a firefighter.

(LEFT) REPRINTED AS COURTESY OF THE NEW YORK POST
(RIGHT) AP/WIDE WORLD PHOTOS/M. SURIANI

I don't wanna hear your justifications but I'm sure they include many or all of these unique reasons: my kid is special / my kid doesn't get along with all the other kids / my kid is smarter blah blubbedy blip.

Your kid needs to be in a building full of other kids so that your kid can figure out how to socialize and play and get beaten up by bullies.

Staying home with mommy full-time is like living in a bubble where there is no crime no tension no sex no fear no trouble no pressure.

Not being on TV or the movies means being a real kid.

Being a real kid means long stretches of homework interspersed with trying to avoid the mean kids or become one of them.

Your job is to drop your kid off into the belly of the beast every morning and then pick them up and take them home and fill 'em up with food and some advice before starting the whole process all over again the very next day.

No home-schooling, no protective bubble, no red carpet.

Will your kid hate you? Yup. And here's a little headline for you: your kids are SUPPOSED to hate you. YOUR KID IS YOUR KID—NOT YOUR GOD-DAM BEST FRIEND.

Believe me—they may hate your fat ass now but they will thank you immensely later on.

Seven million kids have been thrown into the star-making machine and how many made it out?

Two.

Jodie Foster and Ron Howard.

Once known as the twelve-year-old hooker from *Taxi Driver* and fucking Opie.

Now known as two bright and shiny Oscar winners.

That's it. Everyone else died or got arrested or sits in jail or found Jesus or is smoking a big fat bowl of crack while you are reading this and STILL vowing revenge on their filthy, money-grubbing parents.

They don't talk to their moms anymore because they blame their mothers for not protecting them. For not making them stay in the nest. If a bird mom lets a baby bird leave the nest before it's old enough, it crashes to the ground and gets eaten by:

A. A cat.

B. A snake.

C. One of the Culkin kids who skipped the court case bullshit, emancipated himself and now just lives in the woods on his own.

Have you noticed a dearth of sparrows in and around Manhattan ever since Macaulay divorced his dad?

Coincidence? Me thinks not.

CHAPTER 8

NUNS, TITS, BOOZE AND MY MOM

ird moms keep the babies in the nest until their biological clocks tell them it's time to kick them out and let them fly away and start their own families.

That's what Dr. Full should be saying on his show—instead of trying to sneak Britney Spears out of the nuthouse and onto his cheap studio sofa in order to spike his ratings. Where did parents who play with a full deck of cards disappear to?

I called my mom just now—literally, I hung up the phone and started typing the words you are currently reading—because I have some expertise in the area of kids and showbiz. My career began when I was eleven. A nun grabbed me in the hallway at school and told me to show up that night at an audition for the high school musical—there were twelve grades in my school—St. Peter's. So I went home and asked my mom and walked back that night and did a little singing and dancing and some acting as well and the nun said thank you and I headed home. I got the part and it sparked an interest in being onstage or in front of the camera that never went away.

I called my mom to ask if there was ever any discussion about me going into showbiz at that point—real showbiz—and giving up school etcetera etcetera. This is what my mom said:

Hello.

Ma?

Denis?

Hey.

How are you?

Good. Listen, Ma—

Sheila Turbody has bad cancer of the face—it spread all down her neck and into her throat and into her brain.

What?

The doctors say she should never have been spending all that time out in the sun without a hat or sunscreen or anything at all plus she was smoking and—

Ma—who is Sheila Turbody?

You know who Sheila Turbody is. She lived around the corner all her kids got straight A's? Remember?

Oh. Those kids—yeah. Nobody liked them.

Listen, Brian—you had better stop that smoking and wear some sunscreen and—

It's Denis, Ma.

Don't change the subject.

Ma—listen. When I was doing that first play I did—*Mame*—when I was like eleven or whatever I was—was there ever any talk—did I come and ask you guys maybe about leaving school and trying to make it as a kid in showbiz or any—

Good God no, Denis—are you crazy? You were good but you weren't THAT good. We were happy to have you in the show and we went to see them and all but then it was right back to school. Show business. Where did you get that idea?

I was just wondering if I ever asked you if I could leave school and become—

Oh no no no—we would never've put up with that kinda—no one around here knew anything about that. Why?

I'm just writing this section of my book and—

What book?

I'm writing a book about—

You better watch out what you put in that book.

Okay—I gotta go.

(warning-type tone) Denis.

(mocking her warning-type tone) Ma.

What kind of book?

It's funny.

Are they paying you for it?

Yes.

What happened to the TV shows and the movies?

I'm still doing those, I'm just—

None of us thought you'd be doing all this kinda stuff—we didn't know what was going to happen to you. All the cadology and the blighyarding— the vicious blighyarding you would get up to.

Ma—what does blighyarding mean?

You know exactly what it means.

Well—if it is what I think it is—they pay me to do it now.

Well—that's what's great about this country. What's the name of the book?

Never mind.

(with great gravity) Denis.

(mocking her gravity) Ma.

Don't put me in that book.

I gotta go.

Did you go to Mass this week?

No.

You know it's Ash Wednesday?

Really? I just thought people suddenly decided to start putting cigarettes out on their foreheads.

That's not funny.

Yes it is.

Don't you put that in your book.

Okay—I won't. See you on Easter, Ma.

Okay. Thanks for calling, honey. I love you and I'm so proud of you, honey.

CLICK.

(Note—Blighyarding [my spelling]. This one I looked up everywhere once again—INCLUDING World Wide Goddam Words. I could have Googled Galaxy Wide Words and Infinity Wide Words. It absolutely does not exist outside of my mom, my Aunt Bridie and my Aunt Margaret. So my mom and only the two sisters who followed her here to America somehow came up with a term that—as far as I can tell—refers to causing trouble. So we can assume that blighyarding means cursing, pretending to eat horrible overboiled food when in fact you are feeding it to the dog under the table—because even my mom's cats wouldn't eat the stuff—and other minor crimes committed inside or around the house. Vicious blighyarding would seem to mean egging other people's houses and windshields [especially in the winter when the eggs would splatter and freeze], breaking streetlights with rocks, stealing priests' wallets, drinking the holy wine, five-finger discounting booze and baseball cards and making fun of the Mass DURING Mass and ridiculing the nuns and priests behind their backs. In general—just being a wiseass and a troublemaker. I guess I should be proud of the fact that my brother Johnny, my cousins Jerry and Noreen and the New York cousins Terrence and Denis were so off the charts that they had to invent a word to describe our behavior. Anyways—back to why I didn't end up overdosing on heroin when I was fifteen years old.)

I didn't go from a high school production of the musical *Mame* right out to Hollywood to become a giant kid star because of two key words: my parents. I didn't overdose on blow or smack or a combination of both before I was old enough to vote because my stupid mom wouldn't let me.

I was allowed to go hang out with older kids and a nun every night after school for several months and sing and dance and ogle. That's right—I said ogle. Let me explain:

1. When I walked into the hallway outside the room where the audition was—even though I was only eleven—I remember a bevy of beautiful girls—high school girls (translation: they had tits)—who were NOT dressed in their school uniforms but in tight jeans and tops. Man.

2. When I was auditioning—once inside the room—I looked up to realize all eyes were on me. And when I say all eyes—I should say all female eyes—since the room was jampacked full of the girls from the hallway. All staring at *moi*. And *moi* liked it. Girls girls girls. Lips hair hips asses ankles nipples—you name it.

Long story short I got the part of Patrick Dennis—Auntie Mame's nephew—and got my first laugh ever onstage on opening night when I made my entrance and said my line (which wasn't supposed to be funny) and the audience went crazy. When I came offstage, the nun grabbed me and said "No wonder! Zip up your fly!" And something clicked in my head. Every night after that—right before I made my entrance—I made sure to unzip my fly. I got one big laugh when I walked out and another big laugh when I pretended to realize and nervously zipped it up.

What I remember about rehearsals for that play was watching all the high school boys being COMMANDED by the nun to grab the girls by the ass and hold them up in the air—grab the girls around the waist and hold them tight—grab the girls grab the girls. These guys were not only allowed to touch these girls all over their bodies—it was completely and totally allowed. PLUS backstage when there were furious costume changes going on, every once in awhile you'd get to see a girl slip right out of one dress and then climb into another—which meant UNDERWEAR! VAGINA OUTLINES IN PANTIES! GLIMPSES OF TITS! NIPPLE SLIPS! I made many mental notes about all of these things and shared them with all my guy friends—by the time we hit high school every guy I knew was volunteering to be in the fall musical the spring musical and every single fashion and/or dance show in between. It was a perfectly legal chance for an ass grab or a tit rub or a combination of both. Not to mention the occasional free-floating chick undressing and redressing right there in front of you.

When I was doing *Mame* all kindsa high school girls paid attention to me—they hugged me, kissed me, tweaked my cheek, laughed at my jokes—I was surrounded by girls with big tits, small tits, round asses, tight asses—blue eyes, brown eyes—you name it. I even ended up going to the senior prom that year because one of the girls had a boyfriend who was over in Vietnam and she took me instead of another guy. I went to a couple of parties after the prom and got an eyeful of guys french kissing and feeling girls up—funny how I can still remember that almost minute by minute, tongue after tongue and stroke by stroke but I can't make my way through a Hail Mary anymore.

But the reason I bring this up now is to illustrate the fact that kids should be FORCED to stay kids as long as they can.

I saw booze and tits and cigarettes and tongues and other things I wanted to sip, savor, lick, grab and smoke that night and if my mom had let me drop out of school I would've been chasing them 24/7. As it came to be I was smoking and drinking beer within a couple of years anyways but I was also doing my homework and washing dishes in a diner after school and on weekends and hoping desperately to somehow get into college.

My mom always kept our feet nailed hard and fast to the ground. She told us no when we wanted to hear yes and my dad was right there to back her up.

You should not be making money off of your kids, your kids should not be leaving school to act or dance or traipse up and down the runway stages of beauty pageants.

They should be coloring and running and crying and sleeping and feeling safe and warm and fuzzy and all the other things we all know to be what's right for them.

INCLUDING learning how to lose.

AND how to deal with bullies.

You will hear mom after mom and father after father say but she/he WANTS to be in the movies/in a band/on a stage. Hey—join the fucking club. It's all kid code for I don't wanna go to school. I wanna dance and sing and hang around with famous people—who the fuck doesn't? If I could have been singing with The Dave Clark Five on *The Ed Sullivan Show* instead of getting slapped by frustrated lesbians dressed up in religious gear when I was ten I would've done it in a heartbeat. Shit—I'd do it with Cyndi Lauper on VH1 right now.

You choose to be a mom it means you choose to be at home. You choose to be a dad and mom is staying at home? You choose to work and make the money to pay for what mom needs to feed, clothe and shelter the kids. You choose either job? You better pay attention to what the kids do say dream wish puke piss fart think et al.

You don't want the kids watching certain things on TV—watch your kids while they watch TV. I know—SpongeBob's good but most of the other shows really suck and you wanna watch The Big Game/Your Show/ anything that's not a kid show. Tough shit. Don't call the Parents Half-Baked Godforsaken TV Council group so they can legislate shows like *Rescue Me* and *The Sopranos* out of existence—change the fucking channel. WE are not in charge of raising your kids THE NANNY is not in charge of raising your kids THE PRESIDENT WHO GOT A BLOW JOB is not in charge of raising your kids BARRY BONDS is not in charge of raising your kids JANET JACKSON'S LEFT NIPPLE is not in charge of raising your kids—YOU ARE. You wonder why kids have such low self-esteem? Because they have spent enough time around their parents to realize that mommy hates herself and daddy hates her and they both hate each other and it's everyone else's goddam fault.

Ask yourself an honest question: why the fuck did you have the kids in the first place?

Famed *Rolling Stone* magazine and celebrity photographer Annie Leibovitz had her first child at age fifty-one after sticking a turkey baster full of donated semen between her legs because she and her lesbian lover decided they finally wanted kids. Leibovitz claimed the reason it took her so long to consider being a mom was because she "forgot to have children."

Wow.

She forgot to have children.

She didn't forget to travel the world for five decades photographing the rich and the famous.

She didn't forget to put out giant, gorgeous coffee table–sized books full to overflowing with her incredible celebrity portraits.

She didn't forget to become the photo editor for *Vanity Fair*—the magazine for which she shot the controversial cover featuring Demi Moore naked and pregnant in 1991.

She set-dressed, supervised the body makeup for and ultimately captured the beauty of the fully expressed female body in its ultimate state of motherhood and still—somehow—she didn't think it might be nice to have a kid of her own.

Not for another goddam decade.

Sorry, Annie.

I ain't buyin' it.

I think you are a genius with a camera in hand—and I'm sure that as I write this I am forfeiting what little chance I ever had of getting my picture taken by you—but you didn't forget to have a family. You just decided—like a lot of women—that you wanted to do what you wanted to do. A lot. For a really long time.

Then—once you did all the fun stuff—you wanted a kid.

And once you wanted that kid—Mother Nature and the natural course of sexual events and the kid's own best interests should be tossed aside in favor of your "Things To Do At 51" birthday party Post-it note.

Having a kid at forty is considered a dangerous proposition by every available medical expert. After forty it becomes a roll of the baby dice. But fifty? That not only desperately increases the health risk to mother AND child, but also the chances they will both be wearing diapers at exactly the same time.

The reasons nature wants a woman to have her children between the ages of twenty and thirty-five are absolute and incredibly logical:

So the mom remains clear of mind and strong of body.

So your breast milk is full of the nutrients the baby needs to build its necessary immune system.

So when the kid graduates from high school you can be in the audience with a digital camera and a tear in your eye instead of sucking on an oxygen mask from your high-end Stephen Hawking–designed wheelchair.

You have kids when you are young because their lives become your life. That's what a mom is meant to do. You don't have kids because your life is almost over and there's nothing to watch on TV and you've shot all the imaginable cover ideas with every single celebrity still alive.

To make matters worse—four years later? Annie Leibovitz decided to have MORE kids. Twins. When she was fifty-five years old. Only this time with the help of some fertility drugs.

And a surrogate mother.

I guess Annie forgot she had a vagina.

CHAPTER 9

LADIES AND GENTLEMEN, PLEASE WELCOME—IN UTERO

his business of surrogate parenthood reached its peak for me when I turned on *The Today Show* one morning to see Lisa and Brian Switzer. They had tried for eight years to get pregnant—many, many times. No luck.

When that didn't work—they tried fertility drugs. Many many times. Ninety thousand dollars' worth. Still no luck.

They reached the point where the final doctor they saw said to Lisa—no doubt in the nicest way possible—"your uterus is just not up to the task."

Ouch.

So they then approached Brian's sister and she agreed to carry their baby to term—until she was hit by a drunk driver and suffered back injuries that didn't paralyze her but left her unable to physically deal with a pregnancy.

Once again—if there was no bad luck, they wouldn't have any luck at all, right?

Wrong. Here is where I would pose this question—what does God have to do? Write you a personal note? Hit your tits with lightning? Set your dick on fire?

Maybe He just doesn't want you to have a child.

Do the Switzers get that message? No. Do they reconsider what God's plan for them might be? Adoption? Working with special-needs kids? Helping Augusten Burroughs's weird blabbermouth brother?

No no no no.

They deem it must be time to Rent-A-Vadge.

But not even an American vadge.

Apparently a uterus in the United States of America—just like everything else here—costs more to rent. So the Switzers have outsourced a uterus in India.

I believe this is the point at which buying a Chinese baby starts to serve its purpose. There may be as many as a billion kids over there waiting to be delivered to the wide streets of America and renamed from Wang Chung to Colleen or Ida or Louisiana Switzer—as difficult as it may be to grow up different even in the confines of your own house, it's gotta be better than your parents basically purchasing a pussy from overseas just because it's cheaper.

I mean—you may not look like your adoptive parents but at least you're already here on earth.

But then again—this is America. Where we get whatever we want whenever we want it. And if it's not here to be got? Let's buy it from one of those immigrants overseas who we don't want living inside this country's confines. Basically—we don't want your kids coming here—unless we get to buy them.

And this is all a legal process that somehow fits within the confines of our Constitution.

Thomas Jefferson is not only rolling over in his grave right now, he wants to donate some semen.

American Vadge. Good name for a band.

As is Wang Chung.

Lisa Switzer may have been unable to have a baby even if she had started out trying when she was eighteen years old. And you have to give her credit for not stopping in her quest to be a mom. But passing the sperm of her puffy white husband Brian through an egg implanted in an Indian woman has all the potential of producing another kid who looks "different."

Different from its parents when it's dropped off at school.

Puffy? Maybe. White? Probably not.

The bullies and the mean girls and everyone else in between will be lining up to make fun.

And America is already full to popping with kids who don't like the way they look and moms who freak out because they are so concerned about it.

CHAPTER 10

SELF-ESTEEM THIS

 et's face it—kids in Africa and many other piss-poor places are concerned with one thing and one thing only—are flies food? But here in America—the land of plenty—it's all about looks. Kids here get inundated with reasons to hate themselves—skin too dark, nose too big, legs too thin. Magazines, TV, more magazines, more TV—even on the Internet—kids are shown how not beautiful they are and how easy it will be to fix that problem. And moms buy right into it.

Get this through your thick skull—it's okay to hate yourself. Your nose your legs your ass your tits etcetera etcetera. Chicks—moms in this case—seem to think that hating parts of your own body or the way your voice sounds or the way in which you run or dance or sing or whatever is a sign that they have somehow been robbed at birth and therefore have a God-given birthright to have it fixed or somehow praised into the positive by other chicks who will tell them and their kids how perfect they are. Bullshit.

There has always been an unwritten rule among men and boys—nicknames are applied by everyone other than yourself. Women don't understand this. Women call each other by their first names—Ellen and Annie and Steph. Guys call each other by their last names almost from the moment they meet. Then—after they start hanging out—nicknames get invented. In a woman's world, if there are two Ellens in the same group of friends or co-workers—they refer to each as redheaded Ellen or Ellen Insert Last Name Here. Among men—redheaded Ellen would become Red or Carrot Top, shortened to CT or Carrot. Or she'd be Redbush. Or Helen Reddy. Forever. You know the much maligned freaky-looking redheaded prop comic called Carrot Top? That ain't a stage name. He got that moniker in the school yard five seconds after his parents dropped him off on the first day of kindergarten. (If you think Mick Jagger would not have been called Niggerlips if he had gone to grade school in America, you just ain't living in the real world.)

And to break it down even further—among men any physical inability or shortcoming would eventually—on the ice or the playing field or in the workplace—be part of the nickname process. A guy who can't run very fast becomes Pokey or Fatass or Snail. Or the opposite—Speedy or Bullet or Jackrabbit (if his given name is Jack). The unfortunate guy with glasses gets the classic Four Eyes or Xray or Ray Charles (Ray for short). A guy with no left leg becomes Righty.

A buddy of mine knew a kid whose brother was sent to Vietnam in the sixties and only a couple of days after landing there was killed in the line of duty. When the news reached home this kid's reaction was to shake his head no over and over again. For days afterward he walked around shaking his head no. After a few weeks it appeared he was going to do this forever. One day he was walking down the other side of the block—lost in his own thoughts and shaking his head no over and over and over again. That was it. He was nicknamed No No Johnson and even after he got over the loss of his brother and stopped shaking his head he was still called No No. Picking up teams for street hockey? I'll take No No. Going down the railroad tracks to drink beer and smoke cigarettes? Go tell No No. Heading to the beach for a weekend trip—who's driving? No No's got his dad's car. The guy is now in his forties and STILL answers to that nickname at barbecues and golf outings and pickup hockey games.

I've got a friend who's a terrific hockey player—he basically drank his way out of a career on the ice—but clean and sober and in his thirties he's good enough that Cam Neely—who's in the Hockey Hall of Fame—skated a friendly outdoor ice game with him a couple of winters ago and said "that guy's great with the puck." And a guy who gets a hefty mixture of respect, admiration and fear from everyone he plays with. He never even got a nickname—that's how good he was. When guys can't even think of a nickname for you, it means you are pretty much physically and men- tally flawless. This guy is from outside Boston and has a thick Massachu- setts accent and sometimes the other guys might bust his balls about it, but that's about as far as it went.

Long story short—he recently took a puck to his left eye and temporarily went blind—when I say temporarily I mean he eventually gained his vi- sion back, but for the three or four months during which he couldn't see out of that eye but kept on skating you know what his nickname on the ice was? Lefty. And when we started calling him that he started answer- ing to it. With a smile. He finally had a nickname and one—considering the circumstances—that was also funny. Lefty. Girls wouldn't even think of UTTERING that nickname.

We got a guy named Steve we all call Stavros because he looks like he's Greek—even though his childhood nickname was Zippo because he used to set everything on fire, and we also call him Sniper because he can put the puck behind the goalie like he's a Lee Harvey Oswald and the net is John F. Kennedy sitting in a limousine.

We got three Jeffs and a Geoff—so all four had to become last-name nickname guys but one Jeff's last name was too long and sounded like a Polish guy who ran an Irish bar so we shortened it from McCluskey to Clucker.

When his brother joined up a few months later we boiled it all down to Cluck 1 and Cluck 2. We got a guy named Josh who owns a bike shop but was easily confused with another Josh who was friends with another guy named Mike so now we got Bike Josh and Josh Who Knows Mike.

I play hockey with another guy whose name is Jonny. The first time he played with us, instead of using white hockey tape on his hockey socks, he used postal tape. The kind that comes in a big wide roll that the U.S. Post Office uses to seal up large boxes when they ship them. His nick- name that night became Postal. It's what we have called him ever since, on the ice and off. I don't even know the guy's real last name. None of the guys do. He's Postal. When he calls on the phone he says Hey it's Postal. When guys run into him at the mall they say Hey I ran into Postal at the mall. If he snapped and shot sixteen people at work and it was on the news, I'd call up a mutual friend and say Postal just went postal—turn on CNN, they got it live.

If there was a guy on a hockey team whose penis was accidentally sliced off and he continued to play and undress in front of the other guys, his nickname would soon become Dick. Or Ballsack. Or Barbie. And eventually he would answer to that name. Because that's what men do.

I find it hard to imagine women calling a friend who had suffered through breast cancer Titless. Or Nipples. Or Lefty.

When I was growing up—based on the spelling of my name—Denis became Penis which became Penis Man when I went to college. I also got DeeLeerious, D, Learjet, Queerjet, Peen and Pennis. My brother Johnny was called Jumpin' Jack Flash and Kiwi. Which is what everyone still calls him. Kiwi. The reason why involves a long story about him and his friend Mike who everyone calls Pete. Which is another story. Everyone calls my brother Kiwi, including my wife my kids his wife his kids and both of my sisters and their kids. My sister Ann Marie's husband Neil went to high school with me—he was a hockey player who was a very flashy skater. His nickname became Blades. My sister—Blades's wife? No nickname. My sister Betsy? No nickname. My wife? Ann? Leary? No nickname.

Most women discard the nicknames their boyfriend/fiancé/husbands have in favor of—you know the drill—not even the shortened version of the guy's real name. A guy the guys all call Steve is called Steven by his chick. Bobby becomes Robert. Max is always Maximillian. Formal. Serious. Unfun.

It's the same avoid-reality-at-all-costs crap you notice in women's basketball. Listen—in men's sports the coaches are predominantly guys whose faces reflect the game they played. Football coaches have broken noses and bad knees and the ones who don't are short or fat or both. Baseball managers are generally speaking bowlegged and beer-bellied. Hockey coaches have scars all over their faces and fake teeth. Basketball coaches are goofy-looking lanky-assed giants who are almost always wearing ill-fitting suits. And when you watch a game on TV many of the male announcers will mention just exactly what the coach looks like or the coach's nickname or how badly said suit looks. Phil Jackson looks like he failed the audition for a Frankenstein movie because he looked TOO freaky. Bill Belichick looks and dresses like he's two dollars away from being homeless. And every male announcer—and quite a few female broadcasters—remark upon this during every basketball and football season.

Ever hear anyone on broadcast TV mention the paucity of attractive female coaches in all of girls basketball?

Nope.

Any nicknames or mention of oversized skirts or makeup that seems to have been applied with a six-inch brush?

Nope.

Most of the women who coach women's basketball teams look like dykes. As do many of the players. Don't like to hear that fact? It's true. Just ask a man who has no interest in sleeping with you. The LPGA is the other sport chock full of lesbian lookers—it should be called the Lesbian Professional Golf Association. Even the MEN'S golf tour—minus Tiger Woods and maybe seven other guys—is jam-packed with men who look like lesbians. Let's be honest, Phil Mickelson is ten more pounds and two man-tits away from being mistaken for one.

Look—I have no problem with lesbians owning any and all collegiate and professional female sports—it just yanks my chain when we all continue this unspoken agreement not to mention it. We carry on this bullshit approach and pretend they are all so feminine and pretty and dainty and guess what—most of them absolutely ain't. Which is fine. I'll pay them the ultimate compliment—I play hockey and I'm glad I don't have to play against most of these girls because I think they would kick my ass. Hey— there's fighting in hockey.

I take the same approach to female athletes as I do with guys—and I play with and against some girls on the ice from time to time—everyone is expected to do their job. Otherwise—get off the fucking ice. I would do the same with famous female athletes if I was an announcer. For years I have claimed that the reason Randy Johnson—one of the world's ugliest human beings and one of baseball's most dominating pitchers—has had such an overpowering ability to strike out the other side is not necessarily his fastball—it's his face. I think once he comes out of his wind-up and turns the full frontal toward the plate, batter after batter has to avert his gaze. THAT'S how ugly this guy is. He looks like Big Bird from Sesame Street would if he got hit with a frying pan coated with cooking grease.

For years now John Daly has arrived at golf courses around the world looking like a beached whale just back from a four-day bender in the Vodka Tonic Sea. Hair askew, armfat dangling, shirt barely big enough to tuck into the too-tight pants. All I'm asking is the freedom to say the same thing about an aging, overweight lesbian pro golfer without getting dirty looks from girl golf nuts.

The bottom line is that one day there will be a professional football team which will have a defensive line dominated by four giant gay men—due to genetics, performance-enhancing drugs, workout regimens and the increasing openness of our society, it's only a matter of time—and once those guys start winning, the moniker The Four Fags will either become a nickname amongst themselves and their teammates or the way opposing coaches respectfully refer to them during pregame war plans or both. It's the way men are. It's the way men compete. It would just be nice if women did the same thing. Call a crazy point guard from the UCLA Women's basketball team The Witch From The West. Nickname the feisty left wing from the girls USA Olympic Ice Hockey Team a bitch on wheels. Tits Akimbo (can't tell which direction she's going), Vadge On Fire (unbelievably fast), Look Away Lindsay (ugly as sin)—these are nicknames just waiting to be applied.

Flat-chested women go out and get balloon-size fake tits. Guys go to the gym. Fat girls subject themselves to years and years of endless dieting before finally throwing in the towel and getting liposuction. Fat guys go to the gym. Gals with huge noses gaze at themselves in mirrors and shop windows and any other available reflective public surface until finally getting the honker hacked off and replaced by one of a suitable size. Guys just grow a mustache. The chinstrap beard was invented by a husky guy trying to reduce the size of his neckfat. We hate to go to the doctor. We go to the barber instead. Big ears? Leave a little more on the sides. Women often accuse men of not telling the truth or being emotionally dishonest. Meanwhile, the odds are the woman you have just met is not the woman you will see in the bedroom. Once she removes her padded bra and compressive-waisted panty hose and false eyelashes and fake nails, you might be looking at someone other than who you were attracted to. If guys get fat, we just buy bigger pants.

Women have some insane system of numbers when it comes to sizing clothes—6, 8, 4, 2 etc. And even then they seem to have no idea what size they really are—size 10s are constantly trying to suck themselves into size 8s and size 4s are always doing insane acrobatics and extreme yoga positions in changing rooms across the country in vain attempts to fit into size 2s.

Guys know our sizes. We have small, medium, large and extra large. Except of course when it comes to our cocks. Then we are all size large. Which reminds me—why is it whenever plus-size chicks are in denial about their weight, they always claim that their tits got bigger? That's the equivalent of a fat guy claiming that all the fat from the burgers he's been scarfing went right into his penis—which would really be a lie because for any guy the first sign you weigh too much is almost always the same: you wake up one morning and cannot see your penis.

By the way—someone—usually a chick—has to tell a guy he's fat/ugly/smelly. Even though his guy friends may have nicknamed him Slim/Handsome/B.O., he still thinks he's attractive to SOME chick SOME where. Guys don't look at any aspect of themselves as a detriment. No arms? Play soccer. No legs? Wheelchair basketball. No sane chick will have sex with me? They got available hookers on Craig's List. Click on a couple buttons and they come right over. Is this what Al Gore had in mind when he invented the Internet?

CHAPTER 11

MATT DILLON IS A GIANT FAG

en have an innate ability to cut to the goddam chase. There is no let's pretend Johnny is good-looking even though he's got acne scars and one eye facing in the wrong direction. He's called Fugly (short for fucking ugly) or Wall Eye (Wally for short). We don't have the time or inclination to bullshit our way around the reality of life—we put the cards right on the table. It's why guys never know who the good-looking guy in their gang is until they start hanging around with girls and witness which guys the girls go crazy for. It's the truth—we have no idea if a guy we know is handsome and we don't care—as long as he is willing to grab a shovel and go to work or play whatever sport it may be as hard and driven as the rest of us he's an equal member of the team. Once we find out he's good-looking—there is no jealousy. We just immediately go into "what can we get out of this" mode. In other words—the prettiest chick at the party will probably wanna talk to him which means her slightly less pretty friends will need other guys to talk to—which is where we come in.

One of my old friends is Matt Dillon and let me tell you—when it's just the guys hanging around, no one gives a shit what Matt Dillon looks like. He's gotta carry boxes or cover the wide receiver or pass the ball or do an equal amount of driving as the next guy.

Women—however—have this built-in desire to tell even their fat ugly friend that she is pretty. Or funny. Or talented. When in fact she is none of the above. Ask any guy and he'll tell you—when a guy's wife or girlfriend says oh you just gotta meet my friend blah blah blah she is SOOO funny and soooo great, the first thing we ask is—is she hot? The pause right before they answer is all the information you need. No—the pause is telling you—she is not hot. At all. Listed below are the first four things most chicks say about their available friends, followed by the truth:

A. She's really cute, she's got great eyes and she's funny. (She's got cute lips, nice eyes and snorts like a stuck pig when she laughs.)
B. She looks like Michelle Pfeiffer. (IF Michelle Pfeiffer had just been in a car crash.)
C. She's very very pretty. (She's fat.)
D. She's got an amazing body. (But the FACE of Tina Yothers.)
E. She's incredibly smart. (She won't shut up.)

Likewise, if you hear any woman describe another woman using the terms listed below—almost the exact opposite will be true:

A. She's an idiot. (She's got massive tits.)
B. She's anorexic. (She's got great legs and a flat stomach.)
C. She's so self-centered. (Guys love her.)
D. Her ass is huge. (She's Jennifer Lopez.)
E. She's a bitch. (She's gorgeous and funny and will fuck your brains out five minutes after she meets you.)

Chicks will take precious time and carefully chosen words to spend on chubby or homely or big-boned female friends—referring to their bee-stung lips or slow metabolism or zaftig curves. But when they watch Cindy Crawford walk out to greet Jay Leno on *The Tonight Show*? She's too hippy. Julia Roberts in an extreme close-up during a big-budget romantic drama? Her mouth's too horsey. Kate Moss in a magazine? I don't find her sexy at all. Okay—but then again, you don't have a cock. I do—and take it from me when I tell you that four out of five men who HAVE cocks? They would jump into bed with either one of those three in half a heartbeat.

There's a very good reason why most of the girls who star in American-made romantic comedies are considered "cute," "cuddly" or the classic "girl next door" type. Because women are the main audience for these chick-friendly flicks. Women are almost guaranteed to drag their boyfriend/husband/sperm donor out to see it on opening weekend. Women will go see the film several times more if they like it. Then rent or buy the DVD a few months later. As long as the star is not a threat or—at the other end of the same spectrum—represents the hope that normal chicks could possibly land an incredibly handsome and devoted and charming and lovable guy.

That's why you hear women say how cute or cuddly or classically beautiful women like Renée Zellweger, Reese Witherspoon and Sarah Jessica Parker are when—if you ask a guy—the same three girls would be described as elflike, pointy-chinned and "has a killer bod." Could one of these girls land a Richard Gere or Chris Noth or Jake Gyllenfacenhaulen in real life? Sure. Reese Witherspoon DID land Gyllenfashionpuken. Who is considered a good-looking guy. I actually find that guy very funny and really talented which is what he probably likes about her—but let's not pretend she's Michelle Pfeiffer. 'Cause she ain't.

Which is fine. Renée may occasionally resemble a leprechaun from certain angles but as Bridget Jones she was funny and funny goes a long way in my book (the one in my head as well as the one you are reading). Reese Witherspoon in *Legally Blonde*? Big laughs, big points. And Sarah Jessica—well, how often do you get a girl who looks that hot in hot pants AND can honestly make a man giggle.

Giggles, guffaws and shrieks of laughter last a whole lot longer than legs and other assorted things men like to look at. So embrace the actual instead of the virtual.

God knows, men do.

Real men. If you're dating a guy who's more interested in the size of your chest than the length of your laugh—maybe you better start shopping around.

Men don't play the let's pretend about our friends game.

When it comes to a guy like Matt Dillon, the most you'll ever hear another guy say about him is this (followed by what they really mean):

A. Wow. That Matt Dillon's a pretty good-lookin' guy, hah? (Wow. That Matt Dillon's a pretty good-lookin' guy, hah?)

B. Matt Dillon, that guy's a good actor. (Matt Dillon, that guy's a good actor.)

C. My girlfriend's got a thing for Matt Dillon. (My girlfriend's got a thing for Matt Dillon.)

D. Matt Dillon is a giant fag. (My girlfriend's got a thing for Matt Dillon and she won't shut up about it.)

I think it's fair to say that men's interests in the female gender are very much up-front and common knowledge between the sexes. Women however can still be supposedly surprised or befuddled or disbelieving about what makes their motors tick. I've been co-writing and producing a critically acclaimed hit show about New York City firefighters for several years now—one my writing partner and I have based on our own research and the very real lives of my firefighting friends in the Big Apple. It involves lots of smoke and flames and women. Lots of cute, hot chicks who are very attracted to men who run into burning buildings. Time after time in both the press and real life we have been accosted by women who wonder how much action these guys can actually be getting. The answer is: tons. I have witnessed it firsthand in firehouses, on the streets of Manhattan, in supermarkets, bars, parking lots, elevators, nightclubs—you name it. Smart, sensible women—even sometimes one or two who have just finished saying how ridiculous it seems for women to melt just because a man in bunker pants and suspenders with an FDNY T-shirt appears—have melted and fawned and stuttered and flirted and giggled like a little schoolgirl when one suddenly approaches.

It's the "I wanna be saved" syndrome.

It's the "big, handsome he-man" virus.

It makes them wet.

It makes them swoon.

But some of them just don't want to admit it or simply refuse to own up.

Until a big, handsome he-man shows up and glances at them.

I've listened to very smart women I know bemoan the idiotic behavior of girls over twenty-two years of age who go weak in the knees because some half-assed celebrity or middle-aged rock star is supposed to be attractive based on some raggedy-assed magazine's most recent listing of America's Top Fifty Hunks and then—Matt Dillon walks in.

Cue the giggles, the bleats of laughter, the hands gently sweeping Matt's arm, the swishing flip of her hair—you know the drill.

I bring all this up to illustrate a point—women have a power to bullshit and nurture that men do not have. Men have the power to cut right to the chase and make do with whatever weapons they might have in hand.

Women are born with oodles and oodles of empathy. Most men have trouble spelling it. Empathy, I mean. Oodles rhymes with noodles, which men like to eat, and anything they can put in their mouth and may have to—at some point in life—order in. Generally speaking—with food—they tend to learn which letters go where.

Empathy is why two girls on the Central Washington College Girls Softball team carried—I repeat, carried—a member of the opposing team, Western Oregon State, around the bases—repeat, around the bases—after she hit a game-winning home run but tore a knee ligament as she reached first base and was physically unable to travel all the way to home plate in order to make the victorious blast official. As she lay in the dirt, struggling to stand and in danger of having her hit limited to a single, two of the defensive players felt bad and picked her up and did the honors she could not do herself.

Men would never do this. Not in college, not in high school. Such an event would never happen even in a grown men's BEER league softball game.

Even if it happened to your twin brother and you were playing first base and you were and always had been bigger than him—in fact, big enough to carry him around the bases all by yourself—you still would not entertain a minuscule amoeba-sized nose hair of a cell membrane of an iota of a smidgen of the NOTION of carrying him because your testicles would not release the required enzymes from deep inside your scrotum.

Your balls would—however—immediately remind you that his home run was now a single and therefore your team was still in the game and the cold, clammy hand of defeat that was balling into a fist somewhere deep inside your chest would unclench and become a fiery desire to, once again, win at any cost.

No pain no gain.

Women see physical shortcomings and wish to heal, fix or make them disappear. They believe in hope, they believe in helping, they believe in making a difference.

Guys? They believe in roast beef.

It's why women seek out special bras and special panty hose and plastic surgery and shoes shoes shoes. Guys? Slap on a dabful of deodorant, a pair of old Nikes and we're pretty much good to go. Women wanna put pink floaties and life jackets and goggles and ear plugs and flippers on kids just before they climb into the baby pool WITH them. Guys? We pick a kid up and toss him into the deep end of the ADULT pool. He swims back up to the surface? He's a keeper. He doesn't? He's either gonna be riding on a very short bus for a very special school due to the brain damage caused by seven minutes of oxygen deprivation or he's taking a long dirt nap while daddy finds another mommy.

Mom says yes—dad says no.

Mom coos and coddles—dad barks and bites and boots you in the ass.

Mom cries with you—dad screams "what the hell are ya cryin' about?"

The yin is mommy telling you how gorgeous and nice and smart you are—the yang is daddy saying get your giant head out of your evil red ass and stop acting like a retard.

There is no such thing as a helicopter dad. Unless your dad is an actual helicopter pilot.

Three words for all the prospective parents out there in America: give it up. Your money, your plans, your wishes, your clean car—all of it. Even your looks. There was a feature story in an American magazine recently showing moms what makeup was best to wear when giving birth. Which outfit to bring to wear home from the hospital. Not for the baby—the mom. You wanna know what my mom wore home? A smock.

Blue smock, white smock, smocky smock, UNsmocky smock—who gives a shit? Is the baby okay? Does it have ten fingers? What about the toes? The heart lungs kidneys liver? These should be your concerns.

I just read an article in *People* magazine about Jennifer Lopez and her newborn twins. By the way—*People* magazine reportedly paid six million dollars for exclusive rights to the first photos of J.Lo's two kids, which probably made her jump with joy. Until she found out Brad and Angelina got eleven million for photos of their new twins—man, those box-office figures can sure be a bitch.

Anyway—J.Lo and her hubby Marc Anthony plan to raise the kids with the help of two full-time nurses and a butler. How nice.

You know who the butler was when my kids were small? Me. And "Hey—Butler!" was not amongst the appellations I heard my wife use when she needed me to get a bottle or a box of diapers or a bowl of applesauce.

J.Lo also said "I want to accomplish something this year, something to make my babies proud—like, run a triathalon."

Uh-huh.

You wanna make your babies proud? Stay home. Raise them. Kiss them. Hug them until they almost burst.

Forget the triathlon. Run the triathMOM. That's where you breast-feed one kid, then the other—then fuck your husband blind.

Because that's what it's all about. The family. My mom was always home—for better or worse. When you needed her to be there, when you wished she wasn't because you had a bad report card in hand—every time all the time. My wife Ann's first and last thought every single day of her life since the moment we found out she was pregnant with our first child has been this: the kids the kids the kids the kids. We may not have been perfect parents but she certainly made sure the kids were the number one priority.

If you wanna know how to raise children, you no longer even need to consult a medical encyclopedia or a self-help tome. Just watch *The Real Housewives of Orange County*—or its sister Manhattan show—and do the exact opposite of what those self-centered, Botox-bidden, trout pout–pursing, fishnet and finger-skirt-wearing witches do: think about the children. What THEY want, what THEY need. One of the selfish moms on the Manhattan show has a frozen face, a brownstone on New York's Upper East Side and three teenaged kids who almost never see her. She calls herself The Countess because she's married to a Count. Remove one key letter from her husband's title and you will find a word that perfectly sums her up.

It's hard to raise kids right, to work toward being a working family unit. Let's face the facts—all families are dysfunctional. Do you know of a functional one? The Kennedys? Who may not have molested each other but somehow managed to grope their way through half of the Western Hemisphere? Not to mention enough drugs and alcohol to drown a herd of horses. Oops—didn't mean to mention drowning. What about the Bush family? Are they functional? Compared to the Kennedys they would seem to be somewhat normal—just that little matter of the one with Asperger's syndrome. You know—George Junior?

Listen—I look back on how my wonderful wife raised two terrific kids who have grown up with a wonderful sense of humor and two hearts big enough to care openly about each other, their parents and those who are worse off than they are—and I can be proud.

I look back on the way my parents raised us and I am eternally grateful that my mom and dad made us go to Catholic school where we learned to develop a sense of right and wrong and where Sr. Rosemarie Sullivan taught me how to dance and sing and act and ultimately even pointed me toward Emerson College, where I ended up—because of Sr. Rosemarie's training—getting a full scholarship to write and act. I am grateful that my parents supported my dream. I am grateful that my dad told us the truth and my mom always gave us a hug and a kiss and they both never failed to let us know how much they loved us and we all lived under the same roof and always felt like we could turn to them for help and maybe an extra dollar or two. That to me is what a functional family is all about.

And I've got the scars to prove it.

CHAPTER 12

YOUR CAT SUCKS
FISH HEADS IN HELL

 hat's right. Your cat sucks.

Both your cats do.

Or—if you are what's known in the normal human part of the world as Cat Crazy—all fifteen of your cats are simpering, hairball-spewing, self-centered wastes of domesticity.

Need proof?

How many stories have you recently heard about or seen on TV or even read about that involve a cat somehow helping to save its owner?

Answer?

Not one.

Last year?

By my Internet count—exactly zero.

In your entire lifetime?

Think about it for a second.

Zilch.

Which means—not a single, solitary one.

How many stories have you heard about or seen on tv or even read about that involve a dog somehow helping to save its owner?

Countless.

There was a whole television series about a dog who—each and every week—saved its owner or members of the owner's family or even complete and absolute strangers. That dog was named Lassie.

And before you cat owners go off on a tangent about doggie propaganda and media bias and blah blubbedy meow, let me point out the fact that the reason there has never been a TV series about a cat who saves people is because they couldn't find a cat capable of being trained for the purposes of working on camera.

The dog who played Lassie was so good—he played a goddam female dog.

How many times have we all read stories about a strange smell coming from some apartment where an elderly cat owner who hasn't been seen in over a week resides—and when they break the door down they find said owner dead in a chair. Half-eaten by his or her cats.

Ever heard a story like that about a dog?

Nope.

There is one famous tale about a dog whose owner died. They buried him in a cemetery in Edinburgh, Scotland. His dog slept on his gravestone until he himself passed away.

They made a movie about the two of them. It's called *The Greyfriar's Bobby.*

Now there's a statue of the dog in the center of town.

No cat statue.

Matter of fact—I don't think there's a statue of a cat anywhere on this earth. Why?

Because they suck.

We have a cat. He lives in a barn in the country and kills mice. The horses love him. My wife likes him. The kids think he's cute.

Me?

I don't trust him as far as I could throw him—which wouldn't be very far since he's the size of a fat raccoon on steroids. He's the Roger Clemens of catball.

Sneakers is the name the kids gave him but I just call him what he is—Cat. And you know what? He answers to that name just fine. Because he doesn't know he has a name. Because he doesn't care. Because he's a goddam cat. To him, I'm just a giant mouse he doesn't have to kill because I open tin cans with fish and fowl in them and place them on the floor in front of his fat cat face.

But here's my point: after the Twin Towers fell in New York City on 9/11, firefighters and cops began the daunting task of sifting through the rubble for survivors and—eventually—just human remains.

Assisted by—guess who?

That's right.

There were no rescue cats down at Ground Zero.

There are drug-sniffing dogs at airports, dogs who search the woods when you or your kids are lost, hounds who stuff their noses full of serial killer scent and chase down murdering scum, St. Bernards who gambol down steep snowy trails looking for broken-limbed ski fanatics, Belgian shepherds who search snowpacks after an avalanche, postexplosion English terriers, ocean-rescue expert Newfoundlanders and the list goes on and on. Each and every one of them waking up to find, feed, save and savor us.

When's the last time you stood at a street corner waiting for the walk sign to blink to life while a blind guy wearing wraparound sunglasses and carrying a cane sidled up to you—miraculously unafraid and NOT bumping into anything or anyone—because of the efforts of his faithful, dutybound, Seeing Eye CAT?

Never? That would be the universal answer.

There is no Cat Whisperer.

A cat could give two catshits if you are in a good mood or a bad mood. The only time he/she/it decides to rub against your lower leg and purr its purry little purr is when it's

A. Hungry

B. Really hungry

C. Hungry and in heat

Dogs have a snout that breaks into a doggie smile when they greet you.

Cats just sit there and glare.

Dogs dream. They run and yelp and spout muted barks of warning—even as their eyes are closed—probably protecting you from some awful, unknown entity.

Cats nap.

Hoping that you fall into a deep, deep sleep. So they can then begin their secret, evil rounds.

Dogs read your body language like a fine canine encyclopedia—you are a dense, vast, infinite forest of rich and finely discernible tics and tremors. One slightly arched eyebrow on your forehead has your dog translating and reacting, placing a paw on your lap—offering an eager look and willful eyes and that thump thump thumping of a happy and eager tail.

A cat? A cat ain't even aware you just came home. And when a cat does deign to prop its gaze upon you—it's only hoping that if you drop dead right now you do so on the couch so it can have a comfy pillow to knead its perfectly manicured paws into while it gnaws upon your flesh.

Cats do not care who the owner of the house they live in might be, since they don't consider themselves pets. They are cunning and incomparable killing machines who spend all day long preening and fussing and staring at birds.

A dog only knows one owner—you. You are his favorite person or thing on this planet. When you come home the sun shines eternally in his dancing doggy eyeballs. Unlike mere mortal and judgmental human beings, your dog loves you no matter what. How you look, how you smell, sober or clean, sane or crazed, naked or clothed—you are his one and only best friend. You could stumble through the front door bleeding and bound and your dog would help unwrap the ropes and then begin licking your wounds.

You could chop up the asshole next-door neighbor you've been secretly planning to kill—suddenly snap and head over to his house with just a wood ax and twelve years of angst popping out of your carotid artery and all your darling buddy pooch would do is sniff and follow along nipping at your heels, as if to say "We gonna kill that guy now? Hah? Can I help? Hah? We gonna bury the body afterward? Hah? I love you, man."

You can saunter into the house covered in horseshit—which I have actually done, living almost full-time on a horse farm—and the stench emanating from your boots and pants and pores is an absolute buffet for your dog. He can't get enough of you—nuzzling your trousers, licking your face, lingering his nostrils around the nape of your neck—goddammit do you smell good to him. Horseshit is like the finest French perfume for a dog. As is almost any foul, rank, dire, vile or invasive scent you could possibly emit.

As a matter of fact, if there was a Calvin Klein in the canine universe, the carefully designed fragrances he would offer up could include Horseshit, Pit Stink, Damp Towel Rot, Pizza Breath, Ear Aroma, Cheese Foot, Yoga Crack, Just Arrived Home Vagina, Post-Tennis Tea Bag, Crusty Sock, Dried Up Scab, Under Tit Sweat, Nipple Fluff, Ass Lint—the list would be almost endless. Such is the devotion of the dog to all elements of your very being.

(Yoga Crack is another good name for a band, by the way.)

Can you imagine any lover on earth who would say "Go jump in that pile of batshit, then roll around in that muddy field for a while, piss your own pants, puke and then please oh please rush right over here and give me a big long happy hug and a kiss—please?"

You'd have to pay a hooker an extra twenty grand for that. Maybe more.

Just ask Eliot Spitzer. He probably knows.

Which reminds me—just one day after the world burst open with the wicked news of his decade-long, under the radar, sick and expensive liaisons with online ladies of the night—after everyone from Letterman to Leno to the scions of the Catholic Church and Hebrew heads of scholarly study had chastized him in disgust and disbelief—when all of his trusted aides had fallen by the wayside with nasty asides and angry bromides—when even his wife had given up being photographed in the ex-gov's disgraced presence—the paparazzi caught him out for a leisurely walk along Park Avenue with his one and only remaining confidant—his dog.

His dog could care less who he hired to fuck or how he fucked them or where or when or how often. If the dog had been along for the trysts he would have happily sat in the corner of whichever five-star hotel suite whiffing sexy whiffs and playing One Dog Toss with a hooker's bra or Chew Through The Crotch with her discarded panties or seeing how fast he could munch a bunch of sixty-five-dollar-apiece Oreos out of the minibar cabinet.

Dogs don't care if you are a hooker or a hater or even Adolf Hitler—it's all about how you feel to them when they first meet you.

It's not a dog-eat-dog world. It's a dog-eat-cat world.

Why?

Because dogs can't stand cats. And if you have ever known and loved a dog—think about it:

If a loving, caring creature who trusts you with his life doesn't care for someone—don't you get suspicious? Some visitor or friend of a friend who approaches the dog or just enters your house and your dog acts immediately strange and gets his guard up—isn't there something inside that makes you instantly distrust that person? Yes. It's true. Because dogs can smell fear, they can sense danger. If that's the case—why does your dog abruptly wish to kill and/or chase down each and every cat he meets? Let me do the doggie math for you:

Because your dog knows your cat is evil.

Your dog knows that any cat alive is only out for its own interests.

Your dog knows that cats would slink right up to the Devil should he somehow adorn your door, slithering along Satan's leg—unable or unwilling to differ between Beelzebub himself and you.

Which brings us to Michael Vick.

In the dog world, Michael Vick IS the devil.

An All World Star Quarterback famous for his unbelievable speed and agility and highly rewarded for turning the Atlanta Falcons into an exciting NFL team, Vick's jerseys and commercials and assorted other endorsement deals made him a multizillionaire almost overnight.

What was Michael's response to all the money and the spotlight?

Paying the up-front money, the house bank for the bettors and providing the backyard arena for a dogfighting ring that resulted in countless dog deaths and abuse.

Dogs fought to the death and the ones who didn't die but may have been seriously maimed were shot in the head or hung from tree branches or choked until breathless as female dogs were chained to raping posts where the male dogs could have their way.

Do not YouTube the videos.

Vick was arrested and charged and did the expected American stepdance of criminal guilt:

STEP ONE: Deny deny deny.

STEP TWO: Blame it on friends and family.

STEP THREE: Blame the media for blowing things out of proportion.

STEP FOUR: As investigation heats up, blame a "friend gone bad" and a "second cousin."

STEP FIVE: As media glare gets worse—break out "can't a rich black man get some justice?" speech.

STEP SIX: When confronted with irrefutable evidence and testimony provided by said bad friend and second cousin, blame your actions on booze and pot.

STEP SEVEN: Go to rehab.

STEP EIGHT: When rehab stint doesn't faze judge or make looming prison sentence disappear—find Jesus.

STEP NINE: Go to church a lot. Toting a Bible. Even on Tuesdays. Jesus this, Jesus that.

STEP TEN: Convicted and sentenced—and in desperate need to hopefully still be allowed to play football and make millions when you get out of the joint—hold a press conference in which you mention Jesus, apologize to your fans, talk about God, make amends to your family, mention Jesus again and apologize to the owner of the Atlanta Falcons.

That's what he did.

Apologize to everyone he thought was involved in his dirty, filthy, inhumane activities.

Except dogs.

He never mentioned the dogs.

Not once, anywhere along the line.

Jesus, yes. Dogs—nope.

Not even a dog named Jesus.

And there were many members of the media—mostly black—who tried to give Michael Vick an out by saying that people didn't understand the culture Michael had grown up in, where dogfighting is considered a normal sport.

Oh really.

Well, then—here's the culture I come from:

Instead of going to prison for a solid eighteen months—where he is hopefully having footballs forced up his ass by heavily tattooed ex–Wu Tang Clan members (very very DRY footballs, by the way)—I offer an alternative.

Vick—or any other convicted dogfighting czar—doesn't have to do hard time in the big house. He just agrees to perform in a little charity event that I like to call "Strap A Meat Suit On Michael," which consists of this:

1. Sell out Giants Stadium—all proceeds going to buy Snausages, rawhide bones and multicolored squeaky toys.
2. Broadcast it live on international TV.
3. Strap an entire suit made of meat onto Michael Vick OR just have him wear some jogging shorts and a T-shirt and we will attach a sixty-pound pack of assorted juicy beef to him, with a fine filet mignon arranged right around his groin (think of it as an athletic supporter made of steak).
4. Have him run from one end zone all the way to the other—as fast as he possibly can.
5. Watch as he tries to avoid the sixty-seven pit bulls and twenty-three Doberman pinschers who have gone unfed for a week and will be

running full speed right at him from the opposing forty-five yard line.

He makes it from one end to the other alive? He gets to go free.

I'd offer that deal to Michael Vick right now.

Otherwise?

Let him finish serving his time.

And send a feral cat up into his colon to claw the old footballs out.

CHAPTER 13

GRANDE VENTE MOCHA
OPRAH CHAI

 o, this is not an anti-Starbucks rant.

I did that already.

It's called Coffee Flavored Coffee and it's on my second album, *Lock 'N Load*. Buy that or the DVD and listen as I wallop my way through nine minutes about bullshit java recipes—nine minutes of caffeinated cobra spew.

I could update that bit this very second with my thesis on how Starbucks may be responsible for the pussification of America—I reresearch the subject once or twice a week when I stand in line there and listen as some limp-wristed, yellow-Lance-Armstrong-bracelet-wearing, metrosexual-hair-goo-sporting, Hillary-Clinton's-tired-old-ass-worshipping puke spends twelve minutes trying to decide between the Orange Cranberry Vagina Muffin or the Pumpkin Cream Tampon Cake while fingering a Save The Rain Forest Compilation CD featuring Sting, Sheryl Crow, Joni Mitchell, Sting's Abs, That Hot 19-Year-Old Blonde White English Chick Who Sounds Like Janis Joplin, and Sting's Penis—who apparently pops out of his master's yoga pants to sing his new single "How I Have Tantric Sex With Trudie Styler For Seven Straight Hours."

Which is amazing.

Not that the penis can sing—but that he can actually be that horny for Sting's wife. I mean—seven minutes maybe.

I guarantee my wife would not be interested in me physically expressing my love for her over the course of seven straight hours—unless six and a half of those involved getting out of bed and cleaning the house.

Very quietly.

And while we are on the subject of bullshit—let's get rid of the term "barista" right the fuck now.

In the dictionary—not the Starbucks make up your own words dictionary—the Merriam-Webster real life, real words, real definitions dictionary—"barista" is defined as coming from the Italian language and meaning "someone who works behind a bar."

Which is big news for a bevy of guys named Sully and Fitzie and Clyde and Reggie who have been serving soda glasses full of Canadian Club with Budweiser chasers and Jell-O shots and Colt 45 Malt Liquor for decades thinking of themselves as nothing more than trumped-up bouncers with two dishrags and a baseball bat under the counter.

Hey guys—you are no longer just bartenders. Yer *baristas*!

Run down to Starbucks and get a goddam raise, a sixteen-thread Egyptian-cotton apron and a free copy of Mitch Albom's new book *Five Dead Guys Who Are Dating My Dead Mom*!

Barista is meant to conjure up images of a profoundly dedicated coffee sommelier who busies him- or herself with a constant search for the perfect mug of espresso-tinted java with just the right hint of cream combined with enough of the individual bean's aroma to justify its taste on your eager and expensive tongue.

That ain't what it means no more.

Thanks to Starbucks, barista has come to mean an overly friendly, far too kinetic Fall Out Boy fan who chowders up a smirky smile and a loud Welcome To Starbucks Hope You're Having A Great Day So Far What Can We Get For You Sir but then immediately blanches when you mention the actual word "coffee."

He almost always just stands there for a beat—the Fall Out Boy lyrics draining from his Vicodin-rattled veins—before asking if you would prefer to order from the menu.

Then when you say For seventeen goddam bucks a cup I don't wanna read a fucking menu, he begins to blink uncontrollably.

That's what the term "barista" conjures up.

Or a slow, slim-witted, corporate robotron who feels the need to mention that the term "large iced coffee" has to be reconfigured as Grande Vente Ristretto Breve Bullshit Blah Blah Mucho Machiatto Craptalk.

When she is finished and you deliver a long sarcastic stare back at her nose ring and a quick gander at her neck—where the red tendrils of a dragon or a flower or a dragon EATING a flower tattoo are peeking out of her Obama '08 T-shirt—she makes a mental note to blog on her blog later on during her blog break about how she was sexually harassed by a middle-aged celebrity who she's pretty sure was the bad guy in the first *Spiderman* movie.

Her blog is called Rebel Notes From The New Millennium, by the way.

And is read on a daily basis by her, the Fall Out guy and her boyfriend Seth—who's in a band called DysFunktion (they sound like a cross between Pearl Jam and Audioslave, if Pearl Jam sucked and the guys in Audioslave somehow had their hands lopped off) and he actually thinks that drinking any Starbucks beverage with the word "chai" attached to it leads to good karma (plus, like—I'm pretty sure some of the money goes to help improve the environment, dude).

After a decade or so of blighting stares and angry grimaces and trying to set an example to the others by storming out of Starbucks with nothing in hand and the echoes of my brilliantly abusive tirades ringing in everyone's ears—I have come to realize the one weapon we all have just waiting in the wings:

Oprah.

Because Oprah can shame anyone into admitting the truth.

There was an author named James Frey who wrote a book called *A Million Little Pieces*. No one was going to buy the book, besides Frey and the various people in it he blamed for making him a giant, alcohol- and drug-ingesting mess and—of course—the chosen special few who had helped him climb out of that very very dark hole.

Then he appeared on Oprah and voilà—the book became an international best-seller.

After many sales and almost as many months, it became known that most of what Frey claimed to be true in the book was, in fact—lies. Blatant, made-up, totally untrue and fiction-dressed-up-as-factual crap.

So Oprah invited him back onto the show and asked a million little questions about *A Million Little Pieces* and the next thing you know, Frey had crawled away cringing and crying and spewing I'm sorries.

Oprah had used her secret weapon: shame.

Shame shame shame, shame on you.

I wanna drag a barista onto Oprah and have her cross-examine him or her and I know that within minutes she will have an open admittance that Chai and Vente and Breve and all that shiny sugary Starbuck smack is just an excuse to charge mo money mo money for what is—in the end—just another good cup of joe.

Oprah, my friends, is the cure for what ails America.

Too fat, too thin, too out, too in, too dumb, too smart, your skin, your teeth, your ankles, your ass, pregnant man, pregnant man's wife, pregnant man's penis—you name it and Oprah has asked about it, investigated it, researched it, been funny around it, bitten into the middle of it, digested it and spun it out into silken rivulets of golden information that helps to mollify us all.

When I saw the headlines and a front-page picture on the *New York Post* about a woman who became a man but retained his/her womb just in case and then got pregnant I had many many many questions—a million little questions—but the one that bubbled up to the front of my head every time I read about it was "Does this guy have a dick or what?" As expected, no newspaper—not even the *Post*—addressed the issue. And if the *Post* ain't gonna do it—you know it just ain't gonna happen.

But God Bless Oprah.

If the story ran the first time on a Tuesday? Oprah had the guy and his girlfriend on her show that Friday—she found them and flew them in and sat them down and you bet your Oprah-loving fan site she said—about four minutes into the interview—"Let's get to the penis question." Turns out the guy has enough of a clitoris going on that it actually forms a small penis and him and his gal pal can have intercourse. I don't think it's any kind of Sting and Trudy marathon event but it qualifies and obviously satisfies them both. But that's not the point.

The point is Oprah.

Asking anybody about anything.

And always getting an answer.

Pregnant Man, Cancer Dogs, Brad Pitt, Young Millionaires, Great Moms, Archbishop Desmond Tutu, Messy Kids, Tyra Banks, Bad Dads, Bill Clinton, Energy Vampires, The Husband With 24 Personalities—she has dissected and discussed and presented them all.

Jerry Springer and Maury Povich and Montel Williams and Sally Jesse Raphael and all the other dig-up-the-dreggers who pulverized us with drunks and junkies and whiter-than-white-trash trailer trash in their tighty whiteys and cheap lace panties and thong-cracked asses have all died by the wayside—victims of Oprah's ultimate faith in just how smart you can be—no matter how dumb you already are.

Before I started writing this book all I knew of Oprah was The Occasional Guy Click-In—that's where men dial up Oprah on the TV because of The Wife or The Girlfriend—usually in the middle of an argument about a towel that turns into a sudden tornado involving:

  A. Sex
  B. This relationship is going nowhere
  C. You never talk about your feelings
  D. All of the above but not in alphabetical order

And then in the midst of the teardrops and the angst and the stony sidelong looks she finally deigns to mention that Oprah just yesterday said blah blah Find A Better Soul Mate blah or Oprah said a couple days ago blib glib Is He Really The One For You? glub Oprahdey glub.

They talk about Oprah like they spoke to her on the phone on Sunday or she was just here having tea this afternoon.

I clicked in once and saw Oprah's Extreme Makeovers and thought yeah this housewife looks better after being plucked out of the audience and taken backstage and hosed up and wet down and rubbed raw with Loofah pads and trummeled and trammeled with resins and oils and cucumber creams—before being tucked into a designer dress held together with a roll and a half of two-sided fashion tape and some glue but—what happens after the show? She won't make it from the studio to the car without the blow-dry foofing up into a horse's mane and tomorrow when she and her husband wake up she's gonna look the same way she did before she went to see Oprah because there won't be a team of eight gay men and six Korean cuticle experts to cut, paste and paint her into the tart he saw on TV.

What then? Huh?

Before I started writing this book I blamed Oprah for all the damage Dr. Phil has done. He was nothing before her. Just another balding blowhard with endless axes to grind, but she made him into a star and produced The Dr. Full Show which unleashed him onto all of America, where he can say such thick and exasperating things as "Everyone has their own personal Ground Zero."

Oh really?

Does that mean someday two large speeding planes will crash into the side of your insipid, hairless head?

Let's hope so.

I was ready to steamroll right over Oprah—she was the reason so many wives and girlfriends were disappointed and unamused. She was a one-note wonder, fooling feckless women with her Makeovers and Make-unders and a seemingly relentless river of Hope:

Men Can Change!

Children Will Study!

You Can Be A Better You!

What a crock.

Then I sat down and watched a few Oprahs.

I'm not kidding, guys—I got worried.

One day she was angry as she mourned her recently departed cocker spaniel Sophie with a special piece entitled "Lisa Ling Investigates Hidden Puppy Mills."

The next day she was cackling in apparent Full-On Crush Mode as Gorgeous George Clooney detailed a practical joke he had played on his good buddy Brad Pitt. Oprah seemed eagerly enamored as she giggled and swooned.

The next day her brow became creased with intense concern about Security Clutter Foods—admitting how, just like the rest of us, she gorges on snacks she keeps around the house for the sole sake of gorging on them.

Security Clutter Foods? Holy shit.

She turned a harmless box of macaroni and "orange-colored cheese" into something akin to a terrorist attack on her ass and—unlike Dr. Full when he invoked September 11—I did not wish her ill.

Instead—I threw out bags of Cheetos.

One show she was heavy. The next show she was thin. Or thinn-ER.

One show she was happy. The next show? Sad.

The show after that she was five different emotions in between those two before being both of those two—sometimes at almost the exact same time.

I was fascinated. Jay Leno is always Jay Leno. Jon Stewart is always Jon Stewart. The guys on *SportsCenter* might make a dumb pun here and there but they always just give me the scores.

Watching Oprah was like staring into a human mood ring—each day a glint of light from some unseen source shifted her emotional core.

Before I started writing this book I would have guessed that my take on Oprah would have been skewed toward the negative and that—like anyone else twisting a comic turn—I would be focusing on her flaws and foibles. But you know what I came to realize? It's impossible.

Whatever flaws she has, SHE has already found them.

Her weight loss, her weight gain, her impatience, her pretense, her most recent weight loss, her upcoming weight gain, her face her hair her legs her obsession with clothes? Done.

Holier Than Thou Oprah, Down And Dirty Oprah, Black Oprah, White Oprah, Mad Oprah, Sad Oprah, Oprah Outside Hermès, Oprah With Obama, Oprah In A Snit, Skinny Oprah, Acting Oprah, I Was Molested As A Young Girl And Could Have Become A Stripper But Instead I Became Oprah Oprah, Mochiatta Oprah, The Color Purple Oprah, The Oprah Makes Up With David Letterman Oprah, Plump O, Chubby O, O In Size 10 Calvin Klein Jeans, O In A Cashmere Fluffy-Necked Puff Sweater— Oprah On A Couch, Oprah In A Slouch—Oprah Yelling Oprah Laughing Oprah Scowling Oprah Braying Oprah Giving Away Free Cars To Everyone—she has already praised, prodded and taken the piss out of all those Oprahs as she makes her journey forward.

And the new flaws she comes to discover about her always-evolving self? SHE lays out on the table for all the world to see, watch, talk about and touch.

Listen—don't sit there searching for my hidden, ironic tone. There isn't one.

I am way way, way way, Way Into Oprah.

She can do no wrong.

Let me explain:

First off, every single woman you or I know has a place to go to listen to other women talk about what women like to talk about which is pretty much almost any subject you can raise outside of professional sports, removing back hair and inexpensive but sturdy hammers.

Meanwhile—I'm sure Oprah could find a way to touch on even those manly subjects.

Did you see Michael Jordan on Oprah?

Genius.

So here we go:

I just Googled Oprah and Oprah.com came up.

I sped through space to Oprah.com and typed "back hair" into the search engine and guess what I got? Information on unwanted hair and how to remove it and where to go to get it done. Specifically mentioned? Hair on the back. On MEN'S backs.

I did the same with "hammers." I got Oprahed over to Oprah's DIY site, where the toolbox she suggests you keep at home includes a hammer section that—after much testing and research—prefers that you buy an OXO Good Grips 16-ounce rip-claw hammer for $12.98.

Oh. My. God.

Or should I say Oh My Oprah.

Wait. I gotta Google something else.

Hockey sticks.

What do I get?

Dr. Mehmet Oz—one of Oprah's many medical friends—talks to hockey legend Mark Messier about being a role model, how he stays fit and what kind of equipment he uses.

Mark Messier—one of hockey's all-time toughest, meanest, scariest competitors—has been on Oprah.

You cannot beat her, guys. She will Oprah-ize any subject you raise.

I am literally just going to pick random guy-type titles I know that a Million Man March Of Men Of Any Color would not only find funny to type onto an Oprah site, but at some level would have a very basic, slovenly, man interest in:

Semen count?

Ten entries, including Are Vasectomies Dangerous? and Can A Woman Be Allergic To Her Husband's Semen? (The answer is yes, by the way, and not just after a long day left alone with the kids.)

Scrotum?

You get Oprahed over to an interview with author Paul Joannides featuring his book *The Guide to Getting It On*.

Make my penis bigger?

Thirteen thousand two hundred and ninety-four results—including A Man's Dipstick and Treating a Broken Penis. I didn't even know you COULD break your penis. Bruise? Yeah. Scrape? I've done it (there was a girl, half a bottle of cheap vodka and a faulty zipper involved). But break? The mere thought makes me shudder.

Make my penis smaller?

Thirteen thousand two hundred and forty-six. Including Weight Loss And Penis Length—where Oprah says if a man loses 35 pounds he may gain one inch of penis length, which in my case means that in order to gain another five inches I would eventually have to become just a cock with feet.

Now I'm just going to type in words you would never expect Oprah to say:

Tits.

Three entries.

Vagina.

Sixty-seven.

Pussy?

C'mon, man. Oprah doesn't use that word.

Here's a flurry of more practical male topics:

How to hit a baseball—1,755 entries.

How to make a woman come—18,898. (Stop laughing—it's the actual number that's listed right now.)

I'm just spitballing here, guys—flying by the seat of my pants now:

Fixing your truck—700.

Punching a guy in the face? 3,793.

It's amazing. Now I'm just gonna focus on totally silly male fantasy theses:

Big nipples? 3,509.

Nipple hair? 1,383.

Blow jobs? 2,510—including a section called How Sex Is Like Pizza. With one of her male doctor friends. Jesus.

Areola. One entry. Which is one more than ESPN.com.

Remember the potential perfumes for dogs I mentioned earlier in the book? I picked one and stuck it onto Oprah's engine.

Guess what?

Ass lint—36 entries.

I give up. I give in. I give away my subscription to *ESPN The Magazine* in favor of *O*.

It's insane.

Like most men—until this very moment—I had no idea. I didn't know about Oprah.com until I pointed out the Michael Jordan interview—I was only planning on parsing Oprah from notes I had already made, but now?

My life has changed. My Google goggles no longer bear the fog of testosterone-driven prejudice.

I can't get these answers from any existing sports channel. Scores? Yes. Scrotum health headlines? Not a chance.

Has Chris Berman ever mentioned the possibility of a broken penis during *NFL Prime Time*?

Has there been one single president who ever warned the male population of this country about Severe Penile Impairment?

Is there a chapter or verse in the Bible that bemoans a potential de-boning?

No, no and no.

But Oprah tackled it.

Oprah took the time to tell us how it could happen and what to do if it did. Never mind where to get the best rip-claw hammers. (Another good name for a band, by the way.)

I look at ESPN and ESPN.com now and I snicker with a newfound snickularity. Memphis beats Tennessee—so what. The Rangers qualify for the playoffs. Big deal. I wanna watch Sidney Crosby going top shelf with a twisted wrister while the goalie is fooled out of his jock strap and underneath all the action the sports ticker tocks up the really important stuff:

Your penis could break in half!

Big nipples may be more fun!

Rubber deck hammers—the best of!

Details just ahead!

I want an Oprah And Friends round-table section halfway through every episode of *SportsCenter*.

I want Gayle King to co-co-host *Pardon the Interruption*, running down a Twelve Topics In Two Minutes chunk of Man Stuff That Matters—sure LeBron James may be averaging thirty points a game but how are his testicles doing? Has he had them checked? Does he know that Dr. Oz says testicular cancer is the number one form of cancer for men between the ages of fifteen and thirty-five?

I doubt it.

I look at Oprah now and I see why she doesn't want to run for president. Why she hasn't had kids. Why she does what she does day after day after day after day:

We ARE her kids.

She is the be all and end all—the queen bee the queen mum the voice of reason and insanity and hilarity and disparity—becoming president would be a step down for her. It would only suck her power away. Would she be able to ask The Pregnant Man about his clit/penis if she were in the Oval Office? No. Could she discuss the best bras for buxom girls as she sat with visiting heads of state? No. Can she hold a press conference in the Rose Garden and ask a male medical friend to explain how eating pizza can help you get your husband hard? Hell no.

Oprah is where Oprah belongs—right there on the hot plasma rectangle that hangs on each of our walls, illuminating our bedrooms and kitchens with a warm fire of unending, uplifting infotainment.

Celery-Colored Sheets. Wow!

Little League Pedophiles. Oooh!

Cybill Shepherd On Menopause. Train Wreck!

She loves us she feeds us she makes us get fit she sends us out shopping and makes us redecorate she shields us and warns us and reminds us to have good sex bad sex food sex fat sex she gives us a sharp crack across the knuckles about race and religion and rich food and she makes us READ goddammit READ—read new books read old books reread the books she told us to reread last year—she is your teacher your mentor your multidimensional mensch she is actually married to us which is why she has no husband and will never have one:

That's how much she cares about us.

Which is why instead of asking Oprah to become the president I am demanding an amendment to the Constitution—the Oprah Amendment. The people have spoken for decades on end and the results flow in every single day across the world—Oprah is The Ultimate Decider.

Not George Bush not Prick Cheney not the Senate not the Congress—it's The Big O, baby.

I suggest we make every sitting president visit the Oprah set once every three months to listen to a million little questions about how he or she is doing on the job.

There will be no lying.

There will be no deceit.

No man can lie to Oprah and a roomful of Oprah women.

It's the power of O.

You've seen it yourselves with James Frey.

She will roast you and toast you like a fine hamburger bun.

Those gorgeous eyes, those luscious locks cascading down those round, chocolate cheeks—no man can look at her and get away without telling the truth.

I don't care Who You Are, Who You Might Think You Are or how many big, burly guys are calling you God's Gift To Mankind. You get put in front of Oprah—all the bullshit turns to smoke.

And once the smoke begins to clear?

Strap yourself in, stud.

Roger Clemens would Misremember and Disunderstand and wriggle and wraggle until she caught him square in her Cocoa Gaze and then he would try to look away and quote His Heroic Stats and hold up each of his Seven Cy Young Awards and she would still be sitting there—brown glare glaring, arms folded across her aqua turtleneck chest—waiting for the truth to ember its way out of his gimungo, drug-thumping head.

And then it would happen.

He'd realize that women—especially Oprah's women—would trade all those expensive trophies in for twenty pairs of Jimmy Choo shoes.

He'd scratch his itchy, guilty, steak 'n' cheese–eating chin and come to see—there is no escape from Oprah.

He would wilt into a frenzied flopsweat of Dismisremembering and Reunforgetting and finally just break down and admit that his big fat assabscess was in fact the result of a giant set of jet-fueled human growth hormone injections. The Mighty Rocket would fall back to earth in a puddle of his own pretension.

Yay.

Congress couldn't crush him.

The Commissioner Of Baseball couldn't lay a finger on his wide, sneaky back.

But Oprah could.

She would swat him aside like an insect.

Just imagine the other possibilities: con artists, accused murderers and just plain free-ranging dolts.

Speaking of all three:

George Bush would chuckle it up with a smug shrug and some fumble bumble Texas twang pulled out of the bottomless pocket of his nitwit pitter pat before Oprah's glaring brown orbs began to produce long, unlaughing pauses and suddenly—the man in charge of eight bad, ugly, idiotic and financially foolish years for this country—would come to realize he was surrounded by a sea of unimpressed faces bobbing calmly atop Oprah's Angry Ocean.

The guns in the Harpo studio are almost all female and they would be pointed firmly at his prep-school privileged grin as it slowly waned into a grimace and he knew the only way out was owning up to how ridiculous it was for the American people to elect and then RE-elect a guy they thought they could "have a beer with," when in fact that same guy was a recovering white-knuckle alcoholic and would have to have not "a" beer, but six or ten or twenty-three before calling his old coke dealer and getting the Secret Service to pick him up an eight ball, two quarts of Jack Daniel's and a bag of small, nonchokeable pretzels.

It wasn't God who was talking to Him—it was Cheney hiding behind and using a really deep voice.

You saw what happened when Tom Cruise went on the show—picture George Bush hopping around on the guest couch like a circus pet on crystal meth and you'll see where we are going: you work in the White House, you answer to Oprah. Four times a year. I guarantee we'd all be better off.

Men in particular.

We'd know not to lie, cheat and steal.

Because—just like answering to your mom—Oprah and her army would be there waiting for an explanation.

Talk about the ultimate system of checks and balances.

We'd learn to do the things Oprah and the girls put on our "Things To Do This Week" list.

We'd learn to let the woman talk.

We'd learn to listen and stay in the other room and watch TV—let the girls do the shopping and make all the key decisions—from The Best Value In Ball-Peen Hammers to What Color Hammock.

We'd keep our mouths shut and do all the grunt work and expect no credit but get paid back with pizza.

Which might just be a code word for oral sex.

Just ask Steadman.

You punch his name into the Oprah engine and it comes up empty.

Areola 1; Steadman 0.

Doesn't that say it all?

CHAPTER 14

DOES THIS BOMB MAKE
MY ASS LOOK FAT?

hat's what the female terrorist said to her husband minutes before they left home—probably late—to launch a double suicide attack.

Every husband or boyfriend has heard some version of that question—just switch out the word "bomb" and replace it with dress.

Or skirt.

Or blouse.

Or shirt, hat, car, house, sofa, pen, bed, city, country, hemisphere—you get the point.

Every man who lives with a woman has had to sit in that hot seat—in the bedroom, in the hallway, in a hotel suite, almost anywhere—and offer up glowing accounts of an endless stream of outfits that—each after each—apparently "make" her ass look fat. It's never her actual ass that is too big, it's the way the ass looks in some Nightmare Pair Of Designer Jeans or a One Of A Kind Evening Gown or These Goddam Stupid Imported Capri Pants or even Those Old Jeans From Four Years Ago when the ass WAS tiny and looked so incredibly edible you felt like slapping it and throwing her onto the bed right then and there.

Joseph did it with Mary.

Hitler did it with Eva Braun.

Randy Gerber is doing it with Cindy Crawford as you read this sentence.

Trying to divine the best way to—evenly and with a strong, calm voice—discuss her derriere.

Yet—no matter what man you may be—you cannot utter even a sliver, of one tiny teeny slice, shaved off just a corner—of one kernel—of the truth.

It looks fine, honey.

It looks great, sweetheart.

Babe—I love the way your butt looks in that.

Those three alone'll get you into enough trouble.

And even when The Ass Under Consideration does, in fact, measure up to the finest of all Ass Ethics and is, indeed, still sexy and juicy and oh so delectable—she will not hear anything positive that flows out of your mouth no matter how it is offered up. She needs to primp and pose and gape and prowl and turn and frown and gaze over one shoulder and then do the same over the other shoulder and then flip her hair back and start the whole goddam process right from Outfit Number One again.

And you have no choice but to sit and wait and watch and wait and bite your hungry lip.

I'm convinced the burka was not invented by some crazed Arab hell-bent on following religious conventions—it was just a hungry husband who wanted to make his dinner reservation on time. If she's forced to wear only one thing—how hard could it be? (I know I know—even as we speak, Muslim wives around the globe are trying on brown burka after brown burka—wishing that somehow just one of them would make their sacred asses disappear.)

I have spent over twenty-five years going through this exercise two or three or sometimes five evenings a week with the exact same woman—my wife Ann. So at some point a while back I decided to give in and stop swimming upstream and you know what?

Something wonderful happened.

By letting all the anger go, by allowing the distemper and the exasperation to just slip away, by forcing my ire and chagrin and my miff and my tiff and my huff and my puff and my pique and my dander and the speeding express train of torrential goddam curse words about to explode out of my mouth to—instead—evaporate (and by staving off my hunger with a wad of roast beef wrapped in Swiss cheese)—I had a revelation:

Relax, man. Just relax.

It's not your wife.

It's this really hot chick trying on different outfits.

Which means—at its basic, most raw and bottomest best:

You get to see a sexy girl nekked.

And once you embrace that theory—man, have you ever hit the jackpot. 'Cause if you love your wife and she's still got it going on—wow.

Sit back and swoon, brother.

My wife looks better than ever and I gotta tell ya—it's like you're at your own private fashion show.

Wait—it's better than that.

It's like you're simultaneously watching a fashion show AND you get to be backstage at the exact same time.

She tries on an outfit—then she saunters around in her bra and panties looking for another outfit.

She takes that outfit off—and her bra—so now she is topless! Holy shit.

Then she puts on heels and tries on a cocktail dress.

THEN—she decides she has a VPL—Visible Panty Line (ya gotta get the lingo down pronto)—so she slips her panties off and—if you're lucky—decides the dress makes her hips look too full so she takes that dress off and goes in search of another—MEANWHILE you now have her naked and in stiletto heels wandering back and forth right there in front of you—God, what a gift from above.

When I was a teenager, a hot chick strutting her stuff in your bedroom was considered an impossible event and here it is happening multiple times a week for free? I'm telling you, fellas—once you use my system and take what we used to think of as a task and reimagine it as a fun-filled hobby—it just doesn't get any better than this.

What I do now is run downstairs and stuff some beef in my mouth, get changed real quick and then sit on the edge of the bed in the master bedroom and let the games begin:

I don't think that's the right dress, honey.

VPL alert, honey—VPL alert. Let's get those panties off.

I think we're gonna need a bigger set of heels, honey.

I like that top but try it without a bra.

It turns being late for dinner into an entirely different animal. Look—we get ready to go out by grabbing one of our two dinner jackets—check to make sure there are no holes anywhere or at the very least only one or two small pinhead-sized holes and maybe a couple of minor coffee stains that really don't jump out at you because the jacket is brown to begin with PLUS the barely there dollop of mustard that sits in a splotch on the shirt you just grabbed off the floor of the closet is a bigger concern because throwing the thing through a ten-minute cycle of Dewrinkle in the dryer ain't gonna make the yellow disappear from a white shirt but that's why you wear a yellow tie and tie it extra long and voilà—two palm-prints of Aqua Velva 'n you are more than ready to rock 'n' roll.

Her? She likes to linger.

And look.

And linger.

And—here comes the good stuff—primp and preen and reach and flounce and stride and ankle and stretch and parade and—maybe my personal favorite—sashay.

I love it when my wife sashays.

You should feel the same way when your girl does it.

Happy wife, happy life. Not to mention lots of giant boners.

Let's take this theory and run with it.

CHAPTER 15

TESTICLE-COLORED TOWELS

ctually, the proper name for the color is Testicalé.

Testicalé being a fake Spanish word I just made up. It means "ball." As in "my balls hurt." (Hey—I made up the word, I get to make up the definition.)

And a towel that is colored Testicalé is a towel that is pink with a slightly brownish tint and a little bit of peachy peach fuzz along the edges.

And the reason I bring this up is because there is no such thing as a pink towel anymore. Or a brown towel. Nope. Some gay man somewhere—and I'm personally blaming Calvin Klein, married though he may be—decided that women were way more likely to buy way more towels if said towels were in fact saddled with fancy-sounding color names. Thus—instead of pink towels—we now have Salmon. Or Fuchsia. Or Blush.

See? That's why I chose Testicalé. Because the real Spanish word for ball is *testiculo*. Which just sounds too much like testicle, which reminds you of a scrotum and does not make you wanna buy a bunch of towels.

Whereas Testicalé sounds like some kind of smooth, fancy-tasting tequila, which you could sip over ice as you lounged in a soothing hot bath with Cooling Cucumber Bubbles and a Hydrating Skin Mask of Yoga Tea Leaves nestled atop your face.

I bet I could get a shitload of ladies to buy Testicalé towels.

Guys? Not so much.

We couldn't care less what color a towel is.

We don't even care if it's clean.

As long as it wipes the water off our back, head and ass and sops up all the nooks and crannies in between and we can slap on our slacks and get something to eat—we're happy.

But even if pressed into having to pick, the Guy Pie Color Chart For Towels would consist of maybe three—blue, white and red.

Maybe black.

That's it.

I would've thrown gray in there too but for most guys gray would just be another kind of blue.

When did white and blue and black and red become too little too late for most women?

When they got a whiff of Acorn and Heather and Persimmon and Pearl.

I don't even know what colors those are supposed to be—I just saw them listed in a bed-and-bath store catalog I stole out of my wife's office.

Get a load of these:

Moss.

Forest.

Celery.

Guess what color? Green, goddammit. Green. Moss? What the hell. I don't even know a GUY named Moss. Why not go with Mold? Or Yeast? Is yeast green? I dunno. All I know about yeast is that women get infections that are named after it AND I think they might use it to make beer.

More catalog colors:

Mushroom.

Ecru.

Taupe.

Khaki.

Got a guess? Tan. Fucking tan. Which is really light brown but let's not get into that—let's just accept that light brown is tan. Then—years ago—they came up with beige and burnt sienna.

I remember because I was a kid and they added beige and burnt sienna to the Crayola crayons box, so let's accept that tan is tan and beige is lighter tan and burnt sienna is probably some kind of tan that the Indians came up with but is that enough to base a towel selection on? I guess the fuck not because now we have four more bullshit choices, which we will now unbullshit our way through:

Mushroom. Mushrooms are for cheeseburgers, pasta sauces, soup and getting high enough to think that the Grateful Dead were actually a good band when in fact they were just a bunch of spaced-out, balding junkies with two songs they managed to spread out over four hours as a scam to sell tie-dyed T-shirts.

Ecru? Sounds like a cough. (Don't forget—I'm a doctor.)

Khaki? Pants. That's it. Just pants. I don't want a towel named after a pair of pants I wouldn't buy or wear anyways. Christ. Let's make all pant names into colors. How about Cargo. Are those off-white pants, Penis Man? Nope—they're Ski. Hey Lefty—are those pants black or navy blue? The proper name for the color is Tuxedo, asshole.

And Taupe? I looked up "taupe" in a dictionary and here's what it says: "A moderate to dark brownish gray slightly tinged with purple, yellow or green." Jesus Christ. Could there be a less decisive color? Is Taupe running for President Of All Towels?

Orange becomes Tangerine or Pumpkin, red becomes Burgundy, white becomes Alabaster, purple morphs into Plum, Lilac, Aubergine and Mauve.

I knew a pissed-off lesbian from Dublin who was named Mauve and a French-Canadian hockey goon whose last name was Aubergine—neither one brings the color purple to mind. (Although Mauve did give me a purple nurple because she thought I was hitting on her girlfriend when I was—in fact—just asking for a light. Her girlfriend looked like Aubergine, by the way—only he had better teeth.)

The point is—why.

Why do we need these colors why is someone getting paid to create them why are women buying towels and curtains and linens and bedspreads named with them and bringing them home or even worse showing us the choices in the catalog BEFORE they buy them and asking us which one we like better—the Pewter or the Periwinkle? The Topaz or the Azule?

The Milk or the Butter the Cream or the Honey the Egg or the— I don't know if I'm still picking out bed and bath wear or ordering fucking breakfast.

Speaking of which, it's the same thing that's happened with food. My wife and I recently went out to eat on a gorgeous late-winter Saturday evening and after watching her perform an extended version of The Lace Panties And Bare Skin Display and driving twenty-five miles inside an enclosed space as the scent of her perfume arrayed itself around my lips, I had two thoughts in mind: sex sex and more sex.

Actually—that was all one continuous thought, so as we arrived at the restaurant I just wanted to chow down and speed home before tearing her clothes off and manhandling her.

Then—the ponytailed, three-earrings-in-one-earlobe, not black but I'm sure Midnight suit-sporting waiter sauntered up to the table, placed a menu gingerly into each of our hands and—I shit you not—began to re-cite the following special additions:

(I remember because as soon as he was done and excused himself—no doubt to re-buff his nails—I borrowed a pen from my wife and wrote all of this down.)

An Heirloom Tomato Tower Featuring Goat Cheese And A Plum Salsa Dressing.

French Tenderloin Filet With Crab Galette And Israeli Couscous Flecked By Casino Butter.

Pistachio-Encrusted Swordfish With Corn Whipped Potatoes Drizzled With An Asian Fennel Sauce.

For Dessert—Italian Apple Sorbet Sitting Above A Vanilla Wedge And Topped By Belgian Chocolate Glaze.

First things first. A tower of tomatoes is okay by me 'cause it sounds like a tomato sandwich and that seems like it would just be faster to eat, but

FEATURING goat cheese? What is this, a rock concert? And what the fuck exactly is plum salsa—an excuse not to have more tomatoes on the plate? But I digress. Because the tomato tower is normal stuff compared with the French Tenderloin Filet With Crab Galette. You know what the galette was? A crab cake.

It's just a chunk of steak with a crab cake on top, and I've been to Israel—I worked there for a summer once—and I never heard the words "Israeli couscous" in English OR Hebrew and what the fuck is Casino Butter—pads of butter with paper on either side that you stole from the Caesars Palace All You Can Eat Buffet? And let me ask you this—Corn Whipped Potatoes—did you actually whip the potatoes WITH a cob of corn or did you just save me the trouble of having to mix the corn into the potatoes right here on my own plate? I appreciate your deshelling the pistachios for me in advance, by the way, but I don't want them encrusted around my goddam fish. I don't like anything encrusted. Reminds me of that stuff you have in your eyes after you wake up from a deep sleep. Especially when you have the flu. Flu-Encrusted Cod anybody? And drizzled? Let's cut to the goddam chase on that one—poured. Okay? You poured some shit over some other shit. Drizzle means it's raining outside but it's not really raining. And I'm Irish so I'm kind of an expert on this one—anything "drizzled" or poured or splattered or plopped on top of potatoes is gravy—I don't give a good goddam if it's from Asia or the South Bronx—it's G-R-A-V-Y—and you better have a shitload of it. And as far as dessert goes—you ain't fooling me. It's an apple on top of a cookie with hot fudge. Fuck Belgium AND the Italians.

My wife loved it. I closed the menu and let her order for me. It all gets so confusing and long and descriptive and—basically—uses way too much time and far too many words. Here's what the menu at the ultimate restaurant built by, for and WITH men in mind would say:

BEEF

CHICKEN

FISH

SPAGHETTI

BOOZE

CAKE

PIE

That's it. Make them all the same price and you have a done deal—guys will flock there in record numbers.

I bring all of this up to let women all over the world know—once and for all—we don't really care about Amber towels and Auburn washcloths and Claret curtains and Salsified Sea Bass and Crystallized Cocoa Flake Splashed With A Dandelion Brandy Sauce. We'll shower up and rinse our hands clean and sit down and eat the stuff but for one reason and one reason only—we wanna have sex with you. That's it.

That's why I'm extending the argument put forward in the previous chapter, guys—don't go off the deep end about the linen and the menu additions like I just did—sit back and let it all go.

So you have to let some ponce in a ponytail point out food that simply by the length of its title is gonna have a price tag far beyond its actual nutritional value—so what?

So instead of grabbing a red towel and raking it across your ass and your ballsack—you gently dab at your dabbables and remark: "Honey—this towel is so big and fluffy and just so—is it Magenta? It is? It's such a perfect balance with the smaller towels—the hand ones? Lemme guess—are those Puce or Terra Cotta? Oh—Vermillion. I love it!"

That and a slow, gentle slide of your hand—palm down—across the surface of the new Crimson sheets and a quick remark about how much you love the Russet pillowcases will do wonders down unders.

Nowadays, wife wants a cup of tea? Do I grunt and grumble? Nope. I put on my reading glasses and I shuffle down to the kitchen, put on the hot water, open The Tea Drawer and start perusing the titles:

Smooth Move, hon?

Women's Liberty? No? Okay.

Green Ginger it is.

She's got a selection of teas the guys who signed the Declaration of Independence wouldn't have TIME to throw into Boston Harbor:

Azo Passion Tea

Every Day Detox Tea

Yoga Bedtime

Mulling Spice

Yoga Thai Delight

Cinnamon Ease

Yoga Rejuvenatta

Now—they all have their apparent purposes, even though how and when she may need them remains a mystery to me. Does she down a cup of Azo Passion in order to get in the mood? When she needs to loll about on the front porch and ponder the world's problems, does she savor some thoughtful sips of Mulling Spice? Do three and a half ounces of Women's Liberty really set her free? I dunno. But the last couple of boxes I dug out of that drawer are enough to bring any man pause:

Yoga Black Chai and Licorice Root.

This is when teatime can turn into a potential witch's brew—are these the two bags she drops into a boiling mug before telling me to go fuck myself? Is she holding them in reserve in case she one day decides to put me out of her misery? I dunno and I ain't asking.

I just make her the cup of Green Ginger and wonder what kinda teas they make for men.

Oh yeah. I remember:

Lipton.

End of list.

CHAPTER 16

THIS IS YOUR BRAIN ON SEMEN

 think we've done a good job in the last couple chapters with delineating some of the differences between men and women—now it's time for this good doctor to put the final nails into what has become a politically correct coffin in this country:

We don't talk as much as you do.

We just don't.

Keep in mind this is coming from a man who is not only a doctor but—as you must know by now if you've been reading along—a very verbal guy.

I obviously do not have a problem expressing myself.

But you can take all the halfhearted and quarter-assed medical studies done around the world that say men speak just as many words a day as women do and put them in a massive blender and make a giant bullshit shake—I'm here to tell you they are not true.

Go to the gym and watch and listen—guys have headphones on as they run and squat and grimace and grunt—staring up at the TV in between sets.

The women? Paired off on adjacent treadmills or elliptical trainers—yak yakkety yick yak yic, yic yickety, yawbeddy jawbeddy—jic jak yick. Yicketty yacketty blah blah blah.

I don't trust the tests that say women don't talk more than men because I know for a fact these tests are being paid for and urged on if not administered by women who are desperate to find a way to prove one more cliché about them to somehow not be true.

Do I have medical research to back up my claim?

You bet your ovaries I do—fifty years of life on this gabbing glob of rock and gas, all of them surrounded by sisters and Irish aunts and female cousins PLUS twenty-five of those years living in the same domicile with my wife.

She talks on the phone to her sister while she's making dinner and I sit there starving and steaming.

She talks on the phone with her mom while she's making dinner while I still sit there starving and steaming.

She steams vegetables while talking on the phone ABOUT her mother WITH her sister while I try to decide whose temperature is getting higher—mine or the broccoli's.

She talks to her BFF on the phone WHILE she's e-mailing her OTHER best BFF about a THIRD former BFF who's just now calling on the other line.

We don't.

We don't talk when we're hungry—except to say "I'm hungry—let's eat."

We don't talk on the phone when we're hungry unless we are ordering food to be delivered from the place where they make the food right to where we are sitting waiting for some food—still one of the greatest breakthroughs in the history of eating as far as men are concerned.

Once we have the food—no talking—just chewing.

We don't even talk while we're working.

Ever watch a bunch of guys shovel snow? If there's five of them—they say hello and shoot the shit quickly about the game on TV last night or this hot new chick one of them is dating and/or holy fuck did it snow like a motherfucker then they start pointing and dividing up sections of the area that need to be shoveled and then?

They shovel.

For three straight hours.

And the only talking they do is to redirect each other to parts of the area that need to be shoveled again or piles of snow that need to be moved.

That's it.

When they are done they talk briefly about the best shovels in the history of shovels and how to invent an even better shovel and then they get in their trucks and drive away.

All you hear when you walk by a construction site is the sound of machines bamming and whamming and shouts of "Get the fuck out of the way, Tommy!" and "Toss me that hammer, Sal!"

If women did all the shoveling or women were put in charge of actually physically building our buildings we would be left with mounds and mounds of snow-covered streets and sidewalks and a cityscape chock full of lumber, cement bags and steel but a skyline somehow free of skyscrapers. Plenty of recipes would be exchanged and reputations damaged, though.

My studies show that women—on average—use 15,678 words a day.

Men—according to my tests—use about 3,700.

And 2,000 of those are "Uh-huh, honey," "What did she say then?" and "Mm-hmm."

"Yup" and "whatever you say, sweetheart" were also very popular.

Don't bother digging out all the new studies that say men and women speak exactly the same number of words. I've read them all and they are—in one of my daily allotment of roughly 4,000—crap.

As is the BFF idea. And The Frenemy—the female friend who is actually an enemy but still—somehow, incredibly—kept close at hand by your wife or chick.

How many countless times have you heard your girl come home and say "You're not gonna believe what that bitch Suzie said to me today while we were having a nice, chatty lunch at such and such a place" or hang up the phone after a seventy-eight-minute conversation with her "friend" Emily and say "God how I hate her"?

Here's what a guy says to another guy who he KNOWS just insulted him or just even LOOKED at him the wrong way:

What the fuck is your problem, dickwad?

And then the relationship is over.

You know that friend of your wife's who just talks endlessly and not only never shuts up but seems to think every single one of the other women is fascinated by what she has to say when in fact they all wish that somehow she would just stop and take a breath so that they could get a word in edgewise?

Here's what One Angry Guy says to The Big Loudmouthed Guy who All The Other Guys think is talking too much:

Hey—loudmouth. Shut the fuck up and let someone else fuckin' talk.

That's it.

We don't have BMFs.

And while we are on the subject—let's get something else completely set straight—guys don't want their girlfriends or wives to be their best friends. Our best friends are other guys. Guys we hang out with. Guys we play sports and sweat with. Guys we fart openly with and compare coughed-up phlegm with or go to hockey games with or play golf with or watch a heavyweight championship on TV with. Our best friends have beards and balls and hair on their backs and we can watch a sixty-seven-yard touchdown pass from Peyton Manning to Marvin Harrison and just grunt at each other in firm admiration and approval because we know how almost impossible a task that is to pull off. I don't wanna have sex with my best friend or give him a hot-oil massage or kiss him on the back of the neck or sneak up from behind him and quietly cup his right breast in my hand while breathing a low and steamy whisper into his other ear.

Here's a headline—we eat food with our hands when chicks ain't around. And if we do use cutlery, we grab one of those huge serving utensils—a great big spoon or a fork with four massive prongs—so we can shovel whatever the hell it is we're eating into our gaping pieholes with even more speed. Getting to the pitchfork first is key 'cause then you can stab at the hands of the other guys when they try to grab some of what yer eating out of the bowl or dish it sits in.

When chicks ain't around we scratch our asses and tweak our balls and reconfigure our cocks in our pants and spit and moan and stare each other down and call each other pussies and faggot and threaten to kick a guy's ass and elbow him in the face for a rebound and spit and snort and grunt and cackle and high-five and fart and then cackle about the size of the fart and then high-five BECAUSE of the fart and then piss and moan and snot snotrockets. We piss in sinks and sandtraps and on trees and in sandbuckets and into old coffee cans and almost anywhere we can find when the bathroom is taken or there isn't one around and we jerk off a lot and it has nothing to do with whether or not we are in or out of a happy relationship it's just at the very least a release of testosterone and/or a form of target practice because the more we do it the longer we can last and making it last longer is a point of pride when you are trying to make the woman in your life happy in bed. We couldn't care less about *Sex and the City* and we'd really rather stare at a six-color double-page *Road & Track* shot of the engine inside a new Ferrari Testarossa than we would at actresses we don't know in red carpet dresses from *People* magazine or even one of the same actresses tastefully naked but airbrushed into ambiguity in *Playboy* or *Penthouse*. We like to bang shit with hammers but if we hadn't invented hammers we would be just as happy to bang shit with big rocks—we like to drive fast and throw sticks and chuck small rocks and peg acorns or apples or almost anything we can get our hands on.

And we barely talk during any of this. Except to yell "Nice goal, Schiller!" or "Pass the goddam puck, Lombardi!" or "Think I can hit that pigeon with this bottle top?"

As a matter of fact, Think I Can Hit That Tree? is a game even grown men can play for hours on end. All you need is a tree, two men, and some loose stones. One guy says something to the effect of "Think I can hit that tree from here?" and the game is on: two adult males will throw flat stones, round stones, rectangular stones—thin, fat, chubby, chunky, we don't even care—at said tree until they either run out of stones or they see a squirrel. Then they start playing Think I Can Hit That Squirrel? Same rocks, same rules—moving target.

Pretty goddam simple.

We don't do Extreme Makeovers. You wanna know what an extreme makeover for a straight man is? He comes home, takes his suit off and puts on his torn and frayed Red Sox T-shirt from 2003 and complements it with a pair of boxers he bought during the first Clinton administration. He turns on ESPN and thinks about whether or not he should shave. Decides to wait a couple of days.

That's it.

We don't sit around talking about you.

We don't sit around talking about food.

We don't break out acoustic guitars and sing "Viva Viagra" in four-part harmony.

Here's what I have to say about change—we don't do it. We are as God made us. What you see is what you get. You CAN judge a book by its cover—it's called "Big, Hungry, Horny, Simple Guys."

You know that best-selling tome called *Eat, Pray, Love*? It's a memoir written by a thirty-something American chick who gets divorced and travels in well-fed splendor to three different countries to heal her broken heart and oh so damaged self-esteem and in the process find her true inner is-ness and being.

The guy version of that book would be called *Eat, Fuck, Sleep*. And it could be written by any red-blooded American male. In it he would eat, fuck and sleep. And in between those he would work his ass off and also watch documentaries on The History Channel about other men in three different countries and what kind of tools they use and wars they wage and tanks they drive and blah blah history blah until the Red Sox feed from the West Coast away game they're playing against the Angels kicked in around ten p.m. or so.

Let's make this all as scientific as we can—I've included in my study ink and paper scans of the male and female brains. Take a look:

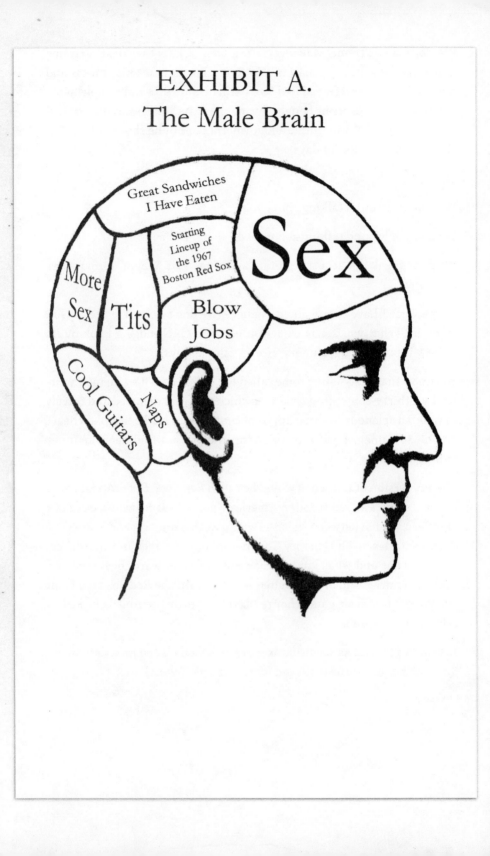

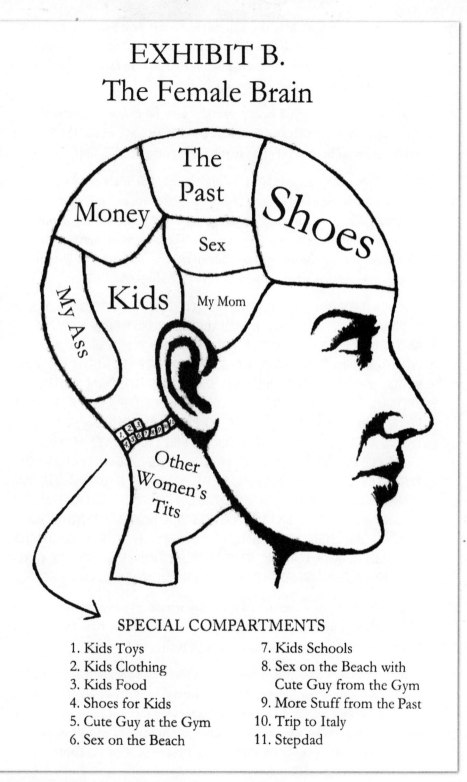

EXHIBIT B.
The Female Brain

SPECIAL COMPARTMENTS

1. Kids Toys
2. Kids Clothing
3. Kids Food
4. Shoes for Kids
5. Cute Guy at the Gym
6. Sex on the Beach

7. Kids Schools
8. Sex on the Beach with Cute Guy from the Gym
9. More Stuff from the Past
10. Trip to Italy
11. Stepdad

Illustrations by Patrick Campbell

In the homosexual male brain, you can replace "Great Sandwiches I Have Eaten" with "Musicals to Die For," exchange "Dicks" for "Tits" and take out "Starting Lineup of the 1967 Boston Red Sox" in favor of "Judy Garland and Her Secretly Gay Husbands."

Also—the Red Sox 1967 lineup section may be interchanged with the starting nine of whichever baseball team may have made the biggest impact on your boyfriend or husband's life during childhood.

These simple diagrams explain many things. For instance—when you sidle up softly and nestle down next to your man and ask that always-upsetting-for-guys question—"honey, what are you thinking about?"—the reason he panics is very very easy to discern. Almost anytime you ask it—except during dinner, sex or sudden death overtime of a Big Important Game—this is what a guy is always thinking—ALWAYS:

SEX SEX TITS FOOTBALL TITS ASS YOUR ASS YOUR TITS HOCKEY BASEBALL PASTRAMI SEX BASEBALL SEX ROAST BEEF NEW SOCKS BLOW JOB MICKEY MANTLE BRETT FAVRE TITS ASS BLOW JOB I WONDER HOW FAR I COULD THROW A FOOTBALL RIGHT NOW NO WARM UP JUST HAUL OFF AND SLING THE GODDAM THING SEX PROBABLY LIKE 40 YARDS CINDY CRAWFORD'S ASS KATE MOSS WITH A RUNNING START I COULD PROBABLY THROW IT LIKE 55 YARDS PIZZA PIZZA WITH A COLD BEER I'M WHAT? MAYBE FIFTEEN FEET AWAY FROM THE WASTEBASKET, BET I COULD TOSS THIS DIET COKE CAN IN FROM HERE WITHOUT HITTING THE RIM JENNIFER ANISTON JENNIFER ANISTON CHEESEBURGER I HAVEN'T SWUNG A BASEBALL BAT IN A LONG FUCKING TIME JENNIFER ANISTON'S ASS JENNIFER ANISTON'S TITS JENNIFER GARNER'S SHOULDERS ARE TOO BIG TITS MY GIRLFRIEND'S TITS MY GIRLFRIEND'S ASS BLOW JOB SEX QUARTER POUNDER WITH CHEESE.

That's why flop sweat sets in when you ask what's on our mind because we KNOW that almost any of these thoughts do not fit the mood you might be in or even make any practical sense. But they're true.

Our emotional makeup is made up of sports and sports memories. We don't cry—unless our favorite player is forced to retire or we're watching a movie ABOUT a sport or a favorite player who retires or any movie connected to baseball—which almost always reminds us of our dads. You may wonder why your man won't shed a tear while you collapse on his shoulder during Leonardo DiPussio's death by freezing ocean in *Titanic*—but stick a *Field of Dreams* DVD in the entertainment center and fast forward to the scene where Kevin Costner plays catch with his dad? That's a different story. Ever hear of *Brian's Song*? Google it. Buy a copy. Slap it in the DVD player. Watch your other half melt into a puddle when James Caan does his deathbed speech to Billy Dee Williams. Guys know what I'm talking about.

Men communicate on a separate plane—almost the way dogs can hear—unless you are one of the species you cannot comprehend. Next time your guy is talking to another guy while they watch a game, listen closely. What they say has a double meaning:

> **GUY #1:** How 'bout those Red Sox, huh?
> (translation: Hey, how you doin'?)
>
> **GUY #2:** Yeah, goddam Ortiz, man—he's killin' the ball.
> (translation: I'm doin' alright.)
>
> **GUY #1:** You see the game last night?
> (translation: How's everything with the wife?)
>
> **GUY #2:** Holy shit. What a catch Ellsbury made.
> (translation: Everything's great.)
>
> **GUY #1:** I TiVoed the game so I was skipping through the commercials and shit, I almost missed it. But then I watched it three times in a row—amazing.
> (translation: Me and the wife had sex so I couldn't watch the game live but I TiVoed it and watched it with the sound down after she went to sleep.)

And so on and so forth.

You will notice a big bisection of The Female Brain contains an overriding interest in children while The Male Brain seemingly contains none.

Look closer. A man's interest in children and work is contained in the giant section labeled "Sex." We go to work to get money to help attract a woman who will want to have sex with us. When we have enough sex with a certain girl for a long enough period of time, our work ethic and the resultant money goes to her to feed and clothe and shelter the kids the sex will produce. It's that simple. And if you die? We will be very, very sad for a long, long time.

Like—three weeks.

Then we will meet another girl who wants to have sex with us and the whole process starts all over again. I know—it enrages you that you could be killed in a car crash or hit by a bus or contract some fatal disease and less than a month after you are placed in the cold, cold ground—the love of your life is bonking a bottle blonde. We all know women who have buried their husbands or lovers and never managed to muster up that same amount of love for another man—sometimes spending decades on their own—a picture of her handsome husband sitting above the fireplace. I know a woman who has had a searing, endless crush on a single guy she works with for over five years now—not only does he have no interest in sleeping with her, he's actually moved in with another woman, who he is now engaged to. The chick I know? Still hoping, still waiting. Doesn't work that way for men.

You have a mega crush on a girl and you make the move and she tells you to take a hike? You move on. More than likely to a girl who kinda looks the same. We don't get picky—we just get busy.

There are countless public examples. Paul McCartney—worth about five hundred zillion dollars. The love of his life Linda dies a long, diabolical death while fighting breast cancer and less than three months later he is banging a one-legged lunatic half his age. Why? Because she offered it. He was horny and hungry and she must have given great head and grilled cheese. Plus, he's a big pothead so he probably figured the fake leg would come in handy for smuggling marijuana on international private jet-set flights.

Why would ex-Beatle Paul pick a gimpy bitch when he could more than likely have had a swarm of two-legged girls to romance and take to bed without having to worry about whether they needed a bedpan or a crutch or maybe even a walker in order to take a piss in the middle of the night? Two reasons: Heather fucked him first and Heather fucked him first.

That's it.

You have to understand the word "smitten." If a guy becomes smitten by you and your body—it's over for him. His money his mind his cock his car—he will give it all up if a girl makes him happy. Her interests become his interests—and I mean pronto.

I live on a farm full of horses. I grew up in the city and the closest I'd ever come to horses were in old western movies and—if I had ever bothered to look close enough—on the ingredient section of some dog food cans. I viewed horses as ten-thousand-dollar lawnmowers. Then I met my wife. She grew up riding and loving and dreaming about horses. So, now I have horses—who I not only love and also dream about—but am learning to ride. If my wife had been into bumblebees, I would stand— as you read this—out in a field full of insects and flowers with a bee-keeper's hat and gloves on shouting "Annie—big motherfucking bee at three o'clock!" I'd have honey stains in my underwear and sting salve sitting on my sink and love every goddam black-and-yellow minute of it.

I met my wife literally across a crowded room twenty-five years ago. When she stepped into the doorway and I first saw her, it wasn't so much that my knees buckled—it was more of total soul collapse. All the blood in my body went into my shoes and then shot straight back up into my brain—twice. Now that was probably a purely visceral response—my penis knew that looks-wise, she was right in my wheelhouse. SO in my wheelhouse that if she was even remotely smart and funny—I was a dead man.

Which I was.

Right after she started talking and making me laugh.

Twenty-five years and two kids and a lot of ups and downs and arguments about everything from how much pepper I put on my potatoes to why I don't bother to put my clothes from today into the laundry hamper tonight (answer? Because I'm planning on wearing them again tomorrow morning) in sickness and in health, in good times and the bad, for better or worse and four marriage counselors later (one was an asshole, one was an idiot and the third one I'm pretty sure was a Yankees fan)—I still wake up and wonder how I got so lucky.

By the way, guys—here's a few quick and easy steps to follow before you enter the first session with your wife and the marriage counselor. I found these to be very, very helpful:

1. It's all your fault.
2. Really. The fault is yours.
3. Still your fault.

Write those down on some five-by-eight-inch index cards and flash-memorize them. Better yet—stick 'em in the glove compartment for safekeeping.

A lot of women I know not only need to be in therapy, they prefer to talk to a male therapist. Why?

Because he's a guy whose JOB it is to listen.

To listen and learn.

About them.

Listen as they register all of their complaints, anxieties, worries, frets, marital woes and relationship friction. Listen INTENTLY as they ramble on and on about their husbands, their mothers, their fathers, their step-dads, their sisters, their bosses—it all gets laid out and the man in the room has to keep two very wide-open ears.

The Man Shrink. The perfect partner.

He nods and squints and murmurs in agreement and when he asks her a question to probe further it's almost always offered up as "How did that make you feel?" or "How did you feel about that?" or "Did that make you feel such and such a way blah blah sympathy blah?"

The Man Shrink takes mental notes and pays rapt attention and is absolutely guaranteed to agree with her. For forty-five minutes. Then—it's time to go.

Man Shrinks are the female version of hookers.

You pay him to provide a necessary service that has a strict time limit and though it involves what seems to be an incredibly intimate exchange—you don't see or talk to him again until the next time you pay him.

Plus, this kind of prostitution is not only legal—it can make your marriage or relationship better. And let's face it—you want her to be happy.

The girl in your life will always be better than a life without your girl. She will make you a finer, more upstanding citizen in our society—and not just in a psychological sense.

Every guy I know has had the experience of seeing another guy he knows amble into a room sporting a fresh new frou-frou haircut, six-hundred-dollar designer jeans and something akin to clown shoes. No one wonders if he joined the circus. No one asks him why his eyebrows no longer meet. They all know he got dressed and groomed by the new girl in his life. Hey— it happens to the best of us. They take your cash and use it to rebuild you.

Which brings up another difference between the sexes. Paul was sixty-something years old, a multibillionaire and incredibly famous when he and Heather hooked up. She was thirty-three and had eight cents in her plastic foot. And claimed she was "in love." Uh-huh. Why is it young chicks—bipeds or single-wheeled—never fall "in love" with sixty-four-year-old janitors. Or hobos?

Would Donald Trump have had such a parade of young pussy pass through Trump Tower over the last five decades if he didn't OWN the fucking thing? Are women at least half his age really that attracted to fourteen strands of dyed blond hair that are teased and tickled and duct-taped into submission until they somehow form a semi-circle of bangs that swoop down like a hair hawk across his forehead before ending up in a nest just above his coat collar?

And the answer is? No. It's the buildings, stupid.

Name the last man in his early thirties or late twenties that you know of who married a rich woman at least twice his age?

Need more time? Go ahead.

Here it is—Donald Trump's first wife, Ivana—listed at sixty years old but you can add a good four or five years to that—and her thirty-six hair-gellin'-megaMetro-sexual-year-old über-Euro-trash-boyfriend Rossano Rubicondi. You make up your own jokes about this union, his name and his motivations and please feel free to insert them right here.

Because guys can't do it. Unless they're gay and there's no sex involved. Ashton Kutcher and Demi Moore is the closest we can come. She was forty-two and he was twenty-seven when they fell in love. That's a difference of only fifteen years. And they may both be fine with it three years later, even as I write this.

But two decades from now—when the kabbalah bracelets and the Botox both stop working their magic, she needs new tits again AND a hip replacement and he's about to hit fifty with a bald spot or two—let's see how much resistance he has when Jessica Alba's daughter is hitting on him during the shooting of *Dude, Where's My Car Part Seven*.

Straight men don't dance, remember birthdays or marry chicks with hearing aids.

We also don't date women who are on death row, which is another compartment in The Female Brain. If you are a guy and you kill your parents or a stranger or your ex-wife or just snap like a twig and take out thirteen of your co-workers—and society decides not to turn you into a human sloppy joe strapped to an electric chair—women will flock to visit you. It happens time and time again. A guy gets life behind bars and the fan mail flounders in. Pretty soon some buxom chick from Biloxi or a local cookbook author from Columbus is getting hitched to a guy she will only be able to have sex with in a five-foot-wide metal trailer once a month for fifteen minutes. Why? I guess because they know where you are. And you love them. They can tell by all the wonderful sweet nothings you write in your letters, which you are only writing because you don't have access to porn (and she sent you a Polaroid of her tits). And she knows you won't cheat on her—unless it's with Mack the Truck from Cellblock B—whose tits might be bigger but have a shitload of hair on them.

This plan would never work for guys. If Brad Pitt had met Angelina Jolie through an exchange of letters while she was assigned to a Federal Penitentiary for her next nine lives—he may have gone to see her in the trailer twice. MAYBE three times.

After that—just too long of a drive.

Two and a half hours there, five minutes of sex, ten minutes of whining about how much the system sucks and how the guards are all talking about her behind her back and how her mother won't stop telling her how she threw her life away and blah blubbedy I'm thinking of getting your face tattooed on my ass but first I have to have Billy Bob's name erased and do you think the fact that I could fit both his first names on my ass means my ass is too big and blub I wanna adopt my Nigerian cellmate blib and then the bell goes off ending the session and Brad still has a two-and-a-half-hour drive back home.

Not really worth the trip.

These are the facts. There is no way around them.

The big chunk of The Female Brain that's called The Past?

That's a gene men don't really carry. When it comes to things that happened five or ten or even eighteen years ago—we have no recollection. Unless we're talking about sports or *The Godfather Part One* and *Two* or the Vanessa Williams issue of *Playboy* magazine. Your old boyfriends? You could have had thirty-seven of them—the only one we care about is the one who came right before us.

But every guy has had the experience of getting into an argument with his chick and she falls off the deep end, spiraling forth from whatever it was you just did wrong to spouting out general admonitions like You Never Listen and You Always Pull This Same Old Shit and the next thing you know she says this:

Remember that time at Stephanie's birthday party four years ago when we were talking in the kitchen to her and you got a beer and went out into the living room and I was talking to Stephanie in the kitchen for like another half an hour and I came out to make sure you were okay and you were talking to that tall blonde with the big tits in the tight white sweater and I gave you a look and went back in the kitchen and Stephanie even noticed it and later when Stephanie was opening her presents and they brought out the cake when we were singing happy birthday to her I saw you say something under your breath to Big Tits and she laughed so I KNOW you were flirting with her and then Big Tits gave me a look like I just made your boyfriend pay attention to me and you denied it all the way home and then we didn't talk for like two days? Do you remember that?

And our response is almost always the same:

Who the fuck is Stephanie?

It ain't personal. It's just the way we are. I think we'd get a lot more done in this country if we finally could put to bed the idea that men need to be a lot more like women and vice versa. It goes against all science, math and common sense about the sexes.

Men claim women are always miserable—stay-at-home moms bitch about having to stay home, working moms bitch about having to work AND raise children, when they are not bitching about not getting paid as much as men.

Listen, let me make this as clear as the clear glass bottom of a just-Windexed—and thus as clear as clear can get—glass-bottomed boat: I'm not talking about single moms who have to work to feed their kids or moms who work as well as the dads because between the two of them they barely manage to feed and clothe and shelter the kids or moms who work a part-time job to help out with the bills that both her and her partner of choice are doing their best to keep from piling up.

My sister-in-law Judy worked as did my brother Johnny as did my sisters Ann Marie and Betsy and both of their husbands and they did so because they needed both incomes and you know who the full-time nannies were? My mom and Judi's sister Janie and any and all available nearby aunts.

I'm not talking about necessity.

I'm talking about the moms—and we all know them—who begrudge the baby and the time they should be spending with it because it's beneath or beyond them.

The moms who are not "fulfilled" by being a mom.

The moms for whom toting a kid is fine—if the kid's outfit matches their own or carrying a kid for twenty minutes or so lends them a worthy amount of caring cachet from the shallow set that follow what's in fashion. If kids are suddenly and ever-so-briefly back in style—then so are they.

Moms who find sitting and talking with other moms while their kids play together so boring that they would rather have a Nicaraguan nanny with no vested interest in the baby other than as a means to stockpile dollar bills change and coddle and burp it while mom is out power-lunching her way to a bigger office with bigger lunches and sleeker desks and seven more assistants they can assault with assorted lists and demands.

If Helicopter Moms are overinvolved and almost ever present—flying into schools and playdates and Little League games and soccer fields to primp and feed and urge and cheer and many times just check to make sure the kid is okay, then the women I'm talking about should be referred to as Jet Pack Moms.

Helicopter Moms fly in.

Jet Pack Moms fly OUT.

As soon as little Ashley shits her pants or toddling Todd erupts with vomit—Jet Pack Mom powers up and disappears. You want her to watch you climb up onto the couch? Sorry. Jet Pack Mom's out shopping. For shoes. For herself. You want her to teach you how to multiply two times two? Sorry. She's busy dividing up dumplings at a Best Friends Who Brunch At Barney's brunch. How about commiserating at the playground while you run and jump and skip and hop? Nope. She's hopped up on low-dose antidepressants to keep her fear of growing slightly older at bay. But when you might need a little extra oomph from the sidelines during your dance recital? If there are other moms attending whom talking to would help shorten or enhance her long walk up the society ladder, Jet Pack Mom will fly in and mingle with fury.

Helicopter Mom found breastfeeding to be a wonderful bonding experience.

Jet Pack Mom briefly loved her larger chest and contemplated augmentation and new dental bonding while the baby was bottle-fed formula.

Helicopter Moms fly in with hugs and extra pencils.

Jet Pack Moms pencil their kids and kid hugs in.

Helicopter Moms fret and worry about bullies and bad grades.

Jet Pack Moms worry about frown lines and labia reduction surgery.

Helicopter Moms dream long baby dreams and wake up thinking baby baby baby all day long.

Jet Pack Moms dream of appletinis and kid-free Caribbean vacations and ponder beachweather workouts all afternoon.

You know that dad you see doting over his daughter down by the plastic slide in the park every day?

He's not a Helicopter Dad.

He's just married to a Jet Pack Mom.

Here's the real deal: men are built for work, kids almost always want their mommies, if you decide to not have kids and just chase your career—hey, not getting promoted happens to almost everybody.

It used to drive me nuts when I was working in comedy clubs and some female comic would say something to the effect of "it's so hard to do this when you're a girl."

Oh really.

And standing up in front of drunken, combative assholes who paid twenty bucks each to get in and just ordered a round of tequila shots and beer that'll cost them another sixty-five bucks—which they think gives them the right to talk out loud while the person onstage tries to talk funny into an electric stick—which only makes THEM talk even louder—yeah, that's oh so easy for the rest of us.

It's a room full of morons who are shitfaced—it sucks for everyone.

It cracks me up when actresses have meltdowns leading to an increase in their medication because some edgy orange frock a wine-and-Klonopin-swilling French designer convinced them to take a chance on led to getting named Worst Dressed Woman At The 14th Annual San Antonio Film Festival. Hey, I got picked as one of *People* magazine's Sexiest Men a few years back—which is a sign that either the apocalypse will shortly be upon us or Willem Dafoe absolutely refused to do the photo shoot—and within a few months the same magazine named me Worst Dressed Man At The Umpteenth Emmy Award Extravaganza. I guess a black shirt and red tie on the red carpet is grounds for getting slammed by Joan Rivers and the five gay men who help to hold her head up. Did I call my shrink? No—my brother saw it in the mag, called me up, we had a good laugh and I was happy they spelled my name right. Who gives a shit?

Women, that's who.

Every job has parts of it that are a giant pain in the ass—whether you carry a penis or a purse.

The Feminist Movement raised the expectations of almost every chick in this country forty-some-odd years ago and over the last few decades women have convinced themselves that men CAN and somehow HAVE changed and WERE willing to be different and more emotionally available and eager to work side by side with them and get paid the exact same amount of money.

No.

We are not changing we are not more emotionally available and we are more than willing to work side by side with you and get paid the same IF you can do the job.

Do you think any race car driver on the IndyCar circuit is in the least bit worried about Danica Patrick's recent win leading to a flock of ladies in flame-retardant pleather jumpsuits taking over their sport?

No.

Danica may eventually be joined by one or three or five more girls but the numbers will stop somewhere shortly after that because:

A. Most women do not know how to merge. And let's face it, if merging at thirty or forty miles an hour freaks you out or makes you even the slightest bit panicky, merging at two hundred and thirty miles an hour while bouncing off other automobiles and fighting for the lead spot just ain't gonna fly. My wife screams and slams on the brakes if a squirrel dashes out in front of her car. It takes her twelve minutes of deep breathing to get past a four-second episode of that—the first six minutes of which involve searching the rear and sideview mirrors to see if the rat with a tail might still be alive. Dale Earnhardt Jr. suddenly swerving in front of her on a banked oily curve? Two words: pulmonary embolism.

B. Talking while driving might seem like a keen attraction to females considering getting behind a race car wheel, but once they find out that all the chatter on the headset is limited to tire updates, fuel tank leaks and loud angry screaming? Not so much. They'd rather go back to forty-five in the fast lane while discussing bikini wax jobs and Barack Obama's teeth on the hands-free.

C. The raw DNA facts I mentioned in the prologue of this book.

Science has proven that women of child-bearing age have an actual biological resistance to taking any extreme risks—Elizabeth Berkley starring in *Showgirls* notwithstanding.

Annika Sorenstam worked out like a maniac and put on ten extra pounds of muscle before trying to challenge Tiger Woods and the top male golfers in the world to a fair-play championship round of golf a few years back and what happened? She hit it long, she hit it hard, she landed on each and every green with a chance to birdie or par and then—she three-putted. Or four-putted. Or five-putted. She pitter-putted her way right out of the tournament and then cried at the sight of the first microphone that popped into her face because she is—in fact—a woman.

She could compete until the pressure got high, and putting on a PGA green? With thousands of people surrounding you and tens of millions watching on TV? It doesn't get much higher than that. It's what men like to call the "Eek! A mouse!" factor. Women react differently to certain things than men do. Mice, blood, gunfire—you name it. My wife is deathly afraid of mice. Me? Bats. Not baseball bats—the ones that fly. They don't make me cry or shriek. No time for that. Too busy fleeing.

Crying, of course, is the chief complaint men have about women in the workplace. Just ask Hillary Clinton. She was way behind in the New Hampshire Presidential Primary—until she cried. Then she gained a bunch of Empathy Points. Mostly from other woman. Not to mention Guilty Husbands Of Empathetic Women—who also voted for her because they were afraid their wives would shut down sexual access if they didn't. Don't laugh—I know at least three guys who voted for Hillary based on that actual situation. Shocking? Not really. I'm only surprised Hillary didn't bawl her way through the remaining forty-eight states. As a matter of fact, if she had changed her campaign motto from Blah Blah Something Change to Vote For Me Or Your Wife Won't Fuck You she would have had the election wrapped up at sunset on Super Tuesday. As Tip O'Neill once said—all politics is local. And for men, it doesn't get much more local than your crotch.

Which reminds me—every woman I have ever known seems to be utterly in an information blackout when it comes time for their period to arrive. They get bloated and angry and snippy and terse and if you ask them if they might be possibly getting their period? First they bite your head off and then they go—ohhh, maybe.

Believe me, if blood came out the end of my penis every month? I'd have the due date nailed down to the exact goddam second and every guy I worked with would know when it was gonna happen. That's another thing about guys—we won't go to the doctor to have our prostate checked—can't stand any man OR machine touching our asses—but we see the slightest beginning of a mole or a growth or even just a stray dot of lint on our penis? Right down to the cock doctor's office. Immediately. So if blood came outta that thing? Forget it. There wouldn't be a war for another seven centuries—unless we could all synchronize our situations. Then we'd bomb and maim and behead each other for three weeks—take ten days off to bloat, whine and moan—then compare notes about who bled how much and go right back to the maiming and the killing.

Who Bled How Much would become a sign of whose dick was bigger, by the way.

Which brings us to shopping, somehow.

Why is it that everything a woman brings home was "on sale." Shoes, coats, gloves, chairs. Anything and everything she buys. "It was supposed to cost eighteen hundred but I got it on sale for a thousand."

That's how she describes a lamp.

Men? We are the exact opposite. Nothing worth having is worth having at all unless it was the most expensive one ever made. "Look at this plasma, Bob—forty-seven thousand six hundred and ninety-nine bucks! Biggest one they make!"

It wasn't enough to have a pill that gave you a hard-on that arrived within half an hour and lasted almost fifteen minutes.

Nope.

We needed an even more expensive pill that bonerizes within seconds and can last up to almost three goddam days.

Cialis—the onus of the trophy wife.

I'll bet Marla Maples filed for divorce from The Donald about eight minutes after she heard Viagra was headed to the open market.

You have to keep a sense of humor about it all, which can be hard in this country nowadays—pun most definitely intended.

One thing that drives men crazy is women who arrive humorless into whatever workplace it might be and then can't understand why none of the men they work with will either flirt, laugh or co-operate with them. The answers are thus:

1. Flirting is now considered a form of sexual harassment.
2. Laughing means you have to have mutual respect, which is earned and not legislated or demanded in a memo.
3. See Flirting and Laughing.

When men work and hang and eat lunch and work and sweat and laugh and work with each other—as explained earlier in this book—there are several things involved: cutthroat challenges, seemingly endless competition, nicknames and a sense of bust-yer-ass for the team camaraderie. You don't get to pick your own nickname—it's given to you based on your performance. This seems to evade most women. They see the competition and ballbusting and direct eye contact as demeaning and sexist and male. It is. If ya don't wanna run with the big dogs then stay on the fucking porch.

Men have no guilt gene about being at work instead of at home with the kids—it's the natural order of things. Nine out of ten kids tested will tell you when they fall down, when they are hungry, when they are tired, when they are just plain in a pissy mood—they want their mommies. Knowing that to be a fact—knowing that it is an actual enzyme in your system—you can't possibly be happy not being at home with your children.

No kids—go ahead and pick a career and chase it down like Lawrence Taylor tearing after an enemy quarterback.

Kids? Your place is with them.

You cannot have it both ways.

Where did the shame in being a full-time, hands-on, always-there-when-they-need-me mom come from?

I know single gay men who are more willing to stay home and raise kids today than half of their female friends. Which means, of course—the kids'll be better dressed and even the boys will carry lip balm, but that's not the point I'm trying to make. This is:

I'd have had a lot more respect for Hillary Clinton if instead of launching an eleven-thousand-page listing of All The Important Things She Did When Her Husband Was President, she just simply said—hey, I spent those eight years trying to shield my only daughter from the international media glare. I'd have stepped right up to support her if—rather than bullshitting her way through imaginary snipers in Bosnian airports and peacemaking meetings with Irish officials that were actually only sitdowns for tea (probably Woman Ends The IRA brand), she had coughed up a couple of good cookie recipes and an itemization of how she helped Chelsea get ready for her SATs.

But no—she wanted to prove that she was more like a man than a mom and that she wasn't just traveling the world in a jumbo private jet to satisfy her own ego—she was out there making a difference. Of course, if she had been at home doting on her husband it may have kept him from trawling for interns.

No mention of interns in the eleven thousand pages, by the way.

It's hard for men to have sympathy for The Feminist Movement when one of its arbiters—Gloria Steinem—took the opportunity of supporting Hillary's bid for White House glory to say being a black man in America was easier than being a woman because at least the black man got the vote thirty years before women did.

Wow. Really?

I wonder how Martin Luther King Jr. would have responded to that quote?

Last time I looked, no one's ever tried to assassinate Gloria Steinem because she has tits.

It's hard to have respect for a woman like Brenda Berkman, who went to court in 1982 to force the FDNY to place her as a member of that department even though she had failed the physical test.

This goes right to the brunt spine of the argument—you wanna be a firefighter—you have to pass the test. Everyone does. Fat guy, skinny guy, black fat guy, yellow skinny guy—fat Muslim, fat Jew, fat Catholic—race, color, creed and sexual equipment have nothing to do with it. It's the same as saying you wanna play professional football—you want Lawrence Taylor's job? Strap on a sports bra, a pair of shoulder pads and a helmet and get out there to kick some ass.

Only difference between football and firefighting is:

A. Fire
B. Life
C. Death

The fire test—among many other feats—requires that you run up seven flights of stairs while wearing and carrying over 100 pounds of equipment, pick up a 150-pound human dummy and carry it all the way back down—within a certain number of seconds. Just like you would in a real fire. Brenda couldn't do it. She had to drag the dummy down by the feet for the last five flights. So her lawyer—the noted feminist Gloria Allred—argued that Brenda, by dragging the dummy, had actually helped save the dummy's life because smoke rises and therefore keeping the head on the stairs the whole way down and below the smoke level was better.

No mention of the fact that five flights of head-banging might lead to a 150-pound quadraplegic. Or the fact that even back then, the only fire victim you're gonna find who weighs less than 200 pounds is either an infant, an anorexic or a crackhead. Unless the fire was in a modeling agency. This is America—most people you are going to rescue in a fire have THIGHS that weigh 150 pounds.

Doesn't matter.

Brenda won the case and was then thoroughly dismayed at the lack of respect she received from the guys on the job. She even went so far as to say—immediately after 9/11—that looking at the names of the 343 firemen who died that day disgusted her—because it didn't have one female name on it. That going to the funerals and hearing the words "firemen" and "fireman" and "the brothers" and "the brotherhood" used during the eulogies was "hard to take after twenty years on this job." Not hard to take because 343 genuine American heroes had given their lives in what goes down on record as the single greatest rescue event in the history of the fire service. No. Hard to take because it wasn't about her and her "cause."

Open vagina—insert head.

I don't know about you but if my kids or my wife or even me and my skinny, hairless Irish ass are trapped inside a burning building, the person I want running in to get us out could be green or black or a Chinese female midget on steroids—I don't give a shit as long as they can carry us out. And I'd like us all to come out alive and not needing wheelchairs to go get the paper.

My cousin Jerry Lucey was a kickass firefighter who gave his life in the line of duty at age thirty-eight while trying to rescue a homeless couple from a burning warehouse building in our hometown of Worcester, Massachusetts, back in 1999. Jerry was a big, competitive guy who loved his job and in his obituary was called "a firefighter's firefighter" by the men he worked side by side with, a phrase that implies the pride and trust and honor and respect his co-workers felt for him. You cannot be given those words by a judge or a legal brief or a team of spin doctors. You have to do it the old-fashioned way—you have to earn it. I believe that system works just fine.

But then again—I'm crazy that way. I actually think you need to actually be able to DO the job if you wanna get paid the same as a man.

And when it comes to equal rights—why are female reporters allowed to roam through men's locker rooms, while the guys are naked and/or toweling off? But guys don't have the same right when it comes to the locker room the girls are in. Hmmm.

Double standard much?

There was a case in Boston recently where a group of male FBI agents cracking a case brought in a whipsmart female D.A. and made her a part of their team. She led them into court and argued a brilliant angle that not only won the day, it apparently almost single-handedly guaranteed a conviction. When they left the courtroom, one of the guys was so happy about the job she did, he grabbed her from behind around the head and gave her a noogie. Now—amongst men, giving a guy a noogie is considered one of the ultimate signs of respect. In fact, if you were gonna chart out what various physical signs between men actually mean, it would break down like this:

Pat On The Ass	way to go
Potato (Fist On Fist)	nice job
High Five	yeah, daddy
Double High Five	you gotta be shittin' me
The Noogie	goddam it I love you, you sonuvabitch

The history of The Noogie and its use by men goes back all the way from that courtroom scene through the Three Stooges and every dad and his son and big brothers and little brothers and Little League coaches and probably even Jesus and certain Apostles (odds being firmly against Judas).

The female D.A. should have considered it the ultimate equal rights tribute. But instead?

She filed a sexual harassment suit.

Open vagina—insert noogie.

Once the suit was filed the three FBI agents—fearing the politically correct era we all slog along in—refused to acknowledge that there was a noogie when they were questioned because they knew by the D.A.'s response when she was given the noogie that she didn't understand the depth and breadth of meaning the noogie brought to the situation.

Noogies aren't politically correct.

This is the era we live in.

No noogies.

Next thing you know—you give one to your kid, it'll be called child abuse.

We live in a country where the fireman coming to save you might be a firewoman who may actually do more damage while trying to pull you out of the fire than if she had never shown up at all.

We live in a country where Don Imus calls the Rutgers women's basketball team a bunch of nappy-headed ho's and gets chastized by former gangbanger and gangsta rapper Snoop Doggy Dogg, who—when someone compared his lyrics to Imus's statement—said "We ain't no old ass white man sittin' on top a MSNBC—some punk—we talkin' 'bout other ho's—ho's that's in the 'hood that ain't doin' shit, that's tryna get a nigga for his money—these are two separate things."

We live in a country in which, when Barack Obama calls some working-class voters in Pennsylvania so bitter and pissed off by the lack of help from their own government that they cling to guns and religion and a hatred of immigrants as a way to vent their frustration, those very same bitter, pissed-off voters who cling to guns and religion and a hatred of immigrants vent their frustration by voting for Hillary Clinton, who was BORN in that part of Pennsylvania and knows that what Obama said is true but decides to just jump on the Bullshit Ourselves In Spite Of Ourselves Joytrain and lacerate Obama for being "elitist."

So that's what they call telling the truth now—elitism.

You know what I wish I could give Hillary Clinton right now, live on TV for all the world to see?

A big, fat, full-blown, elitist goddam wedgie.

Then I'd turn to the camera and say loud and clear:

Can't we all just get along?

Speaking of which.

CHAPTER 17

WE'D HATE YOU EVEN IF YOU WEREN'T BLACK

hen it comes to overbearing, politically correct crapola and the lengths people in this country will go to in order to bullshit each other and try to force the rest of us to toe the same ridiculous line, racial and ethnic stereotyping is perhaps the most ridiculous area of all.

We have decided to try and convince ourselves that anytime a stereotype is mentioned or even pops its ugly head up right in front of our faces—it just cannot be true.

Thus, we are left to believe the following:

The Irish don't like to drink and fight—mostly with each other.

The Italians don't have members of their tribe who like to control the construction and garbage collection businesses and will kill any other Italians who get in their way.

The Chinese are great drivers.

So are the Japanese.

French girls like to shave.

The British have wonderful teeth and no problem at all expressing their feelings.

Polish people are smart.

You never see eight Puerto Ricans inside a hot purple Ford Escort so souped-up with motorhead equipment that the rims, the hood scoop, the hemi and the spoiler on the back are worth more than the car itself.

Black people don't love grape soda, ice cream and fried chicken (although their neighborhoods are full of stores that sell all three from behind the same exact counter).

The Scottish spend money like it grows on trees.

Jews make amazing hockey players.

Canadians don't like ice.

The Russians love wine, Koreans hate math, the Danish are dancers, the Swiss take a stand, the Greeks don't own diners, Australians drink milk all day and the Germans have an incredible sense of humor.

But the Mexicans? They, my friend, are out to take our jobs. And Arabs— they all wanna kill us.

(By the way—the only true false fact in the above batch of bull is the one about Polish people. I've never met a dumb Polack. Every Polack I ever knew had brains and brawn—even my teenaged Polish girlfriend. I think the Polish became victims of a widespread panic when they came to America and showed an outright ability to work hard, attend church and remain polite. All the other immigrant groups felt powerless to slap a label on them so they just picked one they thought you could get away with—dumb. There's gotta be a couple a dumb ones, right? Not in my experience. Besides—the Polish people invented pierogies. And anyone who figures out how to stuff potatoes inside of pasta is okay by me.)

The Irish love the English, the English love the French, the French adore the Spanish—who just worship the ground the Portuguese walk on.

Uh-huh.

And Americans—we just love them all.

In a country built by immigrants—people who sailed here from other places and then when travel by boat was replaced by the plane—flew here in wave after wave—we have somehow tossed all the amazing individuality aside in favor of one big happy melting smelting pot.

No dice, folks.

Take it from a guy whose parents DID come here on a big slow boat—the reason we have stereotypes is because the first four generations of each individual tribe ESTABLISHED that behavior when we all arrived.

I'm Irish.

We drink. And fight.

With each other.

A lot.

Especially at Thanksgiving.

I know a ton of Jewish guys and some of them are terrific athletes—only one of them can skate.

I know a shitload of Canadian guys AND girls—not one of them has the slightest idea how to help me with my taxes.

And we're supposed to act like these things are not true?

Like I said—no dice. Which brings us to the Indians.

Look—we stole this country from the Indians because of two things:

1. We had more guns.
2. They liked to drink.

That's it. Oh—and they had a penchant to trade land for very shiny beads. Thus we get the island of Manhattan and they get five really cool bracelets. Plus—they believed all the lies we told them involving trust and faith and blah blah just keep moving west we're almost done building blah.

So now we give them casinos to assuage our guilt. Casinos filled with statues and displays and historical artifacts explaining the honored traditions of their people.

Which most Americans would be willing to learn about if—when you were staring at the statue of Sitting Bull—you could drop a coin into his mouth, pull his left arm and have Kennedy half dollars pour out of his reclining red ass.

It's time we woke up and smelled the Colombian coffee brewing in the Swedish coffeemaker that sits on our Italian marble countertop, which actually comes from Croatia.

There is no such thing as an American American.

Afro? Yes. Irish? Yup. Anglo? You got it. But American American?

He or she does not exist.

Everyone here came from somewhere else and guess what—they ain't ever going back. The sooner we take a good, long look in the giant American mirror, the sooner we shall see—there ain't no Americans here.

There's barely any American cash or products—never mind people.

We borrow money from Chinese bankers to pay for Arabian oil that we put in Japanese cars that are driven by illegal Mexican immigrants who make the rest of us late because they're afraid to drive above the speed limit in case a Puerto Rican cop pulls them over and calls a Jamaican-born CIS Agent who feeds that information into a South Korean–manufactured computer that is watchdogged by a guy sitting at a desk in Bombay, India.

It's a joke that almost writes itself.

As is the idea of a wall to keep out the Mexicans.

Ich Bin Ein Berliner anybody?

Ronald Reagan taunts Mikhail Gorbachev ring any bells?

This country has the attention span of a gnat on Non-Drowsy Sudafed.

For decades we have sent American commanders in chief trotting off around the globe to vilify and verbally abuse tyrants and tyrannical empires who were so afraid of having their own people escape, they had to build walls to keep them in—as if they were only animals.

So now—well on our way to a bankruptcy both moral and financial—we decide to build one to keep the enemy out.

First off—the only way the wall gets built is if we use illegal Mexican labor. That's the only fiscal possibility. Let 'em come on into America, hand 'em each a hammer and a free pass and let 'em start pounding away. They'll have it done—seventy feet high, ten feet thick, spanning the whole southern hem of the country from So Cal to Eastern Texas—within a week.

The only other choice we have when it comes to illegal Mexican immigrants is this—NOTHING.

Why?

BECAUSE THEY ARE ALREADY FUCKING HERE!

Go to McDonald's or Burger King or Wal-Mart or Costco or a Major League Baseball game or a Catholic Mass or just your local downtown gas station or bus stops any day of the week.

Mexicans.

Everywhere.

Los Angeles, California?

Mexicans.

Vancouver, British Columbia?

Mexicans.

In Scottsdale, Arizona, and downtown Danbury, Connecticut.

Mexicans Mexicans.

On buses in cars on planes in trains bicycles mopeds motorbikes Rollerblades pogo sticks horseback—

Mexicans Mexicans Mexicans Mexicans Mexicans Mexicans Mexicans Mexicans Mexicans and wait a minute now—let me look—let's see—yup—more Mexicans.

You name it they drive ride hop sit or skate on it. Believe me—if Mexicans were out to kill us, we'd already be dead in the ground.

By the way—ever seen a Mexican eating food at Taco Bell? No. Should that be all the info you need to never eat there again? Yes.

Here's the deal—we were lucky enough to steal from the Indians a great piece of land that we have turned into the richest country in the world and one of the reasons is location location location—we have two neighbors on our metaphorical block. One group looks like us and acts like us, they just like to play hockey and drink beer and marry our women. The other group? They DON'T look like us but they just wanna work. And pray. And marry each other.

Wow.

Do you realize that most of Europe, all of the Middle East and everyone who lives anywhere near China would give their nation's left ball to have even ONE of our neighbors next to them? Anyone else would be handing out free skates, beer and beef enchiladas.

Not here, though. Fear and financial worry turn someone who doesn't look or sound like us into the enemy at hand.

I gotta believe if Sweden was located right below Texas and six-foot-tall, long-legged blond chicks in hot pants and halter tops were sneaking over the border just begging to landscape our lawns? Every single senator would be lining up to sign a bill not only allowing them in—but making sure their backyards got worked on first.

My father came here as an illegal immigrant. So did my mom. As did my Uncle Jerry—who wasn't here a year before he got drafted—a couple of weeks after he got his citizenship. What did he do? He went to Korea and got his newly Irish American ass shot at. Then he came home to become a successful member of society.

That's the system our forefathers put in place, folks.

Show up, prove your worth—join in all the fun.

It says so right on the Statue of Liberty.

It doesn't say bring us your tired, your poor—but hey—not those goddam Mexicans.

If anyone has any doubts left—Barack Obama or no Barack Obama— that racism is alive and well in the U.S. of A—the xenophobic attitude toward the twenty million Mexican people already here and the twenty million others trying to get in every single day sends a surefire message to everyone else on the planet—we are not only still racists—we are, in fact, retarded racists.

Fear fear fear fear—that's where it all begins.

No one is born with a racist bone in his or her body. Your parents have to put it there. My son Jack hated a lot of people when he was small—the doctor, the dentist, his even smaller cousin who drooled all over his toys. But you know what he hated most of all? Naps.

When Mel Gibson gets pulled over driving drunk with an open bottle of Patrón tequila planted between his legs and promptly begins to spout anti-Jewish comments at the cops brandishing cuffs before him—are we really gonna buy the argument that it was the alcohol talking?

If that was true—that a few swallows of tequila sends you off on an anti-Jewish tirade—then after happy hour started, Mexico would be a No-Jew zone. Bar doors would fling open and previously friendly Mexicans would start screaming anti-Semitic rants and rambles—until they sobered up.

Not buying it, Mel.

If alcohol were to blame for all the hatred in the world then the bitter blood feud between the Protestants and the Catholics that almost ate up the Irish countryside would have been easily ended by just taking all the whiskey away.

"Wow—now that there's no more booze left—I realize how much I like the other side. Who knew?"

Is Mel Gibson an amazingly talented actor and director with a true gift for storytelling?

Yes.

Do I blame the tequila for what he said?

No. I blame his father. Who runs a splinter-group Catholic church in Malibu that believes the Holocaust didn't happen.

You can go to twenty-five AA meetings a week, folks—it may keep you sober but it won't keep you sane.

Yeah yeah—the Holocaust didn't happen, Nixon was just misunderstood and Mariah Carey doesn't look like a prostitute with that brand-new set of tits.

My father taught me that assholes come in every color—even the ones in our very own family. He didn't give that info over in some kind of Gaelic Martin Luther King speech:

I have a dream. That one day all the idiots in our very own bloodline will actually figure out just how stupid they are and turn over their tools to someone who knows how to use them.

He just believed in judging every man on his own individual merits. So wiping the slate clean in America by pretending we are all the same, all one big, happy family with equal rights and equal abilities just ain't owning up to the facts.

Some people suck. Some people don't. Some people run fast. Some people can't. Some people can sing. Madonna isn't one of them.

I had a reporter one time tell me he thought the FDNY was a racist organization. When I asked upon what information he based this opinion, his response was—"Well, why aren't there more black firemen?" As if there are FDNY officials roaming the streets yelling—"Hey, we need guys to die in fires—but only white guys." I also asked him why there weren't more white people working as traffic cops in New York City—a job populated to almost 60 percent by African Americans. He had no answer.

No one becomes a firefighter because of the money—they get paid a starting salary of approximately $680 a week. You try raising two kids and paying a mortgage on that fee. It's a job you do because you love to do it. Not for the perks.

Listen—people will hate each other for almost any reason. People will break off into separate little groups to point at and gossip about and feed off their fear of other little groups.

If you think tribal warfare only exists in places like Africa and Iraq—pour an equal amount of alcohol into three New York Yankee fans and three Boston Red Sox fans and then lock them in the same room for forty minutes. The only color involved would be blood, ladies and gentlemen. Broken teeth, bruised sternums and lots of blood.

And when it comes to baseball and racism—let's put the Barry Bonds bullshit to bed too. A reporter on the Tavis Smiley radio show delivered a diatribe a while back about how all the negative media coverage of Barry Bonds was due to the color of his skin. Nope. It was due to the fact that he was a huge, gimongous, steroid-popping, lying, thieving ASSHOLE.

Like my dad said—they come in every color.

Barry could have been chestnut, puce, magenta, aubergine, mauve, moss or all six mixed up all together—he would STILL be an asshole. And the more steroids and clear and flaxseed oil and other super-growth hormone chemicals he ingested—literally—he became an even BIGGER asshole.

It's like Naomi Campbell snapping on a British Airways flight after being told one of her bags had been misplaced—she spit on one of the officers who decided to arrest her when she became physically and verbally abusive with them in the first-class cabin.

Naomi claimed they were arresting her because she was black.

No—they were arresting you because YOU SPIT ON SOMEONE AND PUNCHED THEM IN THE FACE.

At that point you weren't a black asshole—you were just A RICH ASSHOLE ON A PLANE.

Naomi claimed they hate her because she's a successful black woman.

No—they hate you because you are a RIDICULOUS black woman who has a history of hitting your maids and your other service staff with cell phones and ashtrays and whatever else you can get your hands on and you've been convicted twice on these charges and served community service in New York a few years back where you had to pick up trash and you decided to do it while parading around in a different designer outfit each one of the whatever number of days it was you were court-ordered to do so. You make fifty grand every time you peel your panties off and slip on a slinky dress and pout—BLACK is the last thing people hate about you. Your legs, your cheekbones, your lifestyle, your money—all of these are way way higher up on the list.

One of the white people involved in the British Airways NaomiGate incident tried to claim reverse racism because Naomi screamed "You white honky bitch!" at her. Sorry. Excuse the pun but—that ain't gonna fly either.

I speak for all white people when I say this—honky don't mean shit to white people anymore. Bitch? Yeah—even I don't like being called a bitch. Nobody does. I'm sure Michael Vick hated that word within an hour of entering prison. He's probably heard every variation of it by now—Atlanta-assed Falcon Bitch, Pro Bowl Bitch, Let's Do It Doggy-Style Bitch.

But honky? That hasn't been an insult to white people since *Starsky and Hutch* was still on TV.

Personally—if you chose to call me a flat-assed stupid Mick, loudmouth honky dumb drunk Irish Donkey Red Sock–lovin' skinny puke? The part that would bother me most would be "flat-assed." I mean—skinny, yeah. Loudmouth—I hear ya. No ass? C'mon.

All the racial and ethnic slurs we can sling all seem to have only the power they get from ourselves. Mick and Donkey and Paddy really don't mean anything to me. I call my other Irish friends stupid micks. I have Jewish friends who call me a donkey. I have one Jewish friend who calls himself Kikey Kikeman—in honor of everyone who knows him considering him to be The Ultimate Jew.

I offer up an idea—let's list all the top ethnic and racial slurs—the ones most commonly used in this country—and see which "team" comes out on top. My research will consist of slurs that have been used against me and those I have overheard being used against other people either in real life or the movies and other slurs I looked up online (www.hate anyonewhoisdifferent.com). I would imagine the group with the most slurs against it would be the one most Americans hate more.

Here we go—let's get them all out in the open now—in no particular order:

Chink, mick, guinea, spick.

Redskin, wop, frog, donkey.

Wetback, polack, spaghetti-bender, coon.

Canuck dago tarbaby jewboy zipperhead spook greaseball panface, bagel junglebunny paddy greaseback, slanty-eye honky dothead jewbag, limey ruskie round-eye kike, hebe gumbah nigger yellowface shylock raisin-head paleface injun porchmonkey and gook.

Whew.

Pretty long, huh.

Kind of gets to sounding like a tone poem about halfway through. Okay— now tallying the final score, I'll break it down into what we should all find obvious.

(I am applying only to the "White" group terms like round eye, honky and paleface. "Asians" will be a listing for all references to people with yellow skin and other physical attributes most racists apply equally to the Japanese, Korean, Chinese etc. "Puerto Ricans" will represent anyone of Latin or Spanish or Cuban or South American descent because—once again—most racists in this country cannot tell them apart, unless they play baseball for the hometown team and the program specifically lists where the guy is from AND the racist fan can read—which is asking a lot.)

White	3
Asians	6
Irish	4
Puerto Ricans	1
Black	7
Italian	6
French	1
Canadian	1
English	1
Russian	1
Polish	1
Jewish	7
Mexican	1
American Indian	1
Indian from India	1

Greaseback is the only slur I came across that no source seemed to have an assignment for—which leads me to believe it is actually an anti-Irish thing and they were just too polite to tell me to my face.

So—if there were such a thing as Racism Playoffs—the Blacks and the Jews would finish tied for first, with Blacks winning out in my book—

which you happen to be reading—because Nigger will always trump Kike, Hebe or any of the other five negative names the Jews received.

The Italians come in tied for the second spot with the Asian group, and the Irish trail by two but lead every other group—except white, which includes them—by a lot. Leaving the Puerto Ricans to feel left out one more time with only one blanket anti–Puerto Rican slur to be hurled after their long presence in this country—not to mention the Mexicans who had only "wetback" to show for all this hatred and fear supposedly surrounding them.

One could make the argument that many racists use "Spick" to refer to Mexicans as well as Puerto Ricans, but that's just gonna make both groups even more pissed off so let's just let it stand the way it is.

Based on this—I'd say the African and Jewish communities—along with the Italians, Irish and Asians—are still making the most headway in this country.

Here's to hoping that—two decades from now when perhaps another twenty million Mexicans have settled in here and begun to legally prosper, vote, work and play—racists will have at least five or six more slurs to shout at them during an altercation. Then our Mexican friends will truly feel as if they are making some progress.

Isn't that the American way?

And listen—all those people on that list, no matter how many racial and ethnic barbs they may or may not have?

Each and every one of them could be called an asshole.

Depends what they're like when you meet them.

And no matter how bad the names they call you might be—at least none of them translates into "pedophile."

CHAPTER 18

THE POPE IS A PIMP

nd not just because his annual budget for Prada Pope shoes is bigger than what many of his Mexican subjects earn in a year.

Or how much money he spends on big, foofy hats and jewel-studded dresses each Easter—his tab for fancy rings alone would make The Queen Of England blush.

No—imagine this scenario:

You run an organization which is in the business of killing and stealing. When one of the guys who works for you gets caught killing and stealing—instead of going to jail or getting the death penalty—you get to send him to a new town where he can kill and steal some more.

And you keep on doing that over and over again with a ton of guys who work for you until—finally—someone in one of these victimized towns decides to stand up and say—hey, who the hell told these guys they can just come in here and kill and steal? Then—and only then—do you submit to the basic laws of humankind and agree to prosecute the guys who work for you and turn them over to the authorities.

Sound like the Mafia?

No—the Mafia would LOVE to have that business plan.

The very same business plan the Catholic Church has used for hundreds and hundreds of years.

Priests have been allowed to kill the trust and faith of young boys and steal their innocence and their souls through rampant sexual abuse and the church's reaction—and the pope is the head of the church—has been to transfer each offending father to a different parish. That way he gets to abuse a whole new set of kids and the church gets to keep all its money.

'Cause that's what it's all about, folks. Moolah.

The Original Popes—good name for a band—were allowed to marry and have sex and produce children but eventually this led to affairs and then Bastard Children—let's call them the pope-arazzi—started showing up unannounced and demanding money and land. The church—realizing what a lousy system this was—decided to declare that all future priests and popes had to remain Celibate—thereby giving them the public rank of monks and thereby allowing the church to exist in a tax-free domain.

So all the real estate and all the money the people gave to the church every time they passed the basket? Cold, hard cash baby.

Priests weren't giving up sex to prove their devotion to God. They gave it up so the church could BUY stuff: more land, more gold, mo' dresses, mo' hats. Could there be a more hat-centric organization on the planet? The priesthood is like a giant army and all the rankings are based on headwear—the bigger the hat, the more important the guy. Regular priests get none, monsignors get nice magenta caps, bishops get bonnets, cardinals each sport a holy red skypiece and the pope's biggest fish-mouth-shaped chapeau is actually called The Tiara.

Let me repeat that—The Tiara.

It's like Tim Gunn went back in time to say—Your Holiness, nothing says Look At Me! more than a shiny crown.

Once they had chosen the No Sex But Plenty Of Elaborate Outfits route, was it any wonder that men with a penchant for other men and free-flowing robes would sign up? And, of course, one thing led to another and one day some priest realized he had an attraction to little boys and—what a surprise—he happened to be in a job where he was SURROUNDED by the little fellas—WHAT A JACKPOT!

And off to the sex abuse races they went.

Until the charges started trickling in.

The Catholic Church avoided cooperating in sex abuse investigations all over the earth until they absolutely had to start coughing up the cabbage. Meanwhile, thousands and thousands of young boys and young men had their lives forever forsaken by these Pedophiles On Parade. And then—to top it all off—they deign to tell young couples on the verge of marriage what it takes to form a long-lasting union or hormone-crazed teenage girls what form of birth control they can or cannot use.

Well the jig is up, jokers.

Two billion dollars in we're-so-sorry payments later on doesn't mean dick to the ex-altar boys who sought your counsel and confirmation but ended up instead committing suicide or sitting on a sofa four times a week spilling their guts out to a shrink—two billion barely cracks the bill for lifelong therapy. Especially in Manhattan. (Four billion might get you through the first two and a half years, not including Hanukkah gifts.)

It's time to take the pontiff and his pontificates to task.

Throw the old commandments out the back door because I proudly present to you:

The NEW Ten Commandments.

(I just got these from Jesus and MAN is he pissed)

1. **THOU SHALT NOT KILL**—unless the priest is much bigger than you and somehow gets the upper hand, then hitting him with a lamp, a heavy gold chalice or even a handy statue of the Virgin Mother is totally allowed. (My suggestion? The statue of my mom will probably get the job done the quickest, plus it's got all kinds of symbolic value—once the story hits the papers.)

2. **DO NOT TAKE THE NAME OF THE LORD THY GOD IN VAIN**—which I still don't like but if the priest quickly pinches your ass or makes googley eyes at you while other people are around, a loud "Jesus Christ, Father—what the hell are ya doin'?" will work wonders.

3. **HONOR THY FATHER AND THY MOTHER**—meaning your ACTUAL father and mother, not the sterling-silver-crucifix-toting

Barbra Streisand fan following you around like a gay cat in heat or the angry lesbian who instead of acting on her sexual urges decided to don religious garb and bust the balls of young bucks like you. Those two you can tell to go fuck themselves. Also—give them this personal message from me—Jesus will see you in hell. Where there are no Melissa Etheridge records or *Sex and the City* DVDs.

4. **THOU SHALT NOT COVET**—any items any priests leave lying around. Like candy, cigarettes, roofies—believe me, these assholes will use anything they can to lure you into their nests. Ignore it all.

5. **THOU SHALT NOT WORSHIP FALSE GODS BEFORE ME**—I should really re-title this one. By false Gods I mean Michael Jackson. Do not go to his house or hotel room or anywhere with this guy—I don't give a shit what Macaulay Culkin says—the guy's a weirdo. That nose? Whatever happened to the old saying "I am as God made me?" I talked to my old man—He don't make noses like that. Believe me when I tell you—Michael Jackson is a priest in pop star's clothing.

6. **THOU SHALT NOT STEAL**—unless it's money from a priest. He leaves his wallet layin' around with a couple hun-gee hangin' out? Consider it yours. Rolex watches, antique clocks, Cuban cigars—hey, you heard about what I did with the merchants at the Temple? Same deal. Consider it all a down payment on the whole church's Big Bad Karma bill. Which I'm tabulating as we speak.

7. **CHARLTON HESTON WAS ALRIGHT BY ME**—this one has nothing to do with the pedophile priest thing, I just wanted to make it official—me and my dad thought Chuck was pretty swell. I mean, yer just not gonna find a better guy to play Moses—even Moses thinks so, and he originally wanted John Wayne to play the part. But Chuck pulled it off with panache. Even if they were gonna remake that picture right now—who could you get who'd be better? Matt Damon? Too wimpy. Clooney? Gimme a break. And I love DeNiro as much as the next prophet but method is the last thing you want in a biblical epic. Remember Harvey Keitel in Scorsese's *Last Temptation of Me*? Yikes. By the way—if Dafoe can play me—why can't Denis? Well—doesn't matter. They'll never let him do it now.

P.S. SPEAKING OF CHARLTON HESTON—that whole *Planet of the Apes* thing? That was a message from Us. You guys don't shape up down there soon—poverty, war, Terrell Owens, etc.—we're turning the whole place over to West African Spider Monkeys. They're good with their hands and they're not easily mollified by the TV, unless Regis and Kelly are on. They love Regis.

8. **THOU SHALT NOT COMMIT ADULTERY**—this one means the same thing it always did. Don't sleep with someone if you're married to someone else. It really sucks. Take my word for it, you get caught? Me and my old man are the least of your worries.

9. **THE MEEK SHALL INHERIT THE EARTH**—what we mean by this is, payback's a bitch. We already said we love Charlton Heston, so you can imagine what our stand on gun control is.

My dad waves his miter a couple of times—miter, cane, wand— same difference—and the next thing you know all the guns fall into the hands of the meek—which in the case of the Catholic Church means the kids the priests were abusing. That's right— when I said turn the other cheek I meant the ones above the neck, you sinbags. Praise my dad and pass the ammunition.

10. **GO SOX**—yeah, that's right. We're all Red Sox fans up here. Every-thing you've heard is true—Evil Empire, Curse Of The Bambino, blah bibleddy blah. Satan controlled all of professional sports unimpeded by Us for the last couple of centuries. We were a little too busy fight-ing off the Black Plague, Hitler and eight years of Richard Nixon to answer any prayers of help being offered up by overpaid wide receivers and Rico Petrocelli. Until the Yankees got that three games to none lead over the Red Sox in the 2004 playoffs. That's when my dad and I decided to step in. I mean, we're not gonna go crazy about it—the Sox won't win EVERY season. But over the next decade or so? Let's just say Fenway Park might have a little invisible halo hanging above it.

11. **THAT'S RIGHT—JUST LIKE SPINAL TAP**—the Ten Command-ments now go all the way up to eleven. This one should already be crystal clear: don't send money to vain, hypocritical preachers you see on TV. The list of smarmy, con artist idiots in that occupation is so long and rife with humdingers—Jim and Tammy Faye Bakker, Jimmy Lee Swaggart—the names alone are supposed to give you a hint. Swaggart? Come on. Rhymes with Braggart? There's a cocky black televangelist currently invoking my name and my Father's

presence as he flies across America from religious gig to religious gig in a five-million-dollar private jet. His name is Creflo Dollar. If I may take my own name in vain—Jesus H. Christ! What do I have to do—draw you a friggin' map? Stop giving your dollars to Dollar. Like I said—we're a little busy up here. Right now we got the whole Darfur thing, the crisis in the Middle East and whether or not to let Nicolas Cage continue to make movies. You guys gotta show a little common sense down there. Speaking of which—my dad wants to put this right out on the table—He does not now, nor has He ever, spoken to George W. Bush about his administration's policies. All He does is lean down and whisper once or twice a day—"Hmmm—a warm glass of whiskey sure would taste good right about now. Do it, Georgie, do it." Of course, Bush is such a moron he thinks my dad is the devil and ends up listening to the other guy. Who wants him to bomb everything. Go figure. See ya soon!

Forever Yours,

JHC.

CHAPTER 19

THE ASSHOLE OLYMPICS

o this is it. I've had it with our whole mess.

Al Sharpton claiming racism every other time Alfonso Soriano gets thrown out at second base.

The five-going-on-six-year Operation Iraqi Freedom, a war that has gone on so long, if George Bush Jr. was eighteen again he'd be calling his dad to find a way NOT to serve.

High-priced American athletes like Latrell Sprewell—who turned down a multiseason NBA contract because "I can't feed my family on 9.5 million dollars a year."

Really? What's your family eating, Latrell—Ferrari Testarossas? Mercedes SUVs?

Asshole after asshole after asshole gets ahold of the microphone and the media's attention in this country and promptly informs the world that we are not a nation of readers.

The drugs we ingest alone contain enough warnings about taking a single series of pills that if we BOTHERED to read the bottles—we'd be operating on orange juice and chicken soup for every ailment in the future. These are the most common side effects of America's favorite new prescription drugs:

Disorientation, apathy, anxiety, hostility, blurred vision, temporary blindness, nausea, vomiting, tremors, anal leakage, coma and death.

Now, granted—death would suck. 'Cause there's no pill you can get to counteract the problem. And even if there was—how are you gonna speed dial your doctor from the afterworld?

But all those other ones? All ya gotta do is get more pills. Maybe it's just me, but—if my ass is leaking? I don't care if liquid gold is flowing out—I'm not taking another pill. I'm filing a lawsuit.

Millions of Americans are so desperate to be drugged they sign up to be saddled with addictions—that's how lazy they are. Why spend the money with a therapist figuring out what your problem is when you can just pop a little pill and feel different? They'd rather spend the day doped up and wearing a diaper than confronting the fact that—most of the time—life just kinda sucks.

Even the threat of a heart attack, blurred vision and temporarily going blind hasn't stopped millions of American men from taking Viagra and its sister pills—which proves that men would rather walk around with a cane, a Seeing Eye dog and a four-hour erection than ever hope to read a book again.

American ingenuity invents new diseases and the new pills required to treat them on a week-to-week basis.

Restless leg syndrome—this is a new disease where you find that your foot or leg—even both legs—will not stop bouncing up and down or otherwise rhythmically moving—especially at night. There are three ways to solve the problem:

1. Buy a set of drums.
2. Join a band.
3. Skip Steps 1 and 2 and take Ropinirole.

The only problem is, Ropinirole apparently has a number of side effects—one of which is an uncontrollable urge to gamble.

Any possibility the Indians are putting some of their newfound casino wealth into prescription drug research? Let's check the labs for free passes to Huey Lewis's next show at Mohegan Sun.

A few years back, doctors announced the "discovery" of a new disease called SAD—seasonal affective disorder. Victims claim the symptoms begin sometime in September and often last until March or April and include depression, despair, misery and guilt combined with a desire to oversleep or extreme napping as well as overeating.

I'm sad to say that—in THIS doctor's estimation—SAD is not a disease. It's called WINTER, asshole. It happens every year right after the leaves fall off the goddam trees.

And you are not a victim—you are a fat, human sloth who wants to suck down boxes of Twinkies and wash them through your cellulite-enflatulated system with a two-liter bottle of Orange Crush and you feel guilty because you slept for nine hours last night but just had a forty-five-minute nap while you were watching Ellen cry about a dog she gave to her makeup specialist who somehow ended up in Paris Hilton's backyard with twenty-seven other Chihuahuas and only half a Snickers bar for all of them to share.

Here's my prescription: get off the fucking couch and buy a set of skis. Or skates. Better yet—buy both. And don't eat the yellow snow.

Case closed.

The car companies are developing corn-fueled cars AND larger seats for fatter-assed Americans at exactly the same time. I say we ignore the irony and indecision implicit in that arrangement and instead plod on with cars that have larger seats that are in fact just comfier versions of toilet seats so you can drive, eat and shit almost simultaneously—the engine built to run on methane which will be produced by the farts you emit as you drive and gorge your way across the country. Fart-fueled automobiles. Short trip over to see Ma? Down a cup of peanuts and some soda. Headed down south to watch spring training? Swallow three hot dogs, put a case of canned pork and beans in the backseat and away we go. Now if we could just come up with a kidney that turns urine back into beer as it passes through your penis, we'd be all set.

I'm tired of the denial. I'm tired of the fat the loud the lazy and the stupid.

We've drugged the fat we've stapled their stomachs we've reinvented the vacuum cleaner so we could attach it to their huge asses and suck out all the fat but still—still—they insist on eating.

Well, eat up.

That's right.

Eat.

Eat as much as you want. I'll explain why in a little bit.

They just announced a study that proves Botox may enter the face, but it settles into the brain stem—not only freezing elements of your visage but some of your thought patterns as well—which explains those pregnant smiling pauses you see every time Sharon Stone gets interviewed on the red carpet.

Botox it up, baby. Shoot your whole goddam body full of that freeze-dried frozen goat sperm.

Steroids—I want the steroid testing to stop. Immediately. The Mitchell Report, the FBI's Roger Clemens Investigation, the Federal Court Trial Of One Barry Bleeping Bonds—end it all and end it now.

I want the biggest baddest baseball players and football maniacs and biking teams this planet has ever seen.

We've had the wrong attitude going on since day one with this stuff. You wanna prosecute athletes for using performance-enhancing drugs? Hey—how about you?

Viagra, Ropinirole, Botox, Advil, NyQuil DayQuil Budweiser Pot Cocaine Emergen-C Xanax Prozac—you name it, someone in this country is taking it right now to improve their sex life, semen count, leg strength, nasal condition, anger management, bowel movements, piss volume or tit size. And you wanna bust a guy for taking some human growth hormone laced with extra ball juice before he rides in the third leg of the Tour de France? Hey—you want me to ride a bike through the French countryside for half a month I'm gonna need a shitload of drugs—HGH and an extra couple bags of testosterone being the least of it. I couldn't ride from one end of Manhattan to the other on a bike without a backpack full of coffee, two bottles of morphine and a crystal meth dealer riding in a rescue car alongside.

I don't wanna hear any arguments about how many more home runs Mickey Mantle or Babe Ruth would have hit if they had used steroids— they were both drunks. Ruth on steroids? He would've gone through three livers and most of the hot dogs in the Western Hemisphere before his heart exploded while he was fucking an elephant in the Bronx Zoo on the night of his twenty-seventh birthday. Mantle had 536 home runs when he retired at age thirty-seven. If he had been able to shoot the juice? He would have hit 538. Before he was old enough to vote. Then his head would have blown apart. Ever seen pictures of the guy with his shirt off at that age? Steroids would have turned him into a walking time bomb.

I want all Americans on steroids—starting now. The athletes the assholes the fat fucks—everyone.

I wanna see baseballs hit 800 feet.

I wanna see footballs tossed 100 yards.

I want heavyweight boxers who weigh 400 pounds and can punch their way through brick fucking buildings.

You don't think the Chinese are already creating a race of giants to eventually dominate the Olympics and from there the world? What—you think Yao Ming is just some crazy freak of nature? No way—Yao Ming is the warning shot fired across the hull. We live in the greatest country in the world with access to the biggest and the best and the brightest—but we ain't gonna be number one for long if we don't start putting the pedal to the ~~medal~~. metal.

Once we get the biggest athletes possible—we monitor the carnage and violence and bone-crunching power they are capable of—and how long before their heart valves turn to cheese—and then we start creating a crew of supersized police and soldiers—meat-eating, man-beating machines we unleash on the rest of the universe.

Meanwhile, the fat people we've been feeding steroids to on the side have now become the fattest animals alive—hippopotami with human hands who wear an old Aerosmith T-shirt on each foot as a sock—we top them off with a couple tons of Twinkies before stuffing them into a specially rigged air force bomber and then—we fly over enemy territory and just drop them out of the sky—it's what I like to call my Fat Fucks Crush Skinny Evil Pricks Program.

I want Ritalin-rattled geeks galore stuck in video game centers all over the country so addled for action that they can't stop inventing new ways to blow shit up at the lightning-fast press of multiplastic buttons.

I want stun guns jam-chocked with Botox we all get for free so that whenever a politician tries to sell us a long line of bullshit we can semi-assassinate him or her—freezing them in place for a solid five minutes. When they melt—they get a do-over until they start to bullshit again and the whole process begins once more.

If models and actresses insist on continuing not to eat—I'm taking the Twinkies away from the Fat Fucks during the prebombing raid flight overseas and replacing them with a steady parade of posers.

Who's hungry for Kate Moss?

I want a new state added to America—The State Of Denial. We clear a bunch of land somewhere out in the middle—Oklahoma or Nebraska or Idaho—and we fill it with cigarettes and alcohol and heroin and cocaine and every other drug imaginable. You move there you get to smoke, snort, swallow, suck and otherwise involve any substance you like into your system. You can drive drunk you can drive high you can do whatever the fuck you want within state borders. You die? Good riddance. You don't die—that's okay too. 'Cause the profit from every dime bag and dollop you buy there goes right into the coffers to pay for medical assistance for the rest of us.

And the governor from The Great State Of Denial will be none other than deposed senator Larry Craig, infamous for the press conference he organized to announce "I am not gay and I never have been gay."

Here's a future clue, Larry: if you have to hold a press conference to announce you don't like having sex with other men? It's too little too late. You might as well take the time to announce just what type of place, guy and cock it is that makes you horny. Although we have a pretty good idea the place is a Minneapolis airport men's room and the guy is who-ever might be sitting in the next stall over. And trotting out your post-menopausal, middle-aged wife was not a particularly good idea either. She looked like she was two knitting needles and one honest confession away from donning a handmade midlife lesbian sweater.

Bobby Brown is moving into downtown Denial City, by the way. He says Whitney Houston turned him on to hard drugs.

Uh-huh.

And David Guest made Liza Minnelli into a heavy drinker.

No more hypocrites and high-toned hype.

And here's another thing—you decide to climb up a snowy mountain on a personal "quest" to achieve some asinine physical goal and you get stuck in a blizzard? We ain't comin' to get you no more. No helicopters no search parties no news coverage no cell phone contact. You climb up, you climb down. Otherwise—see ya. It's called thinning the herd. We invented houses and cars and cable TV so you could stay warm and move around and WATCH bad weather on TV. You decide to go out in that weather? Yer on yer own.

Two guys in California decide to tandem skydive out of a plane using a single chute that doesn't support their weight? I don't call that a tragedy. I call it a test—two less morons to avoid on my way to work.

And I'm sick of hearing about my carbon footprint from Al Goddam Gore. He's gonna lecture me about how many pounds of tree pulp it takes to make the paper box they pack my Filet 'O Fish in?

I don't think so, Al.

How many South African gold miners had to fork their foraged nuggets over to illegal ganglords to make the Oscar, the Emmy and the Nobel Peace Prize Al has hanging on the mantel in his dining room where he must be eating at least four or five organic, free-range chickens a day, based on the size of his current carbon ASSprint. The seats in his house must be made of lead.

I don't wanna hear another word from Rush Limbaugh unless he's gonna explain how to successfully combine illegal Viagra prescriptions, heavy antidepressants and a successful round of golf into the very same afternoon. If he has any news about playing eighteen holes with a hard-on, a big smile and the same Titleist you started with—gimme a ring.

The only Hasselhoff I ever wanna see again is The Drunk Hasselhoff. I'm all for safe driving and a long, healthy life and he does have children to set an example for, but if he's not gonna break out on a bourbon and blow bender once or twice a year and end up on digital video eating a cheeseburger off the floor—what good is he? I don't wanna Hassle The Hoff—but, c'mon, Dave—give the people what they want every once in a while.

Fuck waterboarding—who needs it? You wanna torture terrorists and tyrants we catch in whatever corner we uncover?

Play some American music.

Some REAL American music.

You plant an angry Arab member of Al-Qaeda into a steel chair, tie him down with chains and braces, surround him with twenty-five-foot-high mega Marshall amps and crank up the tunes?

Grand fucking slam, pal.

But you can't play what they always play—heavy metal, hip-hop, Van Halen.

That shit doesn't work—it's exactly what they've been trained to expect.

You gotta hit them with the really hard stuff.

And when I say hard I mean REALLY hardcore:

Clay Aiken.

Hannah Montana.

Celine Dion—in English AND French.

You play that shit for a couple of days—he'll be begging to be waterboarded.

All the info we're looking for will fumble right out of his mouth.

Seventy-two virgins may be what he has in mind—but if Celine hits those high notes long enough? He'll give that dream up as soon as his ears stop bleeding.

The things that make this country great are staring us right in the red, white and blue face, folks—the biggest, the baddest, the best.

The biggest bombs, morons, racists, drunks, hypocrites, fools and assholes.

The baddest movies, music, sitcoms, reality shows, taste, food, fads and educational system.

The best—what?

Laid plans?

Intentions?

Potential?

We got those. No one gives more in charitable dollars, time or prayer than we do. No one has more promise or hope or faith in a better future. All the parts for a bigger, better equation are there. We just gotta figure out the math.

Maybe we can get the South Koreans to lend us a hand.

Scientists have ready research that says if everyone used up resources at the rate Americans do on a daily basis, we would need four more earths in order to survive.

Which means one thing and one thing only:

We gotta kill everyone else on this planet and we gotta do it right fucking now.

Or—we take a good, long look in the mirror and realize most of us can't even physically leave the house because we're too fat or high or freaked out or foolish or a dangerous combination thereof.

Somewhere in between those two possible responses lies the real answer.

Me?

I say we just get the religious right to pray our way onto the extra earths.

Or just ask George Bush Jr. to mention it to Satan the next time they talk. Because unlike most ex-presidents, who travel the one planet we already have getting paid to preach peace and prosperity and friendly co-existence—this guy's gonna have a whole lotta time on his hands.

CHAPTER 20

SOMEONE TELL MY MOM THAT
CELL PHONES CAUSE CANCER

o I decided to wrap up my book by having one more conversation with my mother.

She seems to be a beacon of common sense and working-class creativity, her main interests in life born of the pure family values the Republican Right is always nattering on about—kids, God and country—even though she has voted as a Democrat in every single election since she came to America.

Her sister—my Aunt Margaret—had died a few weeks back, a mere four days after her husband of fifty-something years, my Uncle Connie. It was one of those rare forms of love you don't see anymore—like a baseball player who plays for the same team his entire career—Uncle Connie and Aunt Margaret raise their kids and oversee their grandkids and grow old and get ill together and then when one dies the other can't wait to get to heaven and join the spouse up there in the ever-after. Connie was buried with his beloved Red Sox cap and Margaret with her favorite emerald-green tea mug.

I stood in my mom's driveway the morning of Aunt Margaret's funeral as we waved at the funeral home limo which was picking up Margaret's kids—she had lived a block or so from my mom—to make sure they knew Ma was ready to roll. Then—something strange happened.

My mom's purse rang.

Thinking it must be MY cell, I reached into my pocket just as Ma reached into her bag and produced a cell phone—flipping it open to say:

Okay, Sheila. Can you see us? Okay, sweetheart.

Then she calmly flipped it shut and stuck it back inside the bag.

I stared at her.

What's wrong? she asked.

Ma—when did you get a cell phone? I replied, my jaw dropping.

I dunno, Denis. But it sure comes in handy.

And with that she jumped in the limo and I jumped in my truck and we traveled the eight blocks to the church where everyone in my family— from my father twenty-something years ago to my cousin Jerry The Fire-fighter—had been celebrated and mourned in their passing.

As I followed the limo I considered a world where my mom has been given a portable form of communication—she could now chastise, cajole, re-mind and update us from anywhere on the planet.

Holy shit.

In the church, several of the grandkids got up on the altar and spoke about Aunt Margaret—one of the funniest and sweetest and most de-voted moms of all time. Many little details were brought up—her love of tea and her ability to feed a house full of screaming children without a whisper of a complaint or even breaking a sweat. My favorite little fact emerged from the altar: one of the grandkids remembered a roomful of grandchildren creating such a loud ruckus during a giant kid brawl that Aunt Margaret rushed in and said "If you kids don't settle down right now goddammit I'll sell each and every one of ya's to the Indians!"

We all laughed.

We had heard it before from my ma.

The fear of being sold off to live on a reservation with a tribe of Mohawks or Mohegans would make us sit right down and quietly watch the TV.

Of course, nowadays, being sold to the Indians only means you get a nice cut of casino profits while you live in a McMansion in the Connecticut suburbs.

After the funeral Mass we went to the Catholic cemetery and Aunt Margaret was buried amidst all the others in our American family plot, which sits very close to the edge of the expressway. As trailer trucks and mid-morning traffic sped by we took family shots in front of various headstones belonging to our dead relatives—smiling and throwing our arms over each other's shoulders (as if to say "Look at us! We're still alive!")—and several of us tossed our chewing gum and cigarette butts over the fence into the Protestant cemetery just next door.

Then we all sat down in the nearby restaurant that used to be a diner—still the same ownership, though—and where something like ten of us had worked over the years: my brother Johnny and I as dishwashers, my sisters and many of my female cousins as waitresses. The elders were seated with the four priests who had said the Mass and the kids—which in this case means anyone under the age of sixty—were seated at several sets of tables all pushed together. We naturally began a series of stories remembering all the fights and stitches and stolen money and drunken Irish brawls and interpersonal resentments and we laughed until our tits almost fell off. One of my ne'er-do-well cousins who used to be a short-order cook in the place was confronted with the question why weren't you at Jerry The Firefighter's funeral? He and Jerry had been close in age growing up and when Jerry and the five other firemen were killed it was all over CNN and even President Clinton had come to the memorial service to speak yet this guy claimed he had been in France.

France?

Believe me when I tell you—the closest this guy had ever come to being in France was when he ordered extra fries at the McDonald's five blocks away.

My brother Johnny had the best response, though.

He said: Who'd ya go to France with? The Goddam Coneheads?

We once again laughed our tits off.

Then the actual kids—the ones aged twenty-one and under—began to tell their stories of almost killing each other: setting each other on fire, throwing knives and forks at angry Thanksgiving meals, stealing robbing stomping kicking jabbing jawing from, at, upon and with each other.

I sat there and listened as one young nephew complained about having to be at a funeral during his college spring break. Which led to a huge discussion from the rest of us older "kids" about how spring break for us meant working extra hours in the very diner we were eating in and how no one in this family even knew what spring break was until Denis—me—got hired by MTV to do episodes of the game show *Remote Control* FROM spring break in Florida during the late 1980s.

We screamed and argued and laughed and argued and resented and guffawed and ate and elbowed and pointed and screamed and shrieked and smirked and bellowed and busted balls and it dawned on me just how functional this dysfunctional family actually was—we sit in a diner screaming at each other and laughing about how we have spent decades trying to off one another and then my cell phone rang and I fumbled it out of my pocket and answered with a loud hello—it was my mom calling from the head table asking us to keep the cadology down.

Okay Ma, I said.

Driving home that day I knew I was living in a different world.

Soon a series of calls from what I now refer to as Mobile Mom began to ensue.

She would call to update me on Uncle Angus's hip cancer.

Uncle Sean's bladder cancer.

Eileen found a lump in her breast.

Kiernan has a strange mole on his face.

Several more calls in the next few days about Bridget's Bizarre Blood Clot and Galen's Rotten Gums and Uncle Donal's Deep Chest Cough That Just Won't Disappear made the issue dawn on me:

My mom's new cell phone had become The Official Cancer Hotline.

It was as if the surgeon general had personally asked her to inform her progeny of all medical updates—immediately. Keep them updated and warn them of the dangers.

And every conversation ended with the same admonition: Denis, I'm not gonna say this again—quit that smoking.

Which, of course, she would say again—the very next time she called.

Which might be fifteen minutes later.

So I thought asking my mom a few questions that pertain to subjects in this book would be a nice, neat wrap-up. I prepared a list of six or so things—Politics, The Pope, Raising Children, Coming To America—I wanted to get her final take on and end the book with a little (hopefully) synchronicity. God knows I'd have no problem getting her on the phone—wherever she might be, that goddam phone was sure to be with her.

This is exactly what happened:

[the phone rings three times—as it is answered, the background is full of loud, ear-throttling noise]

Hello.

Ma?

Johnny?

It's Denis.

Oh—hello Denis.

Ma—what is all that noise?

Hang on hang on.

[the phone is placed on a table or something that causes a loud clattering sound—then a moment or so later the noise in the background is lowered and I hear footsteps until I hear more loud clattering]

Is that better, Denis?

Yeah. What was that?

We're just watching Dr. Phil.

What?

Dr. Phil is on.

What's he talking about?

He's talking about Mother's Day and all that crap.

How often do you watch Dr. Phil?

Oh—three or four times a week I suppose. Uncle Denis and Aunt Nell are here from Ireland.

I heard. You guys like Dr. Phil?

He's alright I suppose. His wife gets on my nerves.

His wife?

She's on the show too. Although God knows why. She just sits there like a showpiece just staring up at him. She's a doctor too I think. Who isn't a doctor these days. You know that.

Do you think Dr. Phil makes a difference?

He does I suppose. He's got some idjits [Irish for idiot] on there now— the wife had gained a lot of weight and she's ripping into the husband because he doesn't pay attention to her anymore and now he does like three things at once and never talks to her and Dr. Phil is speechifying about their kids and Dr. Phil's wife is just sitting there. Who knows with all these crazy parents. Neil said you looked up cadology on some computer or something?

Yeah, I did. I found out what it meant but I cannot find a definition of the word "blighyarding" anywhere, Ma. I've looked it up online I've looked in my Irish-English dictionary I've gone through my Gaelic dictionary— can't find it. I had to make up the spelling I think.

Oh Jesus—I don't even know how to spell it. [yelling off the phone] Denis and Nell—what does blighyarding mean? [some mumbling in the background] Uncle Denis thinks it means misbehaving. [to Uncle Denis] Is it Gaelic, Denis? [back to me] He thinks it's Gaelic. Well you know what I meant whenever I said it—you kids were causing trouble and I was telling you to stop it.

Who's yelling now there?

The fat wife is yelling at the husband—Dr. Phil is trying to get them all to shut up.

Ma—I had some questions here I wanted to ask for the end of my book.

Yes.

Did you regret ever coming to America?

No no—I mean, we were brokenhearted when we first came because we had just left home and been on a boat for God knows how long and we come into New York off of a farm and New York was so huge and it was just a big shock to our systems but Denis—we had no choice and we went to work and we raised our kids and this country allowed us to do whatever we could do and we could go to the church we chose and there were no people telling us what to do and you couldn't go home because it was too expensive to fly on a plane then and we were happy and we were able to put our kids through school and get a house and we voted and Jack Kennedy and guys like him who were only the same age as this Obama but they had tons and tons of experience in the war and everything and these people ran the country and as long as you were hardworking everything was available to you and your father always had a good job and he was able to make good money for an honest day's work and you kids got a great education and everything worked out great.

So you would do it the same way all over again.

No way—I'd never leave Ireland now, not with all the money and the jobs they have over there now. No—I wouldn't dream of leaving Ireland now. The only reason to leave Ireland now would be the weather. The husband is being given a good talking to by Dr. Phil now.

So—

Denis, once your children are successful and good citizens—then that's it. You are so lucky that your Ann was such a good mother to raise those two kids and now you'll send them off and you'll find out whether they're going to make their way or not—that's the thing, Denis—you've done all you can do and once you drop them off on those college steps that's it—when Daddy and I dropped you off on that stoop in downtown Boston I was in the car blubbering and he said Nora it will either make him or break him and that's it. That father of that Lindsay Lohan—he was a drunk so what did he expect his daughter to turn out to be? These crazy parents—half the parents are crazy people who shouldn't be parents at all. The damage is done and then you have to do something else to fix it. Anyways, Denis—I need a picture of you for Uncle Denis and Aunt Nell to give to Denis Cronin down in New York when they come down to see you—but you need to write your name on it for them and Jim and Pat Malone saw a woman in the hospital and she said she only smiles when she watches you on *Rescue Me* so—I told this to you when I called you before.

When?

When I called you about the tumor in Angus Grady's neck.

Right right—I forgot.

Well I'm telling it to you again now—this woman she needs to have you sign a picture but not just a picture of your face she needs a picture where you are dressed up like on *Rescue Me*, okay?

Okay Ma.

Okay sweetheart, we have to get back to Dr. Phil now. Thanks for calling. Quit smoking, Denis. I love you.

CLICK.

I can't think of a better ending.

My mom sitting with my Uncle Denis and my Aunt Nell watching Dr. Phil try to calm down an angry, overweight wife as she yells at her disappointed and attention-deficit-disordered husband.

Somewhere on a wall in that room hang pictures of us in America and Ireland as babies and kids and teenagers and adults.

Alongside photos of John F. Kennedy, Jesus and my dad.

Our Irish Trinity.

Nuff said.

THE END.